ETHICAL ISSUES IN ACCOUNTING

Ethical issues in the field of accounting have been previously considered in the UK only in terms of the application of codes of ethics. This unique book identifies accounting as an activity with complex ethical implications for the profession in general and for individual practitioners.

Ethical Issues in Accounting considers several aspects of accounting which have significant ethical dimensions, including creative accounting, the ethical implications of accounting regulation, the dilemmas faced by the accountant in the public sector, the personal and professional issues involved in whistleblowing, auditing, ethical education for accountants, taxation practice, and social accounting, which incorporates accounting for the environment. The role of the professional accounting bodies as guardians of professional accounting ethics is also examined in detail.

Ethical Issues in Accounting provides a stimulating and controversial analysis of the ethical dimensions of a wide range of accounting issues which will be informative reading for accounting trainees, students of business studies and the reflective practitioner.

Catherine Gowthorpe is Principal Lecturer in Accounting at the University of Central Lancashire. **John Blake** is Professor of Accounting at the University of Central Lancashire.

PROFESSIONAL ETHICS
General editor: Ruth Chadwick
Centre for Professional Ethics, University of Central Lancashire

Professionalism is a subject of interest to academics, the general public and would-be professional groups. Traditional ideas of professions and professional conduct have been challenged by recent social, political and technological changes. One result has been the development for almost every profession of an ethical code of conduct which attempts to formalise its values and standards. These codes of conduct raise a number of questions about the status of a 'profession' and the consequent moral implications for behaviour.

This series seeks to examine these questions both critically and constructively. Individual volumes will consider issues relevant to particular professions, including nursing, genetic counselling, journalism, business, the food industry and law. Other volumes will address issues relevant to all professional groups such as the function and value of a code of ethics and the demands of confidentiality.

Also available in this series:

ETHICAL ISSUES IN ACCOUNTING

Edited by
Catherine Gowthorpe
and
John Blake

London and New York

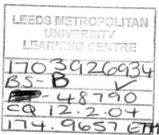
First published 1998
by Routledge
11 New Fetter Lane, London EC4P 4EE

Simultaneously published in the USA and Canada
by Routledge
29 West 35th Street, New York, NY 10001

© 1998 selection and editorial matter, Catherine Gowthorpe
and John Blake; individual chapters, the contributors

The right of Catherine Gowthorpe and John Blake to be identified
as the Authors of this Work has been asserted by them
in accordance with the Copyright, Designs and Patents Act 1988

Typeset in Times by Routledge
Printed and bound in Great Britain by Creative Print and Design
(Wales), Ebbw Vale

British Library Cataloguing in Publication Data
A catalogue record for this book is available from the British Library

Library of Congress Cataloging in Publication Data
Ethical issues in accounting/edited by John Blake and Catherine
Gowthorpe: [contributors, Catherine Pilkington ... *et al.*].
Includes bibliographical references.
1. Accounting – Moral and ethical aspects. I. Blake, John.
II. Gowthorpe, Catherine. III. Pilkington, Catherine. IV. Series.
JF5625.15.E85 1998
98–13837
174'.9657–dc21
CIP

ISBN 0–415–17172–5 (hbk)
ISBN 0–415–17173–3 (pbk)

CONTENTS

CONTENTS

CONTENTS

ILLUSTRATIONS

TABLES

CONTRIBUTORS

Oriol Amat is associate professor of accounting at the University Pompeu Fabra, Barcelona, and has held several visiting professorships at universities in Europe and the USA. He is a committee member of AECA, the Spanish private sector accounting standards setting authority.

John Blake is professor of accounting at the University of Central Lancashire. He has held visiting professorships at universities in Spain and New Zealand, and is currently engaged in several international research projects examining various aspects of international accounting and accounting ethics.

Ray Carroll is an associate professor of accounting at Dalhousie University in Halifax, Canada, and is a fellow of the Certified General Accountants Association of Canada. Professor Carroll has co-authored texts in financial and managerial accounting and is active on several international accounting committees.

Julia Clarke qualified with Ernst & Young in Manchester. She is a lecturer in the department of Accounting and Finance at Leeds University Business School. Her main research interests are in corporate community involvement and social reporting.

Jack Dowds (Ph.D.) is head of the Department of Accountancy and Business Law at Massey University, New Zealand. His academic interest is in the area of financial accounting, particularly the relationship between reported company earnings and underlying cash flows. Dr Dowds was previously a lecturer at the University of Ulster.

Ray Gardiner is senior lecturer, specialising in management accounting, at the University of Central Lancashire. He is also vice-president of the Association of Chartered Certified Accountants. Most of his career has been in industry and commerce ultimately as financial director and managing director of companies in the engineering, paper and construction industries.

Catherine Gowthorpe is principal lecturer in accounting at the University of Central Lancashire. She qualified as a chartered accountant with a Big Six firm and has several years' experience of large company audit. She is currently researching aspects of international accounting and accounting ethics.

Alan Lovell (Ph.D.) is Head of the Department of Accounting at Nottingham Trent University. He has published in a variety of journals and books on the subject of ethical dimensions to accounting practice, including research funded by the Chartered Institute of Management Accountants.

Catherine Pilkington, following a degree in Music and German at the University of Sheffield, qualified as a chartered accountant with Binder Hamlyn at their Manchester office. She worked as a corporate finance manager with Latham, Crossley and Davies, Chorley, before joining the University of Central Lancashire as an associate lecturer in taxation and financial accounting.

Bill Richardson was a research fellow with Sheffield Business School until his untimely death in 1995. He is widely published in the areas of strategic management and crisis management.

Susan Richardson is a senior lecturer and researcher in accounting and management control at Sheffield Hallam University. She has published in such areas as business failure, accounting and organisational change and accounting education, and her research interests cover issues in both the public and private sectors.

Prem Sikka is Professor of Accounting at the University of Essex. He has written extensively on isues of accounting regulation, corporate governance and profession–state relationship. He is currently researching the involvement of accountancy firms in white-collar crime.

SERIES EDITOR'S PREFACE

Professional ethics is now acknowledged as a field of study in its own right. Much of its recent development has resulted from rethinking traditional medical ethics in the light of new moral problems arising out of advances in medical science and technology. Applied philosophers, ethicists and lawyers have devoted considerable energy to exploring the dilemmas emerging from modern healthcare practices and their effects on the practitioner–patient relationship.

But the point can be generalised. Even in healthcare, ethical dilemmas are not confined to medical practitioners. And beyond healthcare, other groups are beginning to think critically about the kind of service they offer and about the nature of the relationship between provider and recipient. In many areas of life social, political and technological changes have challenged traditional ideas of practice.

One visible sign of these developments has been the proliferation of codes of ethics, or of professional conduct. The drafting of such a code provides an opportunity for professionals to examine the nature and goals of their work, and offers information to others about what can be expected from them. If a code has a disciplinary function, it may even offer protection to members of the public.

But is the existence of such a code itself a criterion of a profession? What exactly is a profession? Can a group acquire professional status, and if so, how? Does the label 'professional' have implications, from a moral point of view, for acceptable behaviour, and if so how far do such implications extend?

As the editors of this volume point out in their introduction, accountancy is an area which has been regarded as value-free by some of its practitioners. The editors reject this view, and also point out the drawbacks in defining ethics narrowly in the context of accountancy, because of the widespread influence of the vocabulary of accountancy in our experience of everyday reality. The issues discussed in this book are thus of relevance not only to those engaged in the profession, but also to anyone concerned with the impact of the terminology of accountability and audit on contemporary society.

The *Routledge Series in Professional Ethics* seeks to examine ethical issues in the professions and related areas both critically and constructively. Individual volumes will address issues relevant to all professional groups, such as the nature of a profession, the function and value of codes of ethics, and the demands of confidentiality. Other volumes examine issues relevant to particular professions, including those which have hitherto received little attention, such as journalism, social work and the insurance industry.

Ruth Chadwick

INTRODUCTION

The essays in this book have been collected and are presented here in the belief that ethical issues in accounting merit much more profound exploration and analysis than they have received so far in the United Kingdom. Ethical aspects of accounting have been accorded relatively little attention in either the academic or professional literature produced in the United Kingdom. There are some indications that this position is changing; the Research Boards of the main professional accounting bodies have recently awarded funds for research into accounting ethics and a book promoting understanding of the ethical guide of the Institute of Chartered Accountants in England and Wales (ICAEW) has recently been published (Maurice 1996). We believe, on the basis of anecdotal evidence, that few academic accounting courses in the United Kingdom contain much consideration of ethical issues in accounting, and the syllabuses of the professional bodies contain few specific references to ethics. The absence of ethics in the current discourse of accounting in the United Kingdom does not, of course, prove that it should rightly have a place, but it is our hope that this book will help to provide the requisite proof of its importance.

Accounting is an area of human activity which tends to be regarded by some of its practitioners as neutral and value-free, a reporting function which requires the application of complex technical requirements but no moral involvement beyond adherence to a set of precepts in the form of an ethical code. Practising accountants do not tend to look beyond the narrow confines of the code to consider their roles as moral agents; in fact, it seems likely that they do not consider accounting to be an activity that really has any substantial moral dimension, even though in other areas of their lives they may be deeply concerned with moral issues. This attitude has been identified as 'ethical dissonance' by McPhail and Gray (1996) whose empirical work indicates that accounting students, and by implication accountants, regard accounting as a morally neutral area, a 'separate category of experience'.

However, it is clear to some critics, at least, that accounting is very much more important than the technical standards for undertaking it might imply, and that it has a significant role in the construction of reality in the mainstream (e.g. Hines 1988). It is difficult to overestimate the significance of its role in constructing economic reality because the vocabulary and conventions of accounting permeate our experience of everyday reality so thoroughly. In the United Kingdom of recent years, terms such as 'profitability', 'audit', 'cost-cutting', 'required rate of return', 'UK plc', 'uneconomic', 'bottom line' and 'earnings' have resonated to an unprecedented degree through the lives of many. The vocabulary of the primary accounting statements has acquired a high degree of authority and acceptance, even where the individual terms are unclear or are misunderstood. Moreover, the language of the private sector has entered the public sector, where the ideas and terminology of accountability and audit have been thoroughly absorbed. The idea of audit has been exported from its financial accounting context into an unprecedently wide range of settings (Power 1997), as a means of responding to risk.

These developments may be part of a profound movement in society, the true significance of which may not emerge until we can look back with the benefit of hindsight. Accountants themselves can hardly be expected to bear all the responsibility for the fact that the tools and terminology of their craft have been borrowed and transplanted into so many different organisational and societal contexts. Nevertheless, the outcome is such that accounting's role as a constructor of reality has acquired an unprecedented importance.

ACCOUNTING ETHICS? WHAT DOES ETHICS MEAN?

Because of their potential impact, accounting choices become moral choices, as explained by Francis:

Accounting, to the extent that it is a choice about how to

affect our lived experience . . . is a practice grounded in moral discernment. Accounting is important precisely to the extent the accountant can transform the world, can influence the lived experience of others in ways which cause that experience to differ from what it would be in the absence of accounting, or in the presence of an alternative kind of accounting.

(1990: 7)

It may be argued that accountants are ill-equipped to make the moral choices implied by this perception of the importance of accounting. An important issue in accounting ethics is the wide range of understanding of what the term 'ethics' means, and what might be entailed in ethical action. The profession has tended to define the term narrowly, construing it as a matter of etiquette and professional manners; Plender (1927) recognised that 'the question of ethics' was becoming more important because of the development of the profession, but implied a narrow definition of ethical matters as 'questions of professional conduct and etiquette which frequently arise'. By 1996 another senior representative of the profession was defining 'ethics' in much the same way; from a range of dictionary definitions, he selected 'the rules of conduct recognised in certain limited departments of human life' as being most relevant (Maurice 1996: 9).

Now, in a sense, the narrowness of the definition is quite reasonable, in that relatively few accountants will be called upon to make important policy choices, especially at the 'macro' level of setting accounting standards. However, quite a lot of accountants will be involved in policy choices at the individual firm or audit level, and in any case it may be argued that all should be in a position where they can understand the ethical implication of the choices which are being made by others. A narrow definition of accounting ethics for the profession may be unhelpful in that it delimits a narrow area of concern, but it is nevertheless the approach which is likely to be taken by this or any other profession, in codifying its standards. From a sociological perspective, Durkheim (1957), while arguing for a general moral basis for economic activity, recognised the particular nature of professional ethics: 'Each branch of professional ethics being the product of the professional group, its nature will be that of the group.'

It is clear, then, that there are divergent answers to the question, 'What does ethics mean?', in the context of accounting. The more

3

limited definition involves a narrowly prescriptive approach as exemplified by the ethical codes of the professional bodies. A broader definition brings into the analysis the range of policy and moral choice implied by the pre-eminent position of accounting as the language of much public and political discourse. The content of this book reflects the belief that the broader scope of accounting ethics is a legitimate area of enquiry and interest, not only for students of academic accounting, but also for accounting practitioners.

THE CONTRIBUTIONS

The chapters cover a wide range of aspects of accounting activity, and are written from a broad selection of viewpoints. There has been no attempt to ensure a consistent thrust of argument; the book is intended to stimulate debate among readers and students. The chapters have been grouped, so far as possible, to provide a coherent and logical progression, but they do not, with a couple of exceptions, have to be read in any particular order. In Chapter 1 **Blake** *et al.* introduce some themes related to ethical aspects of accounting regulation, including coverage of the issue of gender-specific ethical approaches. Chapter 2 follows up the closely related area of creative accounting, drawing together some recent empirical evidence on attitudes towards this from three countries.

Richardson and Richardson, in Chapter 3, examine, with the aid of a substantial case study, the ethical dilemma faced by the accountant who is contemplating 'blowing the whistle' on malpractice within the organisation. **Lovell**, in Chapter 4, considers whistleblowing as one aspect of the changing moral atmosphere in the public services, with specific reference to the National Health Service. **Pilkington**, in Chapter 5, examines the ethical issues relating to tax compliance by the taxpayer, and also the range of ethical problems which may face the tax practitioner.

Chapters 6 and 7 are two which should be read in the order in which they are presented in the book. In Chapter 6 **Blake and Gardiner** set out a range of arguments which refute some of the criticisms frequently levelled against the accounting profession by the 'radical' critics. Chapter 7 comprises **Sikka**'s response to **Blake and Gardiner**, in which he provides a detailed defence of his and others' position that the institutions of accountancy are deserving of criticism for their failure to take into account the wider social context of accounting. The two chapters together, then, comprise a debate on the nature of accounting and the bodies which both promote and defend the practices of accountancy.

In Chapter 8 **Gowthorpe** examines some of the recent evidence which points to lax standards of competence and integrity in the auditing profession, and considers the role which education may have in raising awareness of ethical issues in the profession. The theme of education is developed by **Carroll** in Chapter 9 in which he examines the issues surrounding the nurturing of ethical development in the individual and suggests a model for integrating ethics into the accounting curriculum.

The final two chapters of the book deal with aspects of social and environmental reporting. In Chapter 10 **Gowthorpe** presents a summary of the discussions which have taken place in the academic literature and elsewhere about 'deep' and 'pale' green approaches to accounting for the environment. Finally, **Clarke** examines the nature of corporate social reporting (CSR) and its ethical foundations, and provides an overview of the fragmented state of CSR as it has developed in the UK.

Catherine Gowthorpe and John Blake

REFERENCES

Durkheim, E. (1957) *Professional Ethics and Civic Morals*, London: Routledge & Kegan Paul Ltd.

Francis, J.R. (1990) 'After virtue? Accounting as a moral and discursive practice', *Accounting Auditing & Accountability Journal*, 3 (3): 5–17.

Hines, R.D. (1988) 'Financial accounting: in communicating reality, we construct reality', *Accounting, Organizations and Society*, 13 (3): 251–61.

Maurice, J. (1996) *Accounting Ethics*, London: Pitman Publishing.

McPhail, K. and Gray, R. (1997) 'Not developing ethical maturity in acounting education: hegemony, dissonance and homogeneity in accounting students' world views', unpublished paper.

Plender, W. (1927) 'Foreword' to Anonymous, *The Etiquette of the Accountancy Profession*, London: Gee & Co. Ltd.

Power, M. (1997) *The Audit Society: Rituals of Verification*, Oxford: Oxford University Press.

1

THE ETHICS OF ACCOUNTING REGULATION

John Blake, Julia Clarke and Catherine Gowthorpe

ACKNOWLEDGEMENT

This chapter draws heavily on material in the article, 'The ethics of accounting regulation an international perspective', by John Blake, Julia Clarke and Catherine Gowthorpe published in *Business Ethics – A European Review* in July 1996. We thank the editor of the journal, and its publisher, Blackwell (Oxford), for their kind permission to reproduce the material.

OVERVIEW

There is a well-established tradition of ethical guidance for the practising accountant. In this chapter we argue that ethical issues also arise in relation to the accountant's role in the process of accounting regulation. We:

1 Identify the role of the accounting practitioner in different national modes of accounting regulation.
2 Consider the economic impact issues that arise in accounting regulation and the conflicting views on how accountants should react to these.
3 Review the range of ethical perspectives that have been applied to the question of whether accounting regulators should be influenced by economic impact issues.
4 Discuss five cases of economic impact issues considering the relevance of an ethical perspective in each case.
5 Identify the level of representation of women on seven accounting standard-setting bodies and discuss the implications of a possible

limitation in the ethical values informing the debate on accounting standards which arises from under-representation of women.

THE ROLE OF THE ACCOUNTING PRACTITIONER IN DIFFERENT NATIONAL MODES OF ACCOUNTING REGULATION

Accounting regulation can come from either the public sector or the private sector; in many countries there is a combination of the two. Most countries have some form of legislation on accounting, whether in the form of 'company law', as in the UK, 'accounting law', as in Sweden, or 'tax law', as in Germany. In addition some countries have governmental bodies with either delegated authority to regulate accounting, as with the Instituto de Contabilidad y Auditoria de Cuentas (ICAC) in Spain, or with a formal advisory role to the legislature, as with the Bokföringsnämnden (BFN – Accounting Standards Board) in Sweden. Professional accountants may be among those nominated as members of such a body, either by direct governmental appointment, as with ICAC in Spain, or by nomination of their professional body, as with BFN in Sweden.

Private sector accounting regulation tends to have originated with professional accounting bodies. Examples were the Accounting Principles Board (APB), set up by the American Institute of Certified Public Accountants which led the way in setting recommendations from 1959 to 1973, and the Accounting Standards Committee (ASC), founded by the UK accounting bodies, which set accounting standards from 1970 to 1990. In both countries replacement bodies, in the USA the Financial Accounting Standards Board (FASB) since 1973 and in the UK the Accounting Standards Board (ASB) since 1990, have been set up with nominees from a range of interested parties but continued strong representation from the accounting profession.

These private sector standards can be enforced in various ways:

1 In some countries the law may explicitly require companies to comply. Canada is an example. In the UK compliance with accounting standards has effectively been a legal obligation for large companies since 1989.
2 In countries such as the UK, Australia, and New Zealand, which specify some general level of quality that company accounts must achieve such as the 'true and fair view', compliance with

accounting standards may be regarded as evidence of achieving that level (see for example Renshall and Walmsley 1990: 313).

3 A governmental regulatory body may review standards and require companies to comply with them. This is the procedure of the SEC in the USA.

4 The accounting profession may require its own members, acting as company auditors or directors, to use their influence to secure compliance.

5 The technical quality of private sector pronouncements may be so respected that in practice companies choose to comply with them. This is generally true for pronouncements from Sweden's professional accounting body, which are followed by large Swedish companies. In Spain a private body of accountants, the Asociación Española de Contabilidad y Adminstración (AECA), issues recommendations which are commonly adopted by companies and frequently form the basis for subsequent official regulations from the governmental body ICAC (see above).

Thus professional accountants may be involved in the process of accounting regulation as members of public sector or private sector regulatory bodies, appointed by government, a professional body, or some other interest group. In the USA, concern that members of the accounting standard-setting body might be influenced by the interests of their employer led to the structuring of the FASB with seven full-time members, each of whom must sever all links with their previous employer. This contrasts with the previous structure of the APB with part-time members selected to assure a well-defined representation of large international CPA firms, other CPA firms, business and academics. Meyer (1974) examined voting records on the APB and concluded that 'no dominant pattern of voting could be discerned'. Nevertheless Senator Metcalf expressed concern that the (then) 'Big Eight' might dominate the accounting standard-setting process (US Congress 1976). Studies of voting patterns in the APB (Rockness and Nikolai 1977), the FASB (Brown 1981, Selto and Grove 1982) and a study of both (Newman 1981) have failed to identify any pattern of a 'Big Eight' voting block dominating these bodies.

Members of the accounting profession may also become involved in the accounting regulatory process through lobbying the regulators. A former FASB chairman tells us that the large public accountancy firms are regarded as a source of unbiased neutral comment on accounting issues, and so their representations are particularly influential (Armstrong 1977).

Studies of audit firm lobbying to the FASB raise questions as to whether the 'Big Eight' firms are biased in representing accounting regulation. Haring (1979) found a positive, though not statistically significant, association between client lobbying and audit firm lobbying, and also found that the likelihood of FASB support for an accounting rule is statistically related to accounting firms' preferences. Puro (1984), in an examination of audit firm lobbying, found that on standardisation issues, firms tended to favour the position adopted by their clients, while on disclosure issues, firms tended to opt for the approach that maximises their own income, i.e. large firms favour increased complexity, small firms oppose it.

Thus, the evidence seems to suggest that accounting firms do have a bias in their preference for certain forms of accounting regulation that influence their lobbying but do not influence the voting pattern of FASB members with former accounting firm links. In view of the apparent reliance placed by accounting regulators on the representations of these firms, a question arises as to what ethical constraints should affect their lobbying.

ECONOMIC IMPACT ISSUES AND THE ACCOUNTING REGULATOR

Published company accounts are available to a wide range of users. The information that managers provide in those accounts may influence the behaviour of those users. Changes in accounting rules can lead to changes in the information shown in accounts and consequently to changes in the behaviour of the users of the accounts. These changes in behaviour can affect the economy in general and the position of the reporting company and its managers in particular. Thus changes in accounting rules give rise to potential 'economic consequences', a term which has been defined as follows:

> Accounting choices have economic consequences if changes in the rules used to calculate accounting numbers alter the distribution of firms' cash flows, or the wealth of parties who use those numbers for contracting or decision making.
>
> (Holthausen and Leftwich 1983: 77)

The distinction between 'contracting' and 'decision making' is a key point, also termed as 'direct' as against 'indirect' issues (Benston and Krasney 1978), or 'mechanistic' as against 'judgemental' issues (Blake 1992). This arises because accounts are used in two ways.

First, the numbers in the accounts may define the rights and obligations of the company in line with some regulation or contract. Examples are company borrowing power limits which are frequently defined as a multiple of share capital and reserves, and directors' bonus schemes, which may be based on some proportion of reported profit. These are the 'contracting' or 'mechanistic' issues.

Second, the readers of the accounts may take decisions on the basis of the information provided, and managers may change their behaviour in response to their expectations as to users' reaction. Thus, present and potential investors may change their view of share values, governments may change their view as to the tax burden that an industry is able to bear, or employees may adjust their wage demands. These are the 'decision making' or 'judgemental' issues.

The potential economic impact of accounting regulations explains why managers seek to control or influence the process of accounting regulation. As Whittred and Zimmer argue: 'These wealth transfers, the economic consequences of accounting method choice, are ultimately the source of the incentive to possess financial rule making authority, or at least to influence the deliberations of rule making bodies' (1988: 10).

A range of views can be identified on the legitimacy of allowing economic consequences to influence accounting regulation. One is that awareness of these issues can lead to the argument that 'the setting of accounting standards is as much a product of political action as of flawless logic or empirical findings' (Horngren 1973: 61) or the perception of accounting regulation as 'essentially a political process' (Gerboth 1973: 479). Against this view advocates of 'neutrality', a view that accounting rules should not be chosen by reference to how they might influence a decision or judgement, argue that 'the criterion by which rules are to be judged is not the effect they may or may not have on business behaviour' (Solomons 1978). The essential feature of accounting regulation is the provision of 'a level playing field' (Solomons 1989: 37) and any other approach means that 'the credibility of the information being supplied is lost or damaged' (Stamp 1980). Between these two views a compromise can be identified, a 'mixed strategy' (Rappaport 1977), whereby some form of assessment of economic impact is combined with the development of a 'technical solution' based on a conceptual framework.

THE ETHICAL PERSPECTIVE

As Taylor observes:

> One of the most commonly held opinions in ethics is that all moral norms are relative to particular cultures. The rules of conduct that are applicable in one society, it is claimed, do not apply to the actions of people in another society. Each community has its own norms, and morality is entirely a matter of conforming to the standards and rules accepted in one's own culture.
>
> (1975: 13)

The literature on the application of ethical principles to accounting regulation that we consider here has arisen mainly in the context of the USA, with some contribution from the UK and Australia. We will consider the relevance of this perspective to issues arising in other cultures in the next section.

Ruland (1984) identifies three perspectives in philosophy which have a bearing on the question as to whether accounting regulators should be guided by economic consequences issues.

The question of whether ends justify means; that is, in the context of accounting regulation, whether achievement of desirable economic outcomes justifies taking a particular approach to an accounting rule. The deontological point of view is that moral rules apply to the actual actions, the means whereby an end is pursued. The teleological point of view is that an action should be judged on the basis of the moral worth of the outcome. One mechanism that accounting regulators can use to promote a deontological approach is to formulate a conceptual framework, laying down the basis on which accounting regulations are to be formulated, and so providing a basis for assessing the quality and consistency of specific accounting regulations. Collett (1995) points out an interesting inconsistency in the Australian Conceptual Framework Statements issued by the Australian Accounting Research Foundation. While the formulation of such statements implies a deontological approach, the statements themselves specify that all prospective costs and benefits, including by implication issues of economic consequence, should be considered in the formulation of accounting regulations. This implies a teleological approach.

The distinction between positive and negative responsibilities. A positive responsibility holds individuals liable for states of affairs they bring about, while a negative responsibility holds them liable for states of affairs they allow or fail to prevent. Thus positive responsibility holds individuals responsible for the actions they commit, while negative responsibility is impersonal since it makes the individual liable for the acts of others. It is argued that the positive responsibility to produce accounting regulations that result in a fair presentation of business accounts should not be compromised by pursuit of a negative responsibility to avoid certain economic consequences, since these are both uncertain and under the control of other parties.

The distinction between a duty to refrain and a duty to act. It is argued that the pursuit of best accounting practice is the explicit duty of accounting regulator, being a duty to refrain from being distracted by other issues. By contrast those who argue that economic consequences issues should influence accounting regulation are urging a duty to act. The case for pursuing a duty to restrain rather than a duty to act is based on three issues:

(a) *Relentlessness.* There is an infinite range of economic consequences that can flow from an accounting rule. The full range cannot be comprehended, so that a duty to act cannot be fulfilled.

(b) *Certainty of outcome.* Ruland argues that we cannot be certain that, in pursuing a duty to act, the action will achieve or be necessary for the desired outcome, whereas the duty to refrain can demonstrably be fulfilled. Against this, Ingram and Rayburn (1989) argue that many accounting issues do not have a demonstrably superior solution, so that the application of the duty to refrain is as uncertain as the outcome of the duty to act.

(c) *Responsibility.* Violation of the duty to refrain is clearly the responsibility of the accounting regulator. However, where the regulator chooses to ignore an economic consequences issue, so that an adverse consequence arises, then the responsibility rests with those who have made decisions on the basis of the accounts.

Ingram and Rayburn interpret the duty to refrain in a different way. They argue:

We believe that, when it comes to standard setting, the duty to refrain is stronger than the duty to act. Actions, new standards, should be promoted only when there is clear evidence that the benefits to those who are intended to benefit from the standards are greater than the costs.

(1989: 65)

Ijiri makes a similar point:

Stability of the accounting system means that . . . change in the definitions or rules of measurement will not be made unless absolutely necessary. If an accounting system is unstable, the accountor and the accountee sense the risk of relying upon it in developing their agreement and look for other means that are more stable.

(1983: 79)

SOME SPECIFIC EXAMPLES

We now turn to consider a number of economic impact issues that illustrate the application of an ethical perspective.

In the USA the emergence of the accounting rules on foreign currency translation offers an example of how an accounting regulation may be changed in response to intensive lobbying. There are two broad approaches to the translation of the accounts of a subsidiary operating in a foreign country and consequently preparing its own accounts in that foreign currency:

1 The temporal method. In historic cost accounts, this involves translating non-monetary items, such as tangible fixed assets and stock, at the rate of exchange that applied when the item originally entered the accounts, called the 'historic rate'. Monetary items are translated at the rate of exchange at the balance sheet date, called the 'closing rate'.
2 The closing rate method. This involves translating all assets and liabilities at the closing rate.

These two methods can have substantially different effects on a company's accounts. This is down to two factors. First, most companies have total assets in excess of total liabilities – a net asset position – but borrowings in excess of cash – a net monetary liability position. Thus the closing rate method, where the exchange rate applying to all items changes each year, gives the opposite effect to the temporal method, where the exchange rate applied each year only changes in relation to monetary items. Blake (1993) offers a summary of impact together with a fuller explanation. See Table 1.1.

The second reason why the two methods can have markedly different effects on a company's accounts is that the underlying logic of the temporal method tends to identification of the gains or losses on holding individual assets or liabilities as part of the profit or loss for the year. By contrast the closing rate method, which identifies the gain or loss on the net investment in the subsidiary, is similar in character to a revaluation so that it can justifiably be treated as an adjustment to the reserves rather than appearing on the face of the profit and loss account.

The American Institute of Certified Public Accountants, faced with these two contrasting approaches, commissioned a research study. The result was a firm recommendation for the temporal method (Lorenson 1972) based on what has been described as 'one of the best pieces of academic research applied to a major practical problem in accounting' (Flower, 1995: 360). On the basis of this, an accounting standard prescribing the temporal method, FAS8, was issued in 1975.

The standard proved unpopular with US multinationals because:

1 Through the second half of the 1970s the US dollar tended to weaken, leading to reported losses on translation of foreign subsidiary accounts as we have seen above.
2 Companies like to report 'smooth' rather than fluctuating income figures. Alleman (1982) cites the example of how, under FAS8, in 1986 ITT experienced a virtual halving of profit in one quarter and a doubling in the next because of foreign currency losses and gains.

In 1981, in response to vigorous lobbying, FAS52 was issued prescribing the closing rate method. This satisfied US multinationals. However, Ndubizu (1984: 190) points out that there was a

Table 1.1 Impact of two different methods of foreign currency translation

	Temporal method	Closing rate method
Strong foreign currency	Loss	Gain
Weak foreign currency	Gain	Loss

Source: Blake (1993: 40)

negative economic impact on developing countries. This is because such countries tend to have weak currencies. To minimise the loss that this results in under the closing rate method multinationals tend to reduce their net investment in subsidiaries in developing countries by using local borrowing rather than injecting capital directly. Ndubizu argues that a sharp fall in investment in developing countries can be identified following the issue of FAS52 and concludes that 'the advanced countries' accounting standard is argued to discourage foreign investments'.

This example illustrates the issue of relentlessness. In pursuing a 'duty to act' the FASB responded to the concerns of US multinational enterprises but failed to respond to the less apparent consequences for developing countries.

A recent Spanish example illustrates the issue of 'certainty of outcome'. In 1990 a new 'Plan General de Contabilidad' (PGC – general accounting plan) was enacted, revising Spanish accounting law in line with the European Union directives on accounting harmonisation. One feature of the PGC was to require capitalisation of finance lease agreements, so that when a company enters into a lease with an option to purchase at a bargain price at the end of the rental period this should be accounted for as though an asset had been purchased with a secured loan. This is an example of the application of the 'substance over form' concept, whereby a transaction is accounted for in fine with economic substance rather than legal form. Application of this concept is well established in the USA and increasingly applied by the Accounting Standards Board in the UK, but is in contrast to the strong legalistic tradition of Spanish accounting.

When this accounting requirement was proposed it was opposed by the Spanish leasing association on the grounds that it would make leasing less attractive to companies because the increase reported assets and liabilities on the balance sheet would show a higher risk exposure (Vidal 1992); the association successfully lobbied for classification of leased assets as intangible rather than tangible in the belief that this would solve the problem. Following a survey of Spanish financial managers Blake *et al.* report:

> The equipment leasing association appears to have been right in its prediction that a finance lease capitalisation requirement would have an adverse effect on the leasing industry. However, given the distaste that company financial managers show for

the disclosure of leased assets as intangible rather than tangible, the equipment leasing association would seem to have exacerbated their problem as a result of successfully lobbying for such treatment.

(1995: 32)

This example shows how a response to an economic impact issue can have a different effect from that intended.

A number of economic consequences issues arose during the development of an accounting standard on leasing in the UK. The UK and the Republic of Ireland at that time shared a common system for developing accounting standards. In 1981 a proposal by the Accounting Standards Committee to require capitalisation of finance leases included the statement: 'By reason of the law at present obtaining in the Republic of Ireland, this exposure draft is not intended to apply to financial statements prepared or audited in the Republic of Ireland.'

This provision arose because at that time Irish tax law provided that if a lessee capitalised a finance lease a different, and generally less beneficial, tax treatment would follow. In fact publication of a mandatory standard on capitalisation of finance leases was delayed by the Institute of Chartered Accountants in Ireland exercising a veto (as reported in 'Accountancy Age', 26 January 1984: 2) until the 1984 Irish budget changed the position.

In this case the accounting standard-setting body appears to have acted on the basis of a 'duty to refrain' in the sense identified by Ingram and Rayburn (1989) cited above. An interpretation of this kind might seem more appropriate for 'mechanistic' consequences, where a specific outcome can be anticipated, than for 'judgemental' consequences, where the outcome is less certain.

It is interesting to contrast the role of the accounting profession in two cases where the government introduced unconventional accounting legislation to achieve an economic objective, one in Sweden and the other in the USA. At the end of 1977 Uddeholm AB, a major Swedish company in steel and forest products, faced crisis. Major borrowings had been undertaken with a debt covenant provision that total borrowings should not exceed 75 per cent of reported total assets. As a result of a major 1977 loss, the company was in breach of this condition. The Swedish government came under pressure to rescue this major employer, but was barred by international agreement from giving a subsidy to a steel producer. Instead, the government extended a line of credit to Uddeholm, and passed a law effectively requiring the company to treat this line of credit receivable as an asset. The effect was to boost total assets to the point where the company was not in breach of its debt covenant. In the years that followed, the company conducted an orderly realisation of its assets to clear the loans, and in 1985 was taken over by AGA.

Zeff and Johansson report that this legislation was passed 'much to the displeasure of the leaders of the Swedish accounting profession' (1984: 344). In 1980 the opposition in the Swedish parliament called for a report by the parliamentary auditor on this rescue, being concerned with the broad economic issues. Senior members of the accountancy profession drew the auditor's attention to the unconventional accounting treatment and the ensuing report included a recommendation that in future such accounting legislation should not be enacted until the Bokföringsnämnden had given it impartial consideration. The law was repealed in 1983 and the auditor's recommendation was accepted by the government. As Zeff and Johansson note: 'Criticism from the accounting profession had an impact on the political decision makers' (1984: 347).

Margavio (1993) summarises the experience in the USA of special accounting treatment formulated in a vain attempt to protect the savings and loans institutions. During the 1970s these institutions, long favoured by the US government for their role in providing finance to expand home ownership, were badly hit by inflation and consequent high interest rates. Their problems arose from the practice of lending for long periods at fixed interest rates, while borrowing from depositors on a short term basis at what, of necessity, had to be current market interest rates. In the early 1980s a series of accounting regulations from the government were enacted to give these institutions the appearance of viability. For example, in 1981 a regulation permitted losses on the sale of portfolios of low interest loans to be carried forward and allocated over the life of the loans rather than being shown as a loss immediately in the accounts. In evidence to the responsible subcommittee of Congress in 1985 a leading critic of these measures observed, 'The S&L Thrift industry is floating on a sea of tenuous accounting numbers' (Briloff 1990: 8). By the end of the 1980s it had become clear that these measures had failed to give the breathing space necessary for the institutions to recover their stability. Estimates of the cost to the US federal government of underwriting losses in the industry were in excess of $100 billion.

While these regulations come from government rather than the accountancy profession accountants have been criticised for:

1 Failure to publicly identify and criticise the deficiencies of the regulations when they were enacted.
2 Failure, as auditors, to report on the insolvency of the institutions as it arose. (Margavio [1993: 2] reports the example of one large firm which has settled claims against it on these grounds for $400 million.)

To summarise our comparison of the two cases, in the Swedish example an unorthodox accounting regulation was confined to just one company and prompt action was taken to resolve that company's problems, so limiting the issue of 'relentlessness'; the accounting profession was rigorous in pressing for orthodox accounting treatment. In the US case a series of unorthodox accounting regulations allowed concealment of serious underlying problems that continued to grow with consequent major costs. The accounting profession failed to give a lead in tackling the issues, and individual audit firms have become involved in major liabilities for their own failure to act.

SEX DIFFERENCES AND THE ETHICS OF ACCOUNTING REGULATION

Representation of women in the accounting profession has increased steadily in recent years. For example, the membership of the Institute of Chartered Accountants in England and Wales by sex over the last twenty years, set out in Table 1.2. However, as Roberts and Coutts (1992) point out, the age distribution of women accountants is skewed towards the younger age groups because they have only recently started to enter the profession in significant

Table 1.2 Membership of the Institute of Chartered Accountants in England and Wales by sex

	1975	1980	1986	1988	1995
Total	61,718	71,677	84,543	88,918	109,233
Women	1,413	2,971	6,479	8,089	17,136
Men	60,305	68,706	78,064	80,829	92,097
% Women	2.3	4.1	7.7	9.1	15.7

Source: 1975–1988 Roberts and Coutts (1992: 6); 1995 ICAEW

numbers. Therefore they are over-represented at junior levels and under-represented in senior management. It may be, though, that age distribution alone does not account for the level of under-representation at senior levels, and that there are other factors involved: 'While men achieve the career progression that is defined as "success" in accounting, women are constrained to particular specialisms and to the lower ranks' (Roberts and Coutts 1992: 392).

There is some evidence to suggest that there are barriers to women's success in accounting measured in conventional terms of career achievement, such as position and remuneration. Explanatory theories for this imbalance include the suggestion by some authors that unequal relationships are inherent in the nature of accounting which is dominated and defined by a set of values originating from an entirely male world view (e.g. Cooper 1992; Kirkham 1992). In such circumstances women can choose to imitate men by aping their behaviour, and indeed are encouraged to do so (Lehman 1992: 279). Alternatively they may respond to an apparently hostile environment with a set of coping stratagems which may be viewed as deviant and therefore inimical to 'success' by the dominant male hierarchy.

Empirical evidence collected for this study, although limited in scope to a small number of countries, shows that the under-representation of women at senior levels in the profession dwindles to almost no representation at all in the process of standard-setting. In a brief survey conducted in 1996 we found the levels of representation by sex on seven accounting standard-setting bodies shown in Table 1.3.

Table 1.3 Representation by sex on seven accounting standard-setting bodies in 1996

	Men	Women	Total
IASC	43	5	48
ASB (UK)	9	0	9
FASB (UK)	7	0	7
Redovisningrädet (Sweden)	9	0	9
ASB (Canada)	12	1	13
ASB (Australia)	6	4	10
FRSB (New Zealand)	9	3	12
Total	95	13	108

This imbalance of representation by sex in six out of our seven cases is, of course, counter to ideals of equality, and is likely to be offensive to anyone who believes that women should be properly represented at levels where power and influence are exercised. However, in addition, there may be a significant impact on the nature and results of the standard-setting process, in that women might have a different set of ethical approaches to problems than men, and that, in current conditions, male ethical values are bound to dominate.

This view has validity only if it can be proved that women and men approach ethical issues in different ways. Ford and Richardson (1994), quoted in Dawson (1995), noted that preceding studies were split equally between the views that, on the one hand, women were more likely to act ethically than males and on the other, that sex differentiation had no impact on ethical beliefs. Dawson's findings (1995: 67), based upon empirical studies of the attitudes of business managers of both sexes, were that 'men and women bring different ethical standards and values to the work environment', and that 'men and women differ considerably in their moral reasoning processes'.

Two distinct areas of difficulty relating to differing sex-based ethical values suggest themselves in the context of accounting standard-setting. Brown (1987) identifies a general problem in respect of agenda setting: 'Since the proceedings and findings of applied ethics are influenced by the agenda, giving some limited group excessive control of the agenda is giving that group some control over the proceedings and findings' (1987: 83). The agenda for standard-setting boards is set by a male-dominated accounting profession, influenced by other male-dominated communities (e.g. business management, politics and academia).

The second area of difficulty relates to ethical judgement and decision-making processes. We argue earlier in this chapter that ethical perspectives have relevance to debate on accounting issues. Once recognised, an accounting issue could be dealt with by drawing upon a variety of ethical standpoints. The standard-setting boards are missing out a set of alternative ethical perspectives on problems because of the non-inclusion of women in debate.

To summarise, we feel that the imbalance of representation of the sexes in the higher echelons of the accounting profession and in the membership of the standard-setting bodies results in an imbalance in the ethical perspectives which inform the standard-setting process. The subjects for debate and the nature of that debate may be impoverished because of the absence of any significant contribution from women.

CONCLUSION

The role of the accountant in the process of accounting regulation raises an ethical issue as to whether to allow 'economic impact' issues to affect technical judgement. A review of the literature on the application of an ethical perspective to this question indicates a case against this. Specific examples of economic impact issues indicate the relevance of the ethical perspective. Overall we would conclude that:

- The ethical perspective does have relevance to the debate on how the accounting regulator should respond to economic impact issues.
- The ethical perspective would indicate, at the least, a need for care and caution in allowing economic impact factors to influence the development of accounting regulation.
- There is a separate and distinct question as to the ethical principles that should govern accountants in lobbying on issues of accounting regulation.
- There may be an imbalance in the range of ethical debate in the standard-setting process because of under-representation of women.

REFERENCES

Accounting Standards Committee (1981) 'Exposure Draft 29: Accounting for leases and hire purchase contracts', *Accountancy*, November: 117–44.

Alleman, R.H. (1982) 'Why ITT likes FAS52', *Management Accounting*, July: 23–9.

Armstrong, M.S. (1977) 'The politics of establishing accounting standards', *Journal of Accountancy*, February: 76–9.

Benston, G.J. and Krasney, M.A. (1978) 'The economic consequences of financial accounting standards', in *Economic Consequences of Financial Accounting Standards*, Stanford, CT: Financial Accounting Standards Board, 161–242.

Blake, J.D. (1992) 'A classification system for economic consequences issues in accounting regulation', *Accounting and Business Research*, 22 (88): 305–21.

—— (1993) 'Foreign currency translation: a challenge for Europe', *Journal of European Business Education*, May: 30–44.

Blake, J., Amat, O. and Clarke, J. (1995) 'Managing the economic impact of accounting regulation: the Spanish case', *European Business Review*, 95 (6): 26–34.

Briloff, A.L. (1990) 'Accounting and society: a covenant desecrated', *Critical Perspectives on Accounting*, 1: 5–30.

Brown, J.M. (1987) 'On applying ethics', in J.D.G. Evans (ed.) *Moral Philosophy and Contemporary Problems*, Cambridge: Cambridge University Press, 81–93. This volume contains the Royal Institute of Philosophy Lecture Series No. 22, supplement to *Philosophy*, 62 (242).

Brown, P.R. (1981) 'A descriptive analysis of select input bases of the Financial Accounting Standards Board', *Journal of Accounting Research*, Spring: 232–46.

Collett, P. (1995) 'Standard setting and economic consequences: an ethical issue', *Abacus*, 31 (1): 18–30.

Cooper, C. (1992) 'The non and nom of accounting for (m)other nature', *Accounting, Auditing & Accountability Journal*, 5 (3): 16–39.

Dawson, L.M. (1995) 'Women and men, morality and ethics', *Business Horizons*, July/August: 61–8.

Flower, J. (1995) 'Foreign currency translation', in C. Nobes and R. Parker (eds) *Comparative International Accounting*, Hemel Hempstead: Prentice Hall, 348–89.

Gerboth, D. (1975) 'Research intuition and politics in accounting inquiry', *Accounting Review*, July: 475–82.

Haring, J.R. (1979) 'Accounting rules and the accounting establishment', *Journal of Business*, October: 507–19.

Holthausen, R.W. and Leftwich, R.W. (1983) 'The economic consequences of accounting choice: implications of costly contracting and monitoring', *Journal of Accounting and Economics*, 5: 77–117.

Horngren, C.T. (1973) 'The marketing of accounting standards', *Journal of Accountancy*, October: 61–6.

Ijiri, Y. (1983) 'On the accountability-based conceptual framework of accounting', *Journal of Accounting and Public Policy*, Summer: 75–81.

Ingram, R.M. and Rayburn F.R. (1989) 'Representational faithfulness and economic consequences: their roles in accounting policy', *Journal of Accounting and Public Policy*, Spring: 57–68.

Kirkham, L.M. (1992) 'Integrating herstory and history in accountancy', *Accounting, Organizations and Society*, 17 (3/4): 287–97.

Lehman, C.R. (1992) ' "Herstory" in Accounting: the first eighty years', *Accounting, Organizations and Society*, 17 (3/4): 261–85.

Lorenson, L. (1972) *Accounting Research Study No. 12: Reporting Foreign Operations of US Companies in US Dollars*, New York: American Institute of Certified Public Accountants.

Margavio, G.W. (1993) 'The savings and loan debacle: the culmination of three decades of conflicting regulation, de regulation, and re regulation', *Accounting Historians Journal*, 20 (1): 1–32.

Meyer, F.P.E. (1974) 'The APB's independence and its implications for the FASB', *Journal of Accounting Research*, Spring: 188–96.

Ndubizu, G.A. (1984) 'Accounting standards and economic development: the third world in perspective', *International Journal of Accounting*, Spring: 181–96.

Newman, D.P. (1981) 'An investigation of the distribution of power in the APB and theFASB', *Journal of Accounting Research*, Spring: 247–62.

Puro, M. (1984) 'Audit firm lobbying before the Financial Accounting Standards Board: an empirical study', *Journal of Accounting Research*, Autumn: 624–46.

Rappaport, A. (1977) 'Economic impact of accounting standards: implications for the FASB', *Journal of Accountancy*, May: 94.

Renshall, M. and Walmsley, K. (1990) *Butterworth's Company Law Guide*, London: Butterworths.

Roberts, J. and Coutts, J.A. (1992) 'Feminization and professionalization: a review of an emerging literature on the development of accounting in the United Kingdom', *Accounting, Organizations and Society*, 17 (3/4): 379–95.

Rockness, H.O. and Nikolai, L.A. (1977) 'An assessment of APB voting patterns', *Journal of Accounting Research*, Spring: 154–67.

Ruland, R.G. (1984) 'Duty, obligation and responsibility in accounting policy making', *Journal of Accounting and Public Policy*, Fall: 223–37.

Selto, F.H. and Grove, H.D. (1982) 'Voting power indices and the setting of financial accounting standards extension', *Journal of Accounting Research*, Autumn: 676–88.

Solomons, D. (1978) 'The politicisation of accounting', *Journal of Accountancy*, November: 65–72.

—— (1989) *Guidelines for Financial Reporting Standards*, London: Institute of Chartered Accountants in England and Wales.

Stamp, E. (1980) *Corporate Reporting: Its Future Evaluation*, Toronto, Ont.: Canadian Institute of Chartered Accountants.

Taylor, P.M. (1975) *Principles of Ethics: an Introduction*, Encino, CA: Dickenson.

US Congress (1976) *Senate Sub-committee on Reports, Accounting, and Management of the Committee on Government Operations. The Accounting Establishment: a Staff Study* (Metcalf Staff Report), 94th Congress, 2nd session.

Vidal, C. (1992) 'Spain', in A. Hornbrook (ed.) *World Leasing Yearbook 1992*, London: Euromoney, 300–5.

Whittred, G. and Zimmer, L. (1988) *Financial Accounting: Incentive Effects and Economic Consequences*, Sydney: Holt Rinehart and Winston.

Zeff, S.A. and Johansson, S.E. (1984) 'The curious accounting treatment of the Swedish government loan to Uddeholm', *Accounting Review*, April: 342–50.

2

THE ETHICS OF CREATIVE ACCOUNTING

John Blake, Oriol Amat and Jack Dowds

INTRODUCTION

The term 'creative accounting' can be defined in a number of ways. Initially we will offer this definition: 'a process whereby accountants use their knowledge of accounting rules to manipulate the figures reported in the accounts of a business'.

To investigate the ethical issues raised by creative accounting we will:

- Explore some definitions of creative accounting.
- Consider the various ways in which creative accounting can be undertaken.
- Explore the range of reasons for a company's directors to engage in creative accounting.
- Review the ethical issues that arise in creative accounting.
- Report on surveys of auditors' perceptions of creative accounting in the UK, Spain and New Zealand.

DEFINITIONS

Four authors in the UK, each writing from a different perspective, have explored the issue of creative accounting.

Ian Griffiths, writing from the perspective of a business journalist, observes:

> Every company in the country is fiddling its profits. Every set of published accounts is based on books which have been gently cooked or completely roasted. The figures which are fed twice a year to the investing public have all been changed in order to

24

protect the guilty. It is the biggest con trick since the Trojan horse. . . . In fact this deception is all in perfectly good taste. It is totally legitimate. It is creative accounting.

(1986: 1)

Michael Jameson, writing from the perspective of the accountant, argues:

> The accounting process consists of dealing with many matters of judgement and of resolving conflicts between competing approaches to the presentation of the results of financial events and transactions . . . this flexibility provides opportunities for manipulation, deceit and misrepresentation. These activities – practised by the less scrupulous elements of the accounting profession – have come to be known as 'creative accounting'.

(1988: 7–8)

Terry Smith reports on his experience as an investment analyst:

> We felt that much of the apparent growth in profits which had occurred in the 1980s was the result of accounting sleight of hand rather than genuine economic growth, and we set out to expose the main techniques involved, and to give live examples of companies using those techniques.

(1992: 4)

Kamal Naser, presenting an academic view, offers this definition:

> Creative accounting is the transformation of financial accounting figures from what they actually are to what preparers desire by taking advantage of the existing rules and/or ignoring some or all of them.

(1993: 2)

It is interesting to observe that Naser perceives the accounting system in Anglo-Saxon countries as particularly prone to such manipulation because of the freedom of choice it permits. Two features are common to all four writers:

1 They perceive the incidence of creative accounting to be common.
2 They see creative accounting as a deceitful and undesirable practice.

The various methods of creative accounting can be considered to fall in four categories:

(1)   Sometimes the accounting rules allow a company to choose between different accounting methods. In many countries, for example, a company is allowed to choose between a policy of writing off development expenditure as it occurs and amortising it over the life of the related project. A company can therefore choose the accounting policy that gives their preferred image.

(2)   Certain entries in the accounts involve an unavoidable degree of estimation, judgement, and prediction. In some cases, such as the estimation of an asset's useful life made in order to calculate depreciation, these estimates are normally made inside the business and the creative accountant has the opportunity to err on the side of caution or optimism in making the estimate. Grover (1991b) reports on the example of the film industry, where a decision has to be made on how to allocate film production costs. Initially, these are capitalised, and then should be amortised against related earnings. Grover discusses one film company, Orion pictures: 'Some studies are definitely more optimistic than others and Orion was always among the most optimistic . . . . Orion would delay, sometimes for years, taking write-downs on films that didn't measure up' (1991b: 56).

In other cases an outside expert is normally employed to make estimates; for instance, an actuary would normally be employed to assess the prospective pension liability. In this case the creative accountant can manipulate the valuation both by the way in which the valuer is briefed and by choosing a valuer known to take a pessimistic or an optimistic view, as the accountant prefers.

(3)   Artificial transactions can be entered into both to manipulate balance sheet amounts and to move profits between accounting periods. This is achieved by entering into two or more related transactions with an obliging third party, normally a bank. For example, supposing an arrangement is made to sell an asset to a bank then lease that asset back for the rest of its useful life. The sale price under such a 'sale and leaseback' can be pitched above or below the current value of the asset, because the difference can be compensated for by increased or reduced rentals.

(4)   Genuine transactions can also be timed so as to give the desired impression in the accounts. As an example, suppose a business has an investment of £1 million at historic cost which can easily be sold for £3 million, being the current value. The managers of the business are free to choose in which year they sell the investment and so increase the profit in the accounts.

Accounting regulators who wish to curb creative accounting have to tackle each of these approaches in a different way:

(1)   Scope for choice of accounting methods can be reduced by reducing the number of permitted accounting methods or by specifying circumstances in which each method should be used. Requiring consistency of use of methods also helps here, since a company choosing a method which produces the desired picture in one year will then be forced to use the same method in future circumstances where the result may be less favourable.

(2)   Abuse of judgement can be curbed in two ways. One is to draft rules that minimise the use of judgement. Thus in the UK company accountants tended to use the 'extraordinary item' part of the profit and loss account for items they wished to avoid including in operating profit. The UK Accounting Standards Board (ASB) responded by effectively abolishing the category of 'extraordinary item'. Auditors also have a part to play in identifying dishonest estimates. The other is to prescribe 'consistency' so that if a company chooses an accounting policy that suits it in one year it must continue to apply it in subsequent years when it may not suit so well.

(3)   Artificial transactions can be tackled by invoking the concept of 'substance over form', whereby the economic substance rather than the legal form of transactions determines their accounting substance. Thus linked transactions would be accounted for as one whole.

(4)   The timing of genuine transactions is clearly a matter for the discretion of management. However, the scope to use this can be limited by requiring regular revaluations of items in the accounts so that gains or losses on value changes are identified in the accounts each year as they occur, rather than only appearing in total in the year that a disposal occurs. It is interesting to observe that, in their recent draft conceptual framework, the ASB have stated a wish to move towards increased use of revaluations rather than historic cost in the accounts.

We have seen above that creative accounting is seen as a particular feature of the Anglo-Saxon approach to accounting, with its scope for flexibility and judgement, rather than the continental European model, with its tradition of detailed prescription. However, as we show in Table 2.1, each of the two approaches offers greater support for the control of creative accounting in some respects and conversely, therefore, greater opportunity to engage in creative accounting in others. The more prescriptive and inflexible approach of the continental European model makes it easier to reduce the scope for abuse of choice of accounting policy and manipulation of accounting estimates. The less legal orientation of the Anglo-Saxon model is more conducive to the use of substance over form and revaluation.

REASONS FOR CREATIVE ACCOUNTING

Discussions of creative accounting have focused mainly on the impact on decision of investors in the stock market. Reasons for the directors of listed companies to seek to manipulate the accounts are as follows.

(1) Income smoothing. Companies generally prefer to report a steady trend of growth in profit rather than to show volatile profits with a series of dramatic rises and falls. This is achieved by making unnecessarily high provisions for liabilities and against asset values in good years so that these provisions can be reduced, thereby improving reported profits, in bad years. Advocates of this approach argue that it is a measure against the 'short-termism' of judging an investment on the basis of the yields achieved in the immediate following years. It also avoids raising expectations so high in good years that the company is unable to deliver what is required subsequently. Against this is argued that:

- if the trading conditions of a business are in fact volatile then investors have a right to know this;
- income smoothing may conceal long-term changes in the profit trend.

Table 2.1 Opportunities for creative accounting

Opportunity for creative accounting	Solution available to accounting regulator	Accounting tradition where solution is most easily applied
Choice of accounting method	Reduce permitted choice	Continental European
Bias estimates and prediction	Reduce scope for estimate	Continental European
Enter into artificial transaction	Substance over form	Anglo-Saxon
Timing of genuine transactions	Prescribe revaluation	Anglo-Saxon

This type of creative accounting is not special to the UK. In countries with highly conservative accounting systems the 'income smoothing' effect can be particularly pronounced because of the high level of provisions that accumulate. Blake *et al.* (1995) discuss a German example. Another bias that sometimes arises is called 'big bath' accounting, where a company making a bad loss seeks to maximise the reported loss in that year so that future years will appear better.

(2)   A variant on income smoothing is to manipulate profit to tie in to forecasts. Fox (1997) reports on how accounting policies at Microsoft are designed, within the normal accounting rules, to match reported earnings to profit forecasts. When Microsoft sell software a large part of the profit is deferred to future years to cover potential upgrade and customer support costs. This perfectly respectable, and highly conservative, accounting policy means that future earnings are easy to predict.

(3)   Company directors may keep an income-boosting accounting policy change in hand to distract attention from unwelcome news. Collingwood (1991) reports on how a change in accounting method boosted K-Mart's quarterly profit figure by some $160 million, by a happy coincidence distracting attention from the company slipping back from being the largest retailer in the USA to the number two slot.

(4)   Creative accounting may help maintain or boost the share price both by reducing the apparent levels of borrowing, so making the company appear subject to less risk, and by creating the appearance of a good profit trend. This helps the company to raise capital from new share issues, offer their own shares in takeover bids, and resist takeover by other companies.

(5)   If the directors engage in 'insider dealing' in their company's shares they can use creative accounting to delay the release of information for the market, thereby enhancing their opportunity to benefit from inside knowledge.

It should be noted that, in an efficient market, analysts will not be fooled by cosmetic accounting charges. Indeed, the alert analyst will see income-boosting accounting changes as a possible indicator of weakness. Dharan and Lev (1993) report on a study showing poor share price performance in the years following income-increasing accounting changes. Another set of reasons for creative accounting, which applies to all companies, arises because companies are subject to various forms of contractual rights, obligations and constraints based on the amounts reported in the accounts. Examples of such contractual issues are as follows.

Example 1 It is common for loan agreements to include a restriction on the total amount that a company is entitled to borrow computed as a multiple of the total share capital and reserves. Where a company has borrowings that are near this limit there is an incentive to:

* choose accounting methods that increase reported profit and consequently the reserves (Sweeney (1994) reports that companies nearing violation of debt covenants are two to three times more likely to make income increasing accounting policy changes than other companies);
* arrange finance in a way that will not be reflected as a liability on the balance sheet.

An accounting rule change can plunge a company into difficulties with loan agreements. Thus in the USA, when the FASB introduced a rule requiring that income from extended warranties must be allocated over the life of the warranty rather than being recognised at the time of sale, consumer electronics retailers were badly hit:

> The biggest problem could be with the banks that keeps a close eye on debt to equity ratios . . . so stores that borrowed heavily to build inventory and finance expansion could end up in technical violation of bank lending agreements pegged to certain ratios.
>
> (Therrien 1991: 42)

Example 2 Some companies, such as public utilities like electricity and telephone companies, are subject to the authority of a government regulator who prescribes the maximum amounts they can charge. If such companies report high profits then the regulator is likely to respond by curbing prices. These companies, therefore, have an interest in choosing accounting methods that tend to reduce their reported profits.

Example 3 A directors' bonus scheme may be linked to profits or to the company share price. Where the link is to the share price then clearly the directors will be motivated to present accounts that will impress the stock market. Where a bonus is based on reported profit the scheme often stipulates that the bonus is a percentage of profit above a minimum level, and is paid up to a maximum level. Thus:

1 If the profit figure is between the two levels then directors will choose accounting methods that lift profit towards the maximum.
2 If the profit is below the minimum level directors will choose accounting methods that maximise provisions made so that in future years these provisions can be written back to boost profit.
3 Similarly if the profit is above the maximum level directors will seek to bring the figure down to that level so that the profit can be boosted in later years.

The timing of the announcement of gains and losses can have a major impact on bonuses. In January 1991 Westinghouse announced unaudited record earnings of $1 billion and related hefty bonuses; in February 1991 bad debt write-offs of $975 million were announced, putting the legitimacy of bonuses in question (Schroeder and Spiro 1992).

Example 4 Where a part or division of a business is subject to a profit-sharing arrangement then this may affect the preferred accounting methods. In the UK, for example, we know of a local council that had a contract with a company for the company to manage the council's leisure centre. The contract provided for profits to be shared equally between the two parties. At the end of one year, not surprisingly the company's accountants said the centre had made a loss and the council's accountants said it had made a profit. The problem was solved by an agreement for the company to pay a fixed amount of money each year instead of a profit share. In the USA film companies have been notorious for claiming massive expenses against successful films so that writers, producers, and actors on 'net profit' deals receive little or no remuneration (Grover 1991a).

Example 5 Taxation may also be a factor in creative accounting in those circumstances where taxable income is measured by relation to the accounting figures.

Example 6 When a new manager takes over responsibility for a

31

unit there is a motivation to make provisions that ensure that any losses appear as the responsibility of the previous manager. Dahl (1996) reports on a survey of US bank managers that found provisions for loan losses tended to be higher in the year of change in manager.

THE ETHICAL PERSPECTIVE

Revsine (1991) offers a discussion of the 'selective financial misrepresentation hypothesis' which can be seen as offering some defence for the practice of 'creative accounting', at least in the private sector, drawing heavily on the literature on agency theory and positive accounting theory. He considers the problem in relation to both managers and shareholders and argues that each can draw benefits from 'loose' accounting standards that provide managers with latitude in timing the reporting of income.

Revsine discusses the benefits to managers in being able to manipulate income between years so as to maximise their bonus entitlements, as discussed above. He argues that:

> It is reasonable to presume that those who negotiate managers' employment contracts anticipate such opportunistic behaviour and reduce the compensation package accordingly . . . since they (managers) have already been 'charged' for the opportunistic actions they must now engage in them in order to achieve the benefits they 'paid' for.
>
> (1991: 18)

Shareholders also benefit from the fact that managers can manipulate reported earnings to 'smooth' income since this may decrease the apparent volatility of earnings and so increase the value of their shares. Other management action, such as avoiding default on loan agreements, can also benefit shareholders.

At the heart of Revsine's analysis are the implicit views that:

- the prime role of accounting is as a mechanism for monitoring contracts between managers and other groups providing finance;
- market mechanisms will operate efficiently, identifying the prospect of accounting manipulation and reflecting this appropriately in pricing and contracting decisions.

On this basis he argues for freezing all existing accounting standards in the private sector, to be used as 'the basis for all future contracting and reporting'. Instead future FASB work should be applied to the public sector, including institutions such as the savings and loans where publicly funded guarantees underpin their activity. This focus is necessary because 'market discipline is muted in the public sector and perpetrators of financial misrepresentations confront fewer obstacles' (24–5).

In Chapter 1, the literature on the ethics of bias in accounting policy choice is reviewed at the 'macro' level of the accounting regulator. This literature can similarly be applied to the bias in accounting policy choice at the 'micro' level of the management of individual companies that is implicit in creative accounting. If we consider the position taken by Ruland (1984) and compare it to Revsine's analysis, we note the following.

(1)   Ruland distinguishes between the deontological view whereby moral rules apply to actual actions and the teleological view that an action should be judged on the basis of the moral worth of the outcome. Revsine appears to take a teleological view of accounting in the private sector, allowing managers to choose between the alternatives permitted in 'loose' standards to achieve their desired end, but to take a deontological view of accounting in the public sector where he calls for tighter standards to prevent such manipulation. We might ask whether the presence or absence of market discipline justifies such ethical inconsistency.

(2)   Ruland also discusses the distinction between a 'positive' responsibility, which here would be the duty to present unbiased accounts, and a 'negative' responsibility where managers would be responsible for states of affairs they fail to prevent. As we have seen, Ruland gives priority to the 'positive'. Within Revsine's framework, where all outcomes are deemed to be impounded in the process of contracting and price-setting, the distinction is not acknowledged.

(3)   The 'duty to refrain' would imply avoiding the bias inherent in creative accounting while the 'duty to act' would involve pursuing the consequences to be achieved by creative accounting. If we take the three issues where Ruland sees the 'duty to refrain' as the more important:

(a) Relentlessness and
(b) Certainty of outcome: Revsine's arguments, as we have seen, apply to a limited role for accounting as a primarily contract monitoring exercise.
(c) Responsibility: Revsine seems to see compliance with GAAP as

33

the prime responsibility, with no constraint on choice within GAAP. This may be a legitimate approach in the USA, but in a jurisdiction that prescribes an overriding qualitative objective for accounts, such as the European Union with 'true and fair view', Revsine's approach is less defensible.

To the professional accountant creative accounting generally seems to be regarded as ethically dubious. In the USA the then senior partner of Price Waterhouse observed:

> When fraudulent reporting occurs, it frequently is perpetrated at levels of management above those for which internal control systems are designed to be effective. It often involves using the financial statements to create an illusion that the entity is healthier and more prosperous than it actually is. This illusion sometimes is accomplished by masking economic realities through intentional misapplication of accounting principles.
>
> (Conner 1986: 78)

Note the term 'fraudulent' used here to describe creative accounting. In Australia Leung and Cooper (1995) found that in a survey of 1500 accountants the three ethical problems cited most frequently were as shown in Table 2.2.

It is striking that the creative accounting issue ranks above tax evasion as an ethical issue for Australian practitioners. Two surveys of attitudes to creative accounting in the USA both highlight a difference in accountants' attitudes to creative accounting depending on whether it arises from abuse of accounting rules or from the manipulation of transactions. Fischer and Rosenzweig (1995) found that accounting and MBA students were more critical than accounting practitioners of manipulated transactions, whereas accounting practitioners were more critical than students of abuse of accounting rules. Merchant and Rockness (1994) similarly found that, when presented with scenarios of creative accounting, accoun-

Table 2.2 Three most frequently cited ethical problems

	% of respondents
Conflict of interest	51.9
Client proposal to manipulate accounts	50.1
Client proposals for tax evasion	46.8

Source: Leung and Cooper (1995)

tants were more critical of abuse of accounting rules than of manipulation of transactions. Fischer and Rosenzweig offer two possible explanations for accountants' attitudes:

1 Accountants may take a rule-based approach to ethics, rather than basing judgement on the impact on users of the accounts.
2 Accountants may see abuse of accounting rules as falling within their domain, and therefore demanding their ethical judgement, while the manipulation of transactions falls within the domain of management and so is not subject to the same ethical code.

Merchant and Rockness also found a difference in accountants' attitudes to creative accounting depending on the motivation of management. Creative accounting based on explicit motives of self-interest attracted more disapproval than where the motivation was to promote the company.

An accountant, or other manager, who takes a stand against creative accounting faces the same pressures as any other whistle-blower. In extreme cases failure to act could ruin a reputation. As one company accountant who took a firm stand put it: 'It cost me my job, but I don't think I would have gotten another job had I been unethical' (quoted by Baldo 1995).

Schilit (1993) reports the case of one company accountant confronted with such an issue. His employer, a food wholesaler, incurred substantial costs in paying retailers to put new lines on their shelves. This is a common practice, known as 'slotting', and the costs are commonly written off in the year they are incurred. In order to keep within accounting ratios under loan agreements the company president proposed to capitalise the slotting costs and amortise them over ten years. The accountant:

1 Undertook some research on other company practices, and as a result was confirmed in the view that this was not an acceptable accounting treatment.
2 Identified cost savings that would have just kept the company inside its loan agreement.
3 Alerted the auditors to the issue, hoping 'that they would play the role of bad cop and force the company to expense the 'slotting'.

The principal investor in the company tried, unsuccessfully, to put pressure on the auditor to support the capitalisation of the slotting costs. Shortly after the accountant was sacked for taking this stand. The series of actions in this case are revealing:

1 Check that the proposed accounting method is in fact unacceptable. As Hamilton advises:

> First, try to verify your suspicions about what you think is wrong. Some accounting practices that are legal under new laws may look suspect to a non accountant. . . . If you blow the whistle on something that's not illegal, you're really bare and perhaps even vulnerable to defamation claims.
>
> (1991: 138–9)

2 Search for alternative legitimate ways to achieve the desired end and offer these as an alternative approach to management.
3 In the last resort, report the abuse to the appropriate monitor.

IS THERE A SOLUTION?

Questionnaire surveys of auditors' views on creative accounting have been conducted in the UK (Naser 1993) and Spain (Amat and Blake 1996). Table 2.3 shows a substantial minority of auditors in each country taking a tolerant view of creative accounting. In Spain there seems to be more optimism on prospects for resolving the problem. Given that Spain has only had a comprehensive set of rules for auditing and financial reporting since 1990, this may reflect inexperience of the problems. A survey of Spanish attitudes to accounting and auditing reports that they 'appear quite innocent' (Garcia Benau and Humphrey 1992: 313).

New Zealand has acquired, during the 1990s, an accounting regulatory system designed to strengthen accounting standards. In 1974 the New Zealand Society of Accountants (NZSA), now the

Table 2.3 Summary of results of surveys of auditors' attitudes to creative accounting

Agreement with the proposition:	UK%	Spain%
The use of creative accounting is a legitimate business tool	36	31
Creative accounting is a problem that can never be solved	91	38

Source: Taken from Naser (1993) and Amat and Blake (1996)

Institute of Chartered Accountants of New Zealand (ICANZ), started to issue accounting standards which were binding on its members. In 1987 the stock market crash saw the demise of several large and many smaller firms listed on the New Zealand Stock Exchange; in the aftermath the need for a new company and accounting regulatory regime was seen, leading to the Financial Reporting Act and the new Companies Act, both in 1993 (Rahman and Perera 1997: 135–6). The New Zealand Society of Accountants continues to set Financial Reporting Standards (FRSs). These must be submitted for approval to the Accounting Standards Review Board (ASRB), a body appointed by the government. The basic accounting requirement is that accounts should comply with 'Generally Accepted Accounting Practice' (GAAP). Accounts comply with GAAP:

1 When they comply with applicable Financial Reporting Standards.
2 When a matter is not dealt with in an applicable Financial Reporting Standard, they follow accounting policies which:

• are appropriate to the circumstances of the entity; and
• have authoritative support within the New Zealand accounting profession. (See Simpkins 1994.)

The registrar of companies is charged with enforcement of the Act. Noncompliance can render directors liable for fines of up to NZ$100,000. Emery (1994) sees adequate resourcing of the registrar in this role as an essential condition for the smooth running of the new system.

To investigate the impact of this new system on creative accounting we approached both the 'Big Six' firms and those firms with more than four partners having an international association in each of Auckland, Christchurch and Wellington. We undertook fifteen interviews, ten with Big Six and five with other firms.

Table 2.4 shows an almost unanimous view that creative accounting is not now a significant problem in New Zealand, and Table 2.5 shows a similar consensus that there has been a reduction in its practice. Responses to the question of why it was thought that there had been a reduction are shown in Table 2.6.

We have analysed the responses by dividing them into two parts:

1 Reasons brought about by the profession or government. The main factors here is the new regulatory framework, but the

profession's own actions in improving technical standards is also seen as a factor.
2 Directors' own responses, both with concern to litigation risk and to becoming aware that users have 'got wise' to creative accounting.

Both the interviewees who saw some revival in creative accounting were concerned that the lessons of 1987 crash were being forgotten.

Table 2.4 Is creative accounting a significant problem in New Zealand?

		%
YES	1	7
NO	14	93
	15	100

Table 2.5 Is creative accounting becoming more or less common in New Zealand?

		%
Much reduced	11	73
Some reduction	1	7
Unchanged	1	7
Much reduced from past but now slight revival	2	13
	15	100

Table 2.6 Reasons put forward to explain a reduction in creative accounting

The new structure of financial regulation	5	
Use of 'Generally Accepted Accounting Practice' as term	1	
The setting up of technical departments by the big audit firms	1	
New Zealand as a small country, where informal contacts avoid 'opinion shopping'	1	
		8
Directors' response to the stock exchange crash	2	
Directors more sophisticated	1	
Directors more ethical	1	
Users more knowledgeable	1	
No need in a strong economy	1	
		6
		14

CONCLUSION

Creative accounting offers a formidable challenge to the accounting profession. The problem is an international one, with accounting policy choice being a particular problem in the Anglo-American tradition and transaction manipulation a particular problem in the continental European tradition. There is a wide variety of motivations for managers to engage in creative accounting. The justification for creative accounting put forward in the 'positive accounting theory' tradition is:

- In conflict with mainstream thinking on ethics.
- Particularly relevant to the USA, where there is a well-developed stock market and a focus on detailed accounting regulation rather than broad principles, and is considerably less relevant in other countries.

Accountants who accept the ethical challenge that creative accounting raises need to be aware of the scope for both abuse of accounting policy choice and manipulation of transactions.

New Zealand offers an example of a country where a well-designed framework of accounting regulation has curbed creative accounting. However, our interviews raised some concerns as to whether this situation will last.

REFERENCES

Amat, O. and Blake, J. (1996) *Contabilidad Creativa*, Barcelona: Gestion 2000.

Baldo, A. (1995) 'What's right? What's wrong?', *Treasury and Risk Management*, November.

Blake, J., Amat, O., Martinez, D. and Garcia Palau, E. (1995) 'The continuing problem of international accounting diversity', *Company Accountant*, April: 23–5

Collingwood, H. (1991) 'Why K-Mart's good news isn't', *Business Week*, March 18: 40.

Conner, J.E. (1986) 'Enhancing public confidence in the accounting profession', *Journal of Accountancy*, July: 76–83.

Dahl, D. (1996) 'Managerial turnover and successor accounting discretion: bank loan loss provisions after resignation, retirement, or death', *Research in Accounting Regulation*, 10: 95–110.

Dharan, B. and Lev, B. (1993) 'The valuation consequence of accounting charges: a multi-year examination', *Journal of Accounting Auditing and Finance*, 8 (4): 475–94.

Emery, M. (1994) 'New Zealand's new structure – an international comparison', *Accountants' Journal*, 73 (2): 65–8.

Fischer, M. and Rosenzweig, K. (1995) 'Attitudes of students and accounting practitioners concerning the ethical acceptability of earnings management', *Journal of Business Ethics*, 14: 433–44.

Fox, J. (1997) 'Learn to play the Earnings Game', *Fortune*, 31 July.

Garcia Benau, M.A. and Humphrey, C. (1992) 'Beyond the audit expectations gap: learning from the experiences of Britain and Spain', *European Accounting Review*, 1: 303–31.

Griffiths, I. (1986) *Creative Accounting*, London: Sidgwick & Jackson.

Grover, R. (1991a) 'Curtains for tinsel town accounting?', *Business Week*, 14 January: 35.

—— (1991b) 'Dances with debts: why Orion is reeling', *Business Week*, 12 August: 56.

Hamilton, J. (1991) 'Blowing the whistle without paying the piper', *Business Week*, 3 June: 138.

Jameson, M. (1988) *Practical Guide to Creative Accounting*, London: Kogan Page.

Leung, P. and Cooper, B.J. (1995) 'Ethical dilemmas in accountancy practice', *Australian Accountant*, May: 28–33.

Merchant, K.A. and Rockness, J. (1994) 'The ethics of managing earnings: an empirical investigation', *Journal of Accounting and Public Policy*, 13: 79–94.

Naser, K. (1993) *Creative Financial Accounting: Its Nature and Use*, Hemel Hempstead: Prentice Hall.

Rahman, A.R. and Perera, M.H.B. (1997) 'Accounting and its environment in New Zealand', in N. Baydoun, A. Nishimura, and R. Willet, *Accounting in the Asia-Pacific Region*, Singapore: John Wiley (Asia), 127–57.

Revsine, L. (1991) 'The selective financial misrepresentation hypothesis', *Accounting Horizons*, December: 16–27.

Ruland, R.G. (1984) 'Duty, obligation and responsibility in accounting policy making', *Journal of Accounting and Public Policy*, Fall: 223–37.

Schilit, H.M. (1997) 'Is it fraud or just slick accounting?', *CFO Magazine*, August.

Schroeder, M. and Spiro, L.N. (1992) 'Does everything add up at Westinghouse Credit?', *Business Week*, 11 May: 80–3.

Simpkins, K. (1994) 'Financial Reporting Act 1993: key requirements', *Accountants' Journal*, 73 (3): 15–19.

Smith, T. (1992) *Accounting for Growth*, London: Century Business.

Sweeney, A.P. (1994) 'Debt covenant violations and managers' accounting responses', *Journal of Accounting and Economics*, 17: 281–308.

Therrien, L. (1991) 'Electronics stores get a cruel shock', *Business Week*, 14 January: 42.

3

THE ACCOUNTANT AS WHISTLEBLOWER

Susan Richardson and Bill Richardson

INTRODUCTION

In this chapter we explore the concept of 'accountant as whistle-blower'. Our particular focus will be on the opportunities available to accountants working within organisations to observe and report on management malpractices at the highest level. In our view this is an important and underdeveloped aspect of the whistleblowing debate. We suggest that accountants working within organisations occupy special positions that privilege them to the sort of information which has the potentiality to reveal deviant top management behaviour and thus, as a corollary to this statement, it follows that accountants privy to such revelations have the potentiality to 'blow the whistle'.

Deviant top management behaviour can induce huge economic, social and emotional costs for innocent stakeholders and the corporate failures of the last decade have provided examples of this on a grand scale (for instance, the crash of the Robert Maxwell empire and the fall of Asil Nadir's Polly Peck organisation). Contributions from the academic literature in this area also offer examples of deviant top management behaviour and potential whistleblowing situations (for instance, Barton 1995; Dearlove 1994; Kets de Vries *et al.* 1990; Kets de Vries 1993; Lovell and Robertson 1994; Richardson 1993; Richardson *et al.* 1994; Richardson *et al.* 1996; Van Luijk 1994).

Thus, where deviant behaviour is exhibited by top management, and accountants within the organisation are in a position to identify this, then it must be in the public interest for accountants to 'blow the whistle'. If this is the case, then the guidelines for potential whistleblower accountants, set down by the professional accounting bodies, should reflect and support this important potentiality.

Unfortunately, this is not the case. The ethical guidelines of the professional bodies offer little support to latent whistleblowers, particularly those who are concerned about top management behaviour. The expectation, generally, is that top management are the responsible resolvers of ethical issues, rather than the culprit creators of them. For instance, De George (1986) captures this implicit expectation within his three conditions for whistleblowing when he suggests that the employee should exhaust internal procedures and possibilities and that this will usually involve taking the matter up the managerial ladder to the board of directors if necessary and if possible. The Chartered Institute of Management Accountants (CIMA) guidelines do acknowledge the possibility of top management acting in unhelpful ways (to potential whistleblowers) but do not provide much helpful guidance for such situations. They advise that where ethical conflict exists and cannot be resolved internally, the accountant should resign from the company and remain silent on company issues, unless obliged by law to discuss them (Cashmore 1994).

Thus, little help is provided for accountants who find themselves in situations where it is top management behaviour that is unethical and/or illegal, since it is unlikely that ethical conflict will be resolved internally. It seems, therefore, that as things stand, many latent whistleblowing accountants will choose to leave their organisations in preference to whistleblowing. As a consequence of this latency, this silent acquiescence, these accountants are likely to suffer emotional and financial pressures, and deviant managers are allowed to remain *in situ*, their behaviour goes unchallenged and the emotional, social and economic costs which flow from their behaviour continue unchallenged until the point of bankruptcy. In turn, this means that what society perceives, might only be the tip of the iceberg of a problem involving the improper use of organisations by top management.

Nevertheless, for the would-be whistleblower accountant, this strategy may be the safest way out of an extremely frustrating and painful work setting, since there is much evidence to suggest that whistleblowers can generally expect to gain nothing from revealing deviant behaviour. Indeed, according to research undertaken in the United States of America (Soeken and Soeken 1987; Jos *et al.* 1989), whistleblowers can expect retaliation and overwhelming personal and professional hardship as a result of their whistleblowing acts (see also Barton 1994; Dearlove 1994). The words of whistleblower, Maureen Plantagenet, pharmaceutical sales representative, confirm this view: 'I don't think people know what you go through beforehand, but I can understand why there are so few whistleblowers. It's much easier for people just to get out ... ' (quoted in Winfield 1994: 32).

Similarly, Dr Chris Chapman, who blew the whistle on scientific fraud and was shortly afterwards made redundant by his employers, comments that he would think twice about blowing the whistle again, since

> This has taken eight years out of my life. I think it would be very irresponsible to put one's family through that again. You can talk about having a principle, but there is also the money, the stress and the effect on your family. It's just too high a price to pay.
>
> (*Yorkshire Post* 19 February 1997: 3)

(Although Dr Chapman alleged that he was forced out of his job for blowing the whistle, a three-year in-depth inquiry cleared the employer of any conspiracy against Dr Chapman, while at the same time criticising their handling of the affair.)

And Charles Robertson, a former tax accountant who blew the whistle to the Inland Revenue regarding his suspicions of irregularities and was dismissed, describes what it was like for him:

> When I was dismissed the bottom fell out of my world really. I remember it was a lovely weekend, I sat on a lounger in the garden feeling that I had thrown my career away. And I had. . . . It's no good talking about active citizens. You can't have active citizens until you provide the back up for them. Active citizens are left to drown really.
>
> (quoted in Winfield 1994: 32)

The problem seems to be embedded in the paradox of the whistleblower's situation. For some, whistleblowing is an act of subversion, for others it is an act of citizenship (Stonefrost 1990; Vinten 1994). Indeed, the eminent management theorist Peter Drucker (1981) considers whistleblowing to be simply another word for 'informing'. For him, it is impossible to nurture mutual trust, interdependencies and ethics within organisations where whistleblowing is condoned. From this viewpoint, whistleblowing is, therefore, seen as an act of disloyalty. However, this has been criticised as an oversimplistic viewpoint (for instance, Westin 1981), since this implies that silent loyalty to the employer overrides any individual's sense of moral or social duty.

From some perspectives whistleblowers are seen as 'grudge bearers' seeking revenge. Jackson (1992) suggests that whistleblowers cannot avoid criticisms of their act of whistleblowing: if they blow the whistle to outsiders, without first following the recommended internal procedures, they are likely to be branded 'irresponsible'; and if they follow the rules and raise their concerns internally without success, then their ultimate external whistleblowing act is likely to be seen as 'malicious'.

In contrast, supporters of whistleblowing as an act of citizenship are active in attempting to create an environment conducive to employees revealing malpractices by their employers. The report from the Commission on Citizenship (Stonefrost 1990), entitled 'Encouraging Citizenship', suggested the possibility of honouring whistleblowers in the British honours system and a recently created organisation, Public Concern at Work, has set up a 'hotline' for employees who want to 'blow the whistle'. This organisation offers free and confidential legal advice to anyone worried by malpractices at work but who fears being victimised if they complain to their boss. Sir Gordon Borrie, chairman of the organisation, has suggested:

Time and again official inquiries into scandals, disasters and tragedies show they could have been avoided if employees had spoken up in time, or if those in charge had addressed the concerns of staff when they were raised.

(*Yorkshire Post*, 15 October 1993)

In addition, protection for whistleblowers has been sought through legislation via the Public Interest Disclosure Bill, a Private Members' Bill introduced by Don Touhig, Labour MP for Islwyn. Unfortunately, although it was intimated that support for the Bill was high from all parties, the bill ran out of time.

A further problem lies in the lack of a general understanding of what we mean by 'whistleblowing'. Gerald Vinten provides a useful working definition:

The unauthorized disclosure of information that an employee reasonably believes is evidence of the contravention of any law, rule or regulation, code of practice, or professional statement, or that involves mis-management, corruption, abuse of authority, or danger to public or worker health or safety.

(1994: 5)

This provides a broad definition of the act of whistleblowing. However, in reality, employees may find it difficult to assess the extent to which malpractices or deviant behaviour exists. They may not be absolutely sure of the law or accepted practice regarding an issue and, often because of the confidentiality of the information they hold, they are unable to discuss their worries and confirm their suspicions. In addition, they may not know the appropriate procedure for the act of whistleblowing, either internally or externally, or who to whistleblow to. The whistleblowers' 'hotline' goes some way to providing a safe environment in which to check things out. Additionally, and possibly as a result of growing public awareness on the issue of whistleblowing, growing numbers of organisations are setting up their own guidelines for employees who wish to express concerns about the organisation's working practices.

The position of the would-be whistleblower accountant within an organisation is further complicated by conflict between confidentiality on the one hand and the public interest on the other, particularly where it is top management's (the employer's) behaviour that is being challenged. In order for accountants to maintain an acceptable level of professional conduct, they should not be silent on issues of malpractice, because to be silent might suggest condonement and thus implication in the malpractice. However, by raising the issue of malpractice with top management, accountants place themselves in a potential no-win situation if top management refuse to amend their behaviour. They can either resign from the organisation (the route recommended by the professional accounting bodies) or blow the whistle to some external body (and risk the repercussions of losing their job and facing ostracism from the professional bodies and society at large), or accountants can remain with the organisation with the fear of implication when the malpractice is eventually revealed (for instance, accountant employees of the high profile Polly Peck and Robert Maxwell empires, which collapsed under accusations of gross mismanagement, have been summoned to account for their actions). Even when top management purport to amend their behaviour, they may resort to tactics of deceit and cover-up and seek to marginalise the accountant's role in the organisation. Of course, this decision may

45

be taken out of their hands. They may be sacked by top management for raising the issue.

Thus, the issue of accountants acting as whistleblowers is an extremely complex one, involving economic, social and emotional conflicts at a personal and professional level. These conflicts are difficult to grasp at a conceptual level and so in the next section of this chapter we provide a case study that may assist the reader to untangle some of the complexity and to understand the problematic nature of this whistleblowing issue.

What follows is a case study, based on the real life experiences of an accountant working in a small company. Our aim in presenting this case study is to illustrate: first, that accountants in organisations, by the nature of their roles as creators of management control systems and as management controllers, are in privileged positions to uncover deviant behaviour by top management; second, the emotional, social and economic costs imposed upon those who are associated with organisations run by deviant top managers; third, the decisional quandries which the accountant is likely to face in such a context; and fourth, the alternatives that the accountant perceived were available to her and the pressures which existed to influence her ultimate choice of action. By presenting this insight into one accountant's experiences, we hope to provide support for others currently in similar positions and/or those unfortunate enough to find themselves likewise in the future.

MIS LIMITED: A CASE STUDY BASED ON ETHNOGRAPHIC RESEARCH

The company

MIS Limited was a small company with a turnover of £2.5 million. It was owned and managed by a sole director, Philip. Its employees worked on clients' sites around the world and the head office and administration centre was run by a very small staff from offices in the north midlands. Its main source of borrowing was that of a bank overdraft facility and during its comparatively short life the company experienced a constant liquidity problem, the major cause of which was Philip's personal drawings from the company. This cash shortage resulted in Philip finding it necessary to seek an increase in the company's overdraft facility from the company's banker. A new manager, who had recently been assigned to deal with the company's account, was more amenable to Philip's request than the previous manager had been. Consequently, an increase in the facility was agreed and the overdraft limit was raised from £30,000 to £100,000, conditional upon the provision of additional security. A further prerequisite to granting this increase was that more timely and regular management information be forwarded to the bank. Philip subsequently felt the need to recruit an internal management accountant rather than continue to use the external accountant who, at that time, visited the company one day each month to prepare management accounts.

The new management accountant was introduced into the company and began to set up management information systems. The information which these new systems produced highlighted the poor quality of decisions made by Philip on pricing and rate-setting, by focusing on their adverse impacts on profitability and liquidity. The introduction of cash flow forecasts and tighter control over cash flows also highlighted the impact of Philip's continual cash drawings from, and spending of, company funds for personal use. The introduction of the new management accountant thus stimulated a process of change within the company which also included the introduction of new personnel and the departure of some existing employees. These change processes instigated by the management accountant were aimed at creating a new organisa-tional climate more geared towards rational-economic objectives. The new systems and economically oriented organisational climate put pressure upon Philip to act in conformance with more economic organisational objectives. However, Philip resisted this pressure and continued to pursue his own preferred objectives of personal gratifi-cation, to the detriment of the company. Some examples of this behaviour included expensive holidays abroad charged to the company, purchases of high quality clothing, expensive meals and lavish gifts for his girlfriend charged to the company credit card, and transfers of company funds to his personal bank account to cover personal debts that he had incurred.

Eventually, after the company overdraft facility had consistently been breached, the bank intervened and declared that it would reduce the existing facility by £5,000 per month indefinitely and would not tolerate any breach of this new arrangement. This intro-duced an external controlling influence which was much more powerful than the accountant had been able to muster from her position inside the organisation. Together with the impact of the newly instituted control systems and the ongoing efforts of the accountant, Philip's spending habits were kept in check. He was forced into making more rational-economic decisions. This led to greater profitability for the company. After four months, during which time the overdraft limit had been reduced successfully from £100,000 to £80,000, the company was, albeit with some difficulty and careful cash flow management, still maintaining the bank balance below the agreed limit. At this point the bank reviewed the situation and decided to maintain the facility at £80,000 rather than to continue the policy of £5,000 per month reductions. Initially it maintained its close monitoring of the situation but, as the company became clearly more profitable and the cash situation eased as a consequence, the bank began to relax its close control over the company. As the bank withdrew its powerful influence, Philip began his personal spending again and soon pushed the bank balance back up to its limit, eventually breaching it.

As Philip continued to use company money to fund his personal lifestyle, his debt to the company grew and he ran out of personal resources to introduce into the company to cover the loan which had accumulated to it (for instance, he had already introduced his holiday villa in the South of France on to the company balance sheet under the pretence that it would be rented out to earn income for the company). He was personally 'up to his neck' in debt, the company had been bled dry of all its cash resources, employees, creditors and government bodies were clamouring for payment, and clients were losing faith in the company's ability to perform.

A crisis was precipitated following Philip's decision to buy a new house costing over £200,000 (purporting to be the 'southern office', and which was located within a mile of his girlfriend's mother's home). Company funds of over £40,000 financed the necessary deposit, refurbishments and furniture, and the company was charged 'rent' for the 'southern office', which covered Philip's mortgage repayments. This, coupled with the fact that his spending activities had already created a major liquidity problem, meant that the company could not pay its VAT commitments and Customs and Excise officials threatened to wind up the company. Creditors began to get anxious and clients began to move their business elsewhere. The company became the subject of official investigations and subsequently failed.

Philip

Philip was originally in business with two of his brothers. However, (it is said) the brothers were unhappy with Philip's approach to spending the company's money. He spent it as though it were his own. The brothers pressed for the company to be split into three parts, each brother taking one part and commencing to trade separately. Thus, Philip became sole director and owner of MIS Limited. He had never been married but had enjoyed the company of a number of girlfriends – many of whom were employed by his company and all of whom were much younger than himself. These girlfriends occupied much of his attention and the company funds were often called upon to provide holidays, gifts, meals, accommodation, transport and entertainment of a very high standard (and cost) in order to impress them. He did not seem to be particularly interested in working hard for his living but much preferred the life of a playboy. Consequently, he was often absent from the organisation pursuing pleasurable activities instead of dealing with pressing organisational matters. His mood swings at work led to moments of generosity with his employees. For instance, he would suddenly invite his office staff to a lavish lunch (paid for by the company) which lasted late into the afternoon. More generally, however, he was very peevish in his attitude towards them and seemed, for instance, to resent anyone (except himself) taking holidays. He was openly hostile to those who questioned the reckless attitude they perceived him to exhibit in his approach to the financial affairs of the business. The extravagant lifestyle he pursued was always funded by the company's bank account.

The new accountant

The new accountant had been optimistic when she had taken the job at MIS. At the interview Philip had been charming and she had perceived her role to have been one of helping Philip to gain better control of his business and a more professional approach to its management. She had been unprepared for the reality of her role – that of attempting to control Philip's behaviour and, effectively, acting as a relatively powerless surrogate organisational leader. The unrelenting liquidity problem was a major stress creator for the accountant. Under such conditions, much of her time was spent in scheduling payments to minimise adverse responses from irate creditors and clients and in taking steps to ensure payments were received by the company as quickly as possible. Additionally, she had to maintain contact with the bank on a daily (and sometimes hourly) basis when the situation was particularly critical. However, these tasks were made more difficult for the accountant because of her understanding that Philip's behaviour was the main cause of the company's liquidity problem. Each day she was faced with the additional dilemma of whether or not to maintain the cover-up in which she felt entangled. Life became a series of difficult, ethic-laden decisional quandries. For example:

- What should she tell the bank when it asks for reasons why the overdraft limit has been breached? Should she say it is because the owner has decided to refurbish his home at the company's expense?
- What should she say to the Inland Revenue when attempting to negotiate an extension of time to pay monthly contributions? Should she say it is because Philip has used the company credit card for personal items such as holiday accommodation, nightclubs, clothing and expensive meals and the company has to find an unexpected £5,000 to cover this?
- What should she tell a building society manager when he asks for a reference for a company employee seeking a mortgage? Should she tell him that the company is likely to fail and that the long-term prospects for the employee are grim?
- What reason should she give to clients when she is asking if they will pay the company early? Should she tell them it is because the owner has just withdrawn £20,000 to repay a personal debt and the company is now unable to pay the monthly salaries?
- What should she say to irate employees and subcontractors who ask why they have not been paid and threaten to abandon their jobs? Should she say it is because the company has just paid the deposit of £30,000 on the owner's second home?
- What should she say to the auditor, when he is conducting the annual audit? Should she reveal her concerns about the company and Philip's behaviour?

She was also faced with ethical decisions about her own behaviour. For example:

- Should she keep her company car, on hire from a small local company, even though this company has not been paid for over three months?

- Should she ensure that her own salary and those of employees with whom she is working closely are paid in preference to others or should she be prepared to delay payment to herself?
- Should she advise/encourage employees working closely with her to look for other jobs?
- Should she make clear to Philip the consequences of his behaviour on each occasion that it creates repercussions?

The management accountant was obviously in a prime position to identify what she considered to be the deviant behaviour of Philip and the consequences of this. However, she was beset by emotions about how to respond. What now follows is a description of the accountant's attempts to make sense of her position and her reflections on some of the options available to her.

THE ACCOUNTANT'S REFLECTIONS

Impact on personal life

The stressful situation and ethical decision dilemmas she faced during each working day spilled over to affect her private life. For example, she discussed her problems repeatedly and at length with her husband – private time became work-related time. Further, the range of duties, during the periods of cash flow-related crises, were invariably too demanding to be performed effectively only during working hours and so she spent much time working on plans and budgets at home. She often went to bed thinking about her ethical dilemmas, dreamt about them and woke up thinking about them (and sometimes discussing them with her husband). As time progressed she became increasingly despondent and faced each new day not wanting to go to work. The impact of her work-related problems concerned her husband, and the impact of her preoccupation with these problems on her husband concerned her. Days, weeks and months of this type of pressure increasingly called for some action to be taken to reduce or remove the pressure. She could resign from the organisation; she could whistleblow to someone with the power to affect Philip's behaviour (such as the bank or the Inland Revenue); she could try persuasive tactics on Philip once again.

However, the accountant's personal domestic situation held her back. With two children at a cash-demanding age, mortgage repayments to make and a husband in only a reasonably well-paid job, she considered that her family needed her income. There was a sense that the family was beginning to get on to its 'financial feet' and this provided some additional optimism about the future. Having spent a period unemployed while she brought up her children, the accountant was very aware of the difficulties that can be experienced by an unemployed, middle-aged female in obtaining a rewarding job. These sorts of family welfare-oriented pressures served to push her towards 'hanging in' for as long as possible, notwithstanding her understanding of the emotional pain this would evoke and her belief that, given the boss's ingrained behaviour traits, the business would inevitably fold in the not too distant future anyway.

Immoral, illegal or merely biased personal opinion?

In the accountant's opinion Philip's behaviour was at the very least unethical and perhaps illegal. On a personal level she greatly resented his activities in spending the organisation's money selfishly and inappropriately; the effrontery to her personal moral code that his behaviour invoked was a strong motivation to whistleblow.

On the other hand, the accountant was aware that she might be adopting an overly moral stance based on a personal value system which might be out of line with a more generalised, societal view of this sort of behaviour. Additionally, not being a legal expert, she was uncertain about the legality of this type of behaviour. This uncertainty acted as a barrier to her whistleblowing and contributed to a general indecisiveness about an issue of great moral concern to her.

Impact on stakeholders of whistleblowing and of not whistleblowing

The accountant was aware that the bank would not suffer economic costs since it was well-secured in its lendings but other institutional stakeholders might. For example, the Inland Revenue and Customs and Excise had to rely on published information and periodic internal scrutiny of company records to assess the economic position of the company. However, she was uncomfortable with the fact that she had to negotiate extensions of time to pay on numerous occasions when she knew the precarious position of the company and the root cause of this. Her major concern, however, was focused on less powerful stakeholders such as the employees and subcontractors whose livelihoods depended upon the company and its ability to pay on time. There was never enough money to go around and employees were often left anxious about whether they would be paid (some of them were working on the other side of the world, away from their families who relied upon a regular income). She was thus in a quandry as to whether to advise new contractors and suppliers in particular of the organisation's precarious situation and whether to say nothing while existing suppliers increased their accounts due from the company.

However, the accountant was also aware that even informal and covertly helpful attempts to whistleblow about the company's financial situation (whether or not this was accompanied by some commentary on Philip's part in creating it) would cause word to spread and the company would have been in great danger of folding even quicker than would otherwise have been the case, as other stakeholders withdrew or withheld their critical resources from a 'risky' company. Had she formally blown the whistle to some regulatory body, and thus provoked an immediate demand for payment by some of its big creditors, then the company would have certainly folded, since it had insufficient funds to cover its debts and the tax liability due on Philip's loan account (which had reached £140,000 at the point of time covered by the end of the case). Company failure seemed likely to have meant financial hardship to her colleagues and the existing individual and small firm contractors and suppliers. Even at the heart of the worsening cash crisis, too, the accountant could not be sure that, in one way or another, the company might 'pull through'.

In the case of those employees who actually worked with her, some knew of the company's precarious situation and Philip's role in creating this. The accountant felt compelled to ensure that their salaries (and therefore her own) were paid on time. As the company's situation worsened, she also felt she should encourage them to look elsewhere for employment.

During this period of machinations about the contradictory effects of altruistic behaviour her emotions and decisional capabilities were also clouded by a concern for her personal wellbeing and the understanding that either no other stakeholders would care sufficiently about her position should she whistleblow or that those who might seek to help, should help be necessary, did not enjoy sufficient power or position to make protective allies. Her internal supplications to Philip to change his behaviour were muted because of her fear of a powerful adverse reaction on his part.

Interesting, too, while the accountant had empathy with those stakeholder colleagues who were clamouring for payment, she often tended to take their attacks personally and to rationalise the problem being voiced by attributing blame to them and not to the primary source, Philip. For instance, she criticised clients for delaying payments so that she was unable to pay creditors and employees on time and she grumbled when subcontractors were accommodated by Philip's personal intervention as 'special cases'.

'I can see what is going on but I do not have the whole story'

Undoubtedly, the accountant was in a special position in terms of gaining understanding of how the company's money was being spent, and what and who lay at the heart of the organisation's problems. Nevertheless, she was reliant to a great extent on information about potential incomes and about current and past expenditures given by Philip. He played many of his 'cash flow cards close to his chest'. Thus the accountant remained unsure of the cash value of particular company assets and of any personal assets which Philip might have held but hadn't disclosed. She was constantly hoping that he would mend his ways; this hope, together with her incomplete picture of the personal/company financial standing, helped maintain a position of mild indecisiveness.

The accountant also suspected that Philip was involved in activities other than those within the company's sphere of activity and that they might be dubious from a legal standpoint. On the one hand, she pondered whether these might provide a source of life-sustaining income for the organisation and, on the other, was largely unaware of what the activities were. For instance, large amounts were recorded in the books as owing to the company from an overseas associate. When she questioned Philip about these, he said they were bad debts and should be written off. She suspected that this was not the case and that Philip had channelled cash away from the company. However, she had no evidence to support this suspicion. She decided to allow the company auditor to pursue this issue and did not reveal her suspicions. She was surprised that the auditor merely accepted Philip's version about the 'bad debts'.

Unfair behaviour or merely a businessman's right of action and expected management style?

From the point of view of the accountant, Philip's behaviour was unfair to all who were associated with the company. However, she understood that 'entrepreneurs' and those who embark upon business on their own account, often act in unorthodox ways. In the eyes of many, Philip would undoubtedly have the right to do what he liked with his own money (since, after all, he was the sole director of his own company). That the accountant did not see it this way is apparent. From her perspective Philip was actually borrowing the creditors' money, since his personal drawings from the company far outweighed his investment in it. This viewpoint pushed her towards whistleblowing. The understanding that others, particularly uninformed outsiders, might view Philip's behaviour in a completely different light acted as a barrier to the whistleblowing act. In a similar vein, although she resented the risky and thoughtless way in which he operated, she was aware that risk-taking and expensive status symbols are considered by many to be the kind of 'cavalier' behaviour that is expected in particular business contexts.

Moral and professional duty is to whistleblow: moral and professional duty is to not whistleblow, and fear of potential and present culpability

On the one hand the accountant perceived a clear duty to act in the public interest and she considered the behaviour of her boss to be of such unfair, immoral, improper, perhaps illegal proportions that she was almost honour-bound to bring it to the attention of 'someone with power'. Paradoxically, she was also aware that accountants, more than any other type of employee, have a duty of confidentiality and should not be tainted by any collusion in improper or illegal acts. She was also aware that her profession might look askance at one of its members who breaks this aspect of their code and who disloyally works against the interests of the person or firm that employs them. (Indeed, although the accountant was unaware of it at the time, there are a number of examples in the literature of accountant whistleblowers who have been 'sent to Coventry' by their profession, following their acts of whistleblowing – see, for example, Vinten 1994.) This really was a catch-22 situation: the accountant was in danger of having her reputation sullied and future employment prospects damaged whether or not she decided to whistleblow.

A similar paradox existed about the fear of the consequences of the accountant being held culpable for any miscreant practices (and accountants have been seen to share, or even take all the blame in cases involving financial frauds, for instance the cases of Guinness and Brent Walker). On the one hand is the fear of allowing untoward practices to go unchecked to that point where prolonged acquiescence imputes active collusion and the fear of crossing this culpability fulcrum point stimulates the desire to whistleblow. On the other hand, a fear that the point has already been crossed makes the act of whistleblowing more difficult to undertake – the question arises 'have I already connived in it?' (Cover and Humphries 1994). This accountant never believed that she had reached a point close to the culpability imputing one, but neither did she feel comfortable or totally secure with the role of malpractice supporter that circumstances had forced upon her.

'I do not like bullies but that doesn't always stop me being bullied'

Philip's regular office staff of four personnel were all female. He knew how to be a bully. On one occasion, for example, he physically kicked out at Helen (a colleague of the accountant) following a telephone call from the bank drawing his attention to the overdrawn nature of the account. Philip blamed Helen's inadequate cash flow-forecasting skills for the problem with the bank. He would easily become moody, sometimes angry, when things were not going his way or if the accountant attempted to point out to him what she perceived as the error of his ways. Further, he was quite a big man and thus, to some extent, his physical presence could be intimidating. His ability to manipulate situations in the office was also facilitated by the simple fact that he was, of course, 'the boss'.

For her part, the accountant resolved not to be bullied but to behave professionally, notwithstanding, perhaps even because of, these personal power-based pressures. One side to her nature provoked her to fight bullies. Nevertheless, she accepts that, overall, the total context in which she worked was one that was stacked towards her adopting a strategy of protestation from a base position of acquiescence rather than one of forceful and decisive change-invoking activity.

A growing conviction that the boss will not change versus the eternal hope that he might

As time progressed and the accountant observed Philip's actions she became increasingly convinced that he was incapable of changing his personality, and thereby his organisation-destroying lifestyle and associated spending behaviours. The consequences of his actions on the liquidity and precarious position of the company had been repeatedly pointed out to him and yet his personal demands on the financial coffers of the organisation became even greater. The bank had only recently threatened to liquidate his company – to 'cut off the hand that fed him' (Richardson *et al.*1994) – and it had pointed out the very real possibility that his style of management placed him in jeopardy of trading illegally. Nevertheless, as soon as the bank had relaxed its stringent, day-to-day, controls he had reverted back to this very same dangerous practice. From this point of view, the accountant was clear that if Philip would not or could not change, then some other aspect of the system in which she was embroiled would have to.

Despite this growing conviction about the intransigence of her boss and the associated need for some kind of action on her part the accountant kept hoping and half-expecting that Philip would change his behaviour, which she perceived as clearly irrational. The hope that such a change might occur acted against her attempting to make change happen.

A perception that nobody else will intervene versus a sense of 'why should it have to be me?'

The accountant had witnessed the bank's attitude towards Philip and his organisation. She felt that the bank did not realise the importance of its position as a controller of Philip's crisis-inducing behaviour nor of its need to monitor his performance closely. It was most concerned to ensure that its position as lender was secured. The Inland Revenue and VAT officials were helpful and to a large extent flexible in terms of granting extensions to the due dates by which payments should have been made to them, but they had no understanding or interest in the causes of the need to delay payment. Seemingly it was beyond their remit to investigate such issues or to intervene in the way the organisation was managed. External accountants-cum-auditors appeared to have ignored the basic strategic problem facing MIS, at best, and, at worst, contributed to its development. Other personnel inside the organisation did not have the accountant's close understanding of the dire situation the company was in, and the driving forces which underpinned it. Clearly none of them had the power to influence positive change (Philip's girlfriend might have possessed such power but, in the assessment of the accountant, would not be disposed to wield it). This covert, mental assessment of the power and motivational positions of stakeholders in and around MIS left the accountant clear in her mind that if beneficial change was to take place, other than through the consequences of bankruptcy and liquidation proceedings, then she was the one who would have to instigate it.

She was comparatively new to senior management and to the post of accountant and did not feel sufficiently experienced or expert to be confident about her ability to facilitate actions which would lead to desirable outcomes. She also felt a sense of inequity about the fact that many other, more powerful stakeholders, however inadvertently, had left the job of changemaker to someone in her relatively disadvantaged and impotent position (the role of the law and the professions in matters of disclosure about the financial activities of companies and their top managements is the subject of growing debate, internationally – Dearlove 1994; Barton 1994, 1995; Kalathil 1994; Pratten 1991; Kets de Vries *et al.* 1990; Kets de Vries 1993; Townsend 1994; Van Luijk 1994). These thoughts acted to persuade her against meaningful action.

Who to whistleblow to? Someone, somewhere should be interested, but who, where and how will they respond?

The accountant felt that the bank was the stakeholder with the most potential influence over Philip's behaviour, and she had many opportunities to disclose in clear fashion, to the bank, Philip's role in creating the liquidity problems in which it shared an interest. However, she lacked confidence that the bank would respond in a manner which protected her or, indeed any interests other than its own. Instead, therefore, she relied on the bank to interpret the management accounts she furnished in a way that drew attention to Philip's spending behaviour. So far as she was aware, the bank never emphasised this aspect of the information she provided to it. At a particularly critical time she was invited to a meeting between the bank manager, Philip and the company's auditor. Here she was torn between her role as a supporter of the company and her role as a professional who should report her views honestly. She chose to respond honestly to any questions put to her but did not volunteer any further opinions. In the event, no awkward questions were asked and the bank agreed to continue supporting Philip. However, the auditor refused to attend the meeting and submitted his resignation. It would appear that the blame for the fact that Philip had not separately declared his loan account in the latest audited accounts (a particular concern for the bank) was laid at the feet of the resigning auditor!

She was still a relatively inexperienced accountant and although she understood, in general, the regulatory role of government departments such as the Inland Revenue, the Value Added Tax Office and the Department of Trade, she was unaware of any processes provided by these sorts of bodies to help people in her position as a potential whistleblower. Neither did she consult with any legal expert. The most recently employed auditor, with whom she did feel she might be able to discuss the situation, also, independently, had refused to attend the meeting with the bank, referred to above, and shortly after resigned his position without making contact with the accountant. At the time of these crises the accountant was a student member of a professional body of accountants and was studying related topics at a local university on a part-time basis. On reflection she feels that little help emanated from these avenues. Advice and/or practical help might have been available from these sources; she simply did not know. To have found out would have required her to make overt and specific enquiries of her tutors and of her professional association and she did neither.

At the back of her mind, during this time, was a fear that her 'confessions' to these sorts of stakeholders might be ignored, or perhaps discounted as over-reactions from an employee with an inexperienced or biased view of organisation and leadership. Even worse, she feared that a dialogue with these types of stakeholders might lead to confrontation-invoking investigations in which her own position and motives became prime suspects.

All in all, the accountant felt very lonely in the role of concerned professional.

Whistleblowing is not the only strategy for change

The above discussion conveys a sense of the frustration experienced by our ethnographic informant as she sought to decide how to achieve change towards a fairer, more professional and more economically viable system of organising at MIS. During all her deliberations 'whistleblowing' remained but one from a selection of strategies she could have selected. Indeed, 'whistleblowing' remained a least-favoured option and while at any one time particular factors might have held greater force for 'whistleblowing' than their opposing counterparts, the total force of all the 'fors' combined never outweighed the combined 'againsts' to provoke the act of 'whistleblowing'.

The accountant would have been happiest had a simple persuasion strategy worked. She would also have preferred more powerful external stakeholders to have intervened to control Philip's behaviour. In the event, after coming to terms with the likelihood that none of these preferred strategies would work she chose to leave the organisation. She tendered her notice (without offering the real reason for her leaving, but rather providing a less confrontational one) and shortly afterwards joined the ranks of the unemployed.

CONCLUSION

In our view, accountants working within organisations do occupy privileged positions which allow them the opportunity to detect and observe deviant managerial practices at the very highest level. Although the example we have provided is of a small firm, we feel that this illustrates the typically problematic nature of this type of situation for accountants. We describe the options that the accountant at MIS perceived were available to her, her rationalisation of these and her ultimate decision. We suggest that, given the current support in the UK for accountants in potential 'whistleblowing' situations such as the one described here, most accountants are likely to take the 'quiet way out', thus allowing managerial malpractices at the highest levels within organisations to continue until the organisation fails. Our example at MIS provides a unique insight into what it is like to work in and associate with such organisations while they are led by deviant top managers and the media has provided us with vivid accounts over the last decade of the economic, social and emotional costs involved for innocent stakeholders of these organisations at the moment of failure.

We feel that the story we recount at MIS is not a unique one and we would suggest that, based on our own research in this area and that of others it is, in fact, commonplace in organisations of all sizes. (See, for instance, Barton 1995; Dearlove 1994; Kets de Vries *et al.* 1990; Kets de Vries 1993; Lovell and Robertson 1994; Richardson 1993; Richardson *et al.* 1994; Richardson *et al.* 1996; Van Luijk 1994.)

REFERENCES

Barton, L. (1994) 'Whistleblowing as an emerging business crisis', in L. Barton (ed.) *New Avenues in Risk and Crisis Management*, published conference proceedings, Las Vegas, NV: University of Nevada Press, 3–10.

—— (1995) 'Embezzlement and the new wave of financial crimes', in L. Barton (ed.) *New Avenues in Risk and Crisis Management*, published conference proceedings, Las Vegas, NV: University of Nevada Press, 9–18.

Borrie, G. (1993) *Yorkshire Post*, 15 October.

Cashmore, C. (1994) 'Some preliminary considerations on ethics in management accountancy', London: London Guildhall University: Occasional Paper.

Chapman, C. (1997) *Yorkshire Post*, 19 February.

Cover, M. and Humphries, G. (1994) 'Whistleblowing in English Law', in G. Vinten (ed.) *Whistleblowing: Subversion or corporate citizenship*, London: Paul Chapman Publishing Limited: 89–105.

Dearlove, D. (1994) 'Help for whistleblowers?', *The Times*, 10 February: 14.

De George, R.T. (1986) *Business Ethics*, New York: Macmillan, 2nd edn.

Drucker, P.F. (1981) 'The public interest', reprinted in A.P. Iannone (ed.) *Contemporary Moral Controversies in Business*, Oxford: Oxford University Press, 1989.

Jackson, J. (1992) 'Motive and morality', *Business Ethics: A European Review*, 1 (4): 264–6.

Jos, P.H., Tompkins, M.E. and Hays, S.W. (1989) 'In praise of difficult people: a portrait of the committed whistleblower', *Public Administration Review*, November/December: 552–61.

Kalathil, S. (1994) 'Chinese style corporate governance', *Administrator*, ICSA, October: 26–7.

Kets de Vries, M.F.R. (1993) 'Doing a Maxwell: or why not to identify with the aggressor', *European Management Journal*, 11 (2): 169–74.

Kets de Vries, M.F.R., Dick, R. and Petrie, J. (1990) 'Ernest Saunders and the Guinness Affair', Fontainebleau, France: INSEAD (case available from European Clearing House, Cranfield).

Lovell, L. and Robertson, C. (1994) 'Charles Robertson: in the eye of the storm', in G. Vinten (ed.) *Whistleblowing: Subversion or corporate citizenship?*, London: Paul Chapman Publishing Limited.

Pratten, C. (1991) *Company Failures*, The Institute of Chartered Accountants Financial Reporting and Auditing Group, May.

Richardson, B., Nwankwo, S. and Richardson, S. (1994) 'Understanding the causes of business failure crises', *Management Decision*, 32 (4): 9–22.

Richardson, S. (1993) 'Descriptions of some selfishly-led organisation realities', in B. Richardson (ed.) *Managing in Enterprise Contexts*, Sheffield: Pavic.

Richardson, S., Cullen, J. and Richardson, B. (1996) 'The story of a schizoid organisation: how accounting and the accountant are implicated in its creation', *Accounting, Auditing and Accountability*, Bradford: MCB University Press, 9 (1): 8–30.

Soeken, K. and Soeken, D. (1987) *A Survey of Whistleblowers: Their stresses and coping strategies*, Laurel, MD: Association of Mental Health Specialities.

Stonefrost, M.F. (1990) *Encouraging Citizenship. Report of the Commission on Citizenship*, London: HMSO.

Townsend, P. (1994) 'Non-executive directors – better times ahead?', *Administrator*, ICSA, June: 7–9.

Van Luijk, H.J.L. (1994) 'From monitor to master? Ethical comments on the regulation of fraud notification by accountants', a paper presented at the Fourth International Conference on Ethics in the Public Service, Stockholm, 15–18 June.

Vinten, G. (ed.) (1994) *Whistleblowing: Subversion or corporate citizenship?*, London: Paul Chapman Publishing Limited.

Westin, A.F. (1981) *Whistleblowing: Loyalty and dissent in the corporation*, McGraw-Hill.

Winfield, M. (1994) 'Whistleblowers as corporate safety net', in G. Vinten (ed.) *Whistleblowing: Subversion or corporate citizenship?*, London: Paul Chapman Publishing Limited, 21–32.

4

ASSUMPTIONS, VALUES AND PRINCIPLES: ACCOUNTING IN THE PUBLIC SERVICES

Alan Lovell

INTRODUCTION

The broad subject of ethics has many categories and areas of contention, and professional ethics may be presented as one of those categories. However, if dismissed as just that, namely as just one of the ethics categories, not only would this 'category' have been grossly over simplified, a rich possibility would have been missed to study some of the more troublesome and problematic areas that comprise the ethics spectrum.

Any group of individuals possessing 'expertise' invariably seeks to protect its expertise base by creating two things. The first is an image of value and importance in the eyes of the public, or at least that portion of the general public that is its client base. The second is barriers to entry, the ultimate of which is the granting by statute of a monopoly over that area of expertise claimed by the group. In order to be granted a monopoly by the state, a 'profession'[1] must satisfy certain criteria, the two central elements being:

1 To always work in the general public interest if ever a conflict of interests arises; and
2 To operate within a code of ethics.

There is common ground between these two elements, but both in their own ways are slippery and troublesome. Within UK law, the term 'the public interest' is not defined by statute. Its malleability possibly explains both its longevity and its unreliability in a court of law. As a defence, when employees seek to justify their actions in

63

bringing to public notice organisational practices about which the employees believe to be either immoral or illegal and possibly both, the public interest can prove inadequate against charges of stealing corporate property (such as critical information), or breaching aspects of confidentiality.

The existence of a professional code of ethics can also prove to be the flimsiest of shields if employees endeavour to justify actions of resistance to corporate (mal)practices. The protection that codes of ethics might appear to offer members of professional bodies is invariably illusory. Essentially codes of ethics are designed to offer the appearance of protection to the general public that should a member behave in an 'unprofessional manner' (however that is defined), sanctions will be taken, the ultimate of which would be expulsion from the professional body. If the area of expertise represented by the professional body is protected by statute, such an expulsion would remove the ex-member's ability to practice. In accountancy, the only area of practice protected by statute is that of external audit. However, to act in accordance with a code of conduct while under pressure from an employer to do otherwise, and to look to one's professional body for support in such circumstances, is likely to lead to disappointment for the member.[2] A spokesperson for the Chartered Institute of Management Accountants is quoted as saying that if members cannot achieve satisfactory responses from their employing organisations to their concerns over particular corporate practices, they should leave their employment (*Accountancy Age*, 13 February 1997: 2). The fact that the corporate practices remain is totally ignored. The notion of the public interest in this type of case does not seem to apply. The more intriguing issue, however, and the one explored in this chapter, is where the codes of conduct of members of differing professional bodies clash, that is, where they challenge the *a priori* assumptions of the other.

Whether public service organisations are in the private or public economic sectors, they represent arenas of potential conflict, for here we will find professionals in the form of social workers, probation officers, nurses, doctors, educationalists and others, who are responsible for delivering the primary service of the organisation, and who often have very strict codes of professional conduct. Within the same organisations, however, other professionals will be charged with the responsibility of managing those organisations in as cost-effective a way as possible, a charge not always compatible with the service objectives of the organisations. This is particularly so since the early 1980s when the Financial Management Initiative (FMI) first began to develop. Since then the vast majority of government administration in the UK has been subject to forces of commercialisation. By the close of 1997, in excess of 80 per cent of central government administration has been transferred to executive agencies, trading funds, or has been contracted out to the private sector. Departmental relationships within these organisations are often required to employ the notion of an internal market, even where the creation of such markets is highly contrived.

Within some of these organisations the senior managers will have professional backgrounds reflecting the nature of the organisation's primary role, for example they might be qualified social workers, doctors or nurses, and this raises new opportunities for potential conflicts of interest. However, given the focus of this book, it is the role of accountants, accounting information, and the nature of ethics of and between the various professional groupings within public service organisations, that is our concern.

Public service organisations represent some of the most emotive and contentious arenas for the development of a commercial orientation. All government departments and executive agencies are required to become more business-like, although this is not the same as 'like business'. The former carries connotations of being resource-aware (that is, efficient and economic in the use of resources) and customer focused (assuming being 'customer-focused' is more than mere rhetoric for profit-seeking organisations). Being business-like, however, carries a much wider remit and could encompass those practices that fly close to the distinction between that which is acceptable (legally, socially, commercially) and that which is not.

Although this chapter displays an emphasis towards healthcare scenarios, other public service contexts are considered. Indeed many of the issues are generic, healthcare merely being the setting chosen to consider the issues.

THE DOMAINS OF CONSCIENCE AND CARE

It is tempting to stereotype managers in general and accountants in particular as hard-nosed, amoral, driven by the logic of economic reason, and the root of the problems that face all public services as the end of the twentieth century approaches. The rise of accounting technologies are clearly evident within public services, and McSweeney

65

(1994, 1996) has argued that management accounting has moved from a largely managerial support mechanism to management being *by* accounting. Twisting terms, as McSweeney has done, can be both powerful and helpful, but such claims must exist outside of the anecdotal, possessing substance beyond myth. It is the intention in this article to consider some of the tensions inherent in the *raison d'être* of the functions of accountancy and the caring professions, particularly nursing.

That accounting technologies were and remain a central tenet of the Financial Management Initiative, which was introduced during Margaret Thatcher's first administration, is a question of historical fact. In certain areas that have traditionally been part of public service delivery, such as the 'delivery' of school meals, or the administration of social welfare payments, few claims can be made that these tasks carry commitment to a higher authority, or that the roles performed reflect a form of 'calling'. In this sense the delivery of school meals, the administration of road fund licences, or the administration of social welfare payments might be grouped with the production of, say, motor vehicles, or the development and selling of insurance products. This is not in anyway to denigrate or belittle such organisational activities or products. The comparison is made merely to differentiate them from other forms of endeavour where the notion of a calling and public service carry differing depths of meaning and values. In areas such as healthcare, education and justice, for example, we are entering the field of human or individual rights. While there is no unanimity on how far such 'rights' extend, there can be few arguments that we are dealing here with issues of principle, issues which help define the value base of a society. However, to suggest that, *ipso facto*, care and conscience are elements that are optional to the ethical base of organisations involved in the production of motor cars, issuing of road fund licences, development of insurance policies and so on, would clearly be a gross error. It is just that when we are dealing with organisations involved in the provision of services such as healthcare or education, we are dealing with roles that potentially carry meaning and value for both provider and beneficiary beyond the price attached to the service. For example, when standards (however assessed) in healthcare or education or justice are deemed to be falling, any associated debates address the very nature of societal values and social priorities.

In such areas we find not only individuals who choose to work because of some notion of personal commitment to a cause or belief, despite conditions of work or pay which in other contexts would pose fundamental problems for recruitment, we also find examples of codes of practice which require the professionals concerned to be champions of those for whom the service is provided. The most noted example of this phenomenon is the requirement of nurses to act as patient advocates and react to any practices that put patients at risk or disadvantage patients. Under the terms of their professional code of conduct nurses can be struck off their professional register for failing to report concerns about standards of care. The sixteen-point Code of Professional Conduct issued by the United Kingdom Central Council for Nursing, Midwifery and Health Visiting (UKCC) states:

> Each registered nurse, midwife and health visitor shall act, at all times, in such a manner as to justify public trust and confidence, to uphold and enhance the good standing and reputation of the profession, to serve the interests of society, and above all to safeguard the interests of individual patients and clients.

The code also includes the following directives:

> Act always in such a way as to promote and safeguard the well being and interests of patients/clients. The registered nurse, midwife and health visitor must make appropriate representations about the environment of care:
>
> (a) where patients or clients seem likely to be placed in jeopardy and/or standards of practice endangered;
> (b) where the staff in such settings are at risk because of the pressure of work and/or inadequacy of resources (which again places patients at risk);
> (c) where valuable resources are being used inappropriately.
>
> (UKCC, 1989: 8)

The code goes on to state:

> It is clearly wrong for any practitioner to pretend to be coping with the workload, to delude herself into the conviction that things are better than they really are, to aid and abet the abuse and breakdown of a colleague, or to tolerate in silence any matters in her work setting that place patients at risk, jeopardise standards or practice, or deny patients privacy and dignity.
>
> (UKCC, 1989: 9)

Throughout the 1980s and 1990s the financial constraints within which the National Health Service in the UK has been required to operate have posed enormous challenges for all concerned. As the end of the millennium approaches the situation is little changed, and the tensions that such conditions exacerbate are reflected not just in cases of nurses or doctors 'going public' with regard to their concerns for patient care (for instance, the cases of senior charge nurse Graham Pink and Doctor Helen Zeitlin (Lovell 1992)) but also the cases of alleged suppression of concerns and the suffocation of expressions of concerns by medical staff. The Royal College of Nursing (RCN) operates a confidential and anonymous help line for troubled members and the following quotes are extracted from a report by the RCN.

I am so ashamed that the professional care for whatever reason has sunk so low. I just had to get it off my chest . . .

I do not know what you or anyone else can do, but thank you for allowing me to tell someone in safety.

I am writing to the 'RCN Whistleblow' service because I don't really know what else to do. I have become so concerned about the future of the nursing service in my unit that I am quite literally, at a loss to know who to turn to for advice . . . my colleagues feel the same but are too insecure to say or do anything.

There are two recurring issues in the report. The first is the grave concern of nurses over the quality of patient care. The second is the fear of reprisals against nurses who speak out against what they feel to be falling standards.

Anyone who attempts to rectify the situation by approaching management is labelled a troublemaker.

I have recently spoken up . . . the experience was unnerving. This makes me question speaking up about standards of care or any complaint in the future.

We are well represented by our sister, but we are subject to bullying tactics by management.

Two colleagues wrote official letters outlining their very deep concerns about cuts (in nursing staff numbers). Neither received a reply for two weeks but now they have both been informed that they are being moved from their wards, one going to elderly care, the other might be put onto another medical ward. . . . Personally I find it all rather suspicious that the two who complain are being moved.

Possibly the most moving contribution to the RCN's report is recorded below. While the nurse's letter can be challenged as playing on the emotive nature of the subject, it captures one side of the debate in a profound and compelling fashion.

I did my early shift from 7.00 a.m. and the staff who came in the afternoon were not trained or experienced enough each to give out the medication. I worked an extra three or four hours to try and help the other staff who were totally stretched and under pressure. In the end, I left the ward in tears, too tired to do any more, and afraid of what would happen to the patients later. [. . .] I am worried that a management decision will have dire consequences but feel incapable of halting the resulting damage . . . management are interested only in budgets, not patient care or staff welfare.

What happens when someone in the terminal phase of their illness wants you to sit and hold their hand at night because they are frightened and the ward is too busy as there are too few nurses on duty? It's almost a case of saying, 'Sorry, could you be scared or want to talk when we are a little less busy or have more staff.' My patients and staff deserve better than this – my patients have been through two world wars and deserve quality nursing care. Morale is low . . . and staff are frightened and intimidated by a defensive, ingrained management style.

To avoid the accusation that healthcare is a an extreme example of the problems of low morale and funding problems, it is worth considering other areas of public service. The UK prison service is another public service wrestling with mounting problems and financial resource constraints. Derek Lewis, when being first interviewed for the post of Chief Executive of the Prison Service had the organisation described to him as 'the Cinderella of the public services for as long as anyone can remember . . . not only was the prison service failing to perform . . . it was inefficient and trapped in a tangle of bureaucracy' (Lewis 1997: 2).

While punishment is an important element of prison terms, so too must be rehabilitation. There are demands and dangers associated with 'delivering' an effective prison environment which place it apart from many other challenges to be found in organisational life. At the time of writing, incidences of suicide and attempted suicide are increasing throughout the prison service to unprecedented levels and while the availability of drugs inside prisons is a problem for prison officers and management, it is also a way of keeping a lid on the potential for even greater prison disturbances. A report by Her Majesty's Inspector of Prisons (October 1997) identified serious breakdowns in control and management at Lincoln Prison. Staff in the jail's 'A' wing had virtually given up patrolling the landings while 'thugs, bullies and [drug] dealers were able to roam without interference'. Sir David Ramsbottam stated that, 'little patrolling was taking place and inmates were clearly running their own culture' (*The Guardian*, 16 October 1997: 11). Bullying was said to be rife with twenty-one serious assaults on inmates in three months. At Nottingham Prison there had been twelve attempted suicides in the three-month period between June 1997 and September 1997 and two actual suicides in a seven-week period (Beaumont 1997). Much of the trauma leading to the suicides was said to be due to remand prisoners being locked up for twenty-three hours at a time. The problem in all cases was seen as one of resourcing, yet the Minister for Prisons made an immediate announcement following the publication of the 'Lincoln' report that no additional finance would be made available to the Prison Service.

MANAGING DISSENT

While public service organisations maintain a public position of acting first and foremost on behalf of their patients/clients and encouraging freedom of communication with and among their employees, practice offers images of different worlds. Whistleblowers, irrespective of the sector of the economy in which they are to be found, or the nature of their employing organisation's work,[3] tend to suffer personally as a consequence of their actions, even when the concerns that lead to the individual going public with their concerns are later seen to be 'proven' (Butler and Hunter 1994; De George 1990; Glazer 1983; Lovell 1994; Near and Miceli 1986; Soeken and Soeken 1987; Winfield 1990). The case of Graham Pink is informative in this respect (Lovell 1992). After trying and failing over an eight-month period to generate what he felt was an adequate response from management to his concerns about patient care on the geriatric wards where he was a senior charge nurse, Pink went public. He was suspended and ultimately dismissed when a local newspaper published an account of his anguish over a particular incident on his ward. Pink lodged a case for wrongful dismissal, but before the court was able to give a verdict, the hospital trust settled out of court.

To counter the risk of whistleblowing acts, it is not uncommon to now find employees of hospitals being required to sign 'gagging' clauses if they wish to be employed by the hospital trust. The following are two examples of such clauses:

> In the course of your normal work with the Trust you will come into the possession of confidential information concerning patients, the Trust and its staff. Such information must always be treated as strictly confidential and further, must not be divulged to any individual or organisation, including the press, without prior written approval of the Chief Executive or his nominated deputy.
>
> (Kingston Hospital Trust, UK)

> During the course of your employment you may see, hear or have access to information on matters of a confidential nature relating to the work of the hospital or to the health and personal affairs of patients and staff. Under no circumstances should such information be divulged or passed onto any unauthorised person(s) or organisations. Disciplinary action will be taken against any employee who contravenes this regulation.
>
> (Mount Vernon Trust, Uxbridge, UK)

While the notion of confidentiality is normally associated with commercially sensitive information, it is difficult to use this defence in the context of a hospital, particularly when actions by doctors or nurses that are injurious to patients are already subject to disciplinary action by their professional associations – the British Medical Association (BMA) and the UKCC respectively. The 'gagging' clauses thus seem to extend doctors' and nurses' 'duty of care' with regard to knowledge and information about other employees (including senior management) and about the hospital itself.

The picture that emerges is of a sector of the economy that does not naturally exist in a market environment, yet has one 'created' for it to handle the severe problems of resource allocation. On the one hand there are examples of members of particular professional groupings (such as doctors and nurses) expressing either grave concern over the state of patient/client care, or expressing grave concern over the gagging and suffocation of their concerns. On the other is the *bête noire* in this scenario – the general grouping of 'professionals' known as management, but in particular, *the financial constraints*, and thus, by association, the accountants.

THE TENSIONS AND CONFLICTS INHERENT WITHIN PUBLIC SERVICE MANAGEMENT

The practice of accounting resides within the broader framework of management and the role required of management within the healthcare environment in 1997 is filled with ethical dilemmas. Accounting, both in principle and in practice, assumes a low level of trust on the part of those who are being monitored by the accounting systems, probably only stage 1 of Kohlberg's hierarchy (see Chapter 8 of this book for an examination of Kohlberg's hierarchy and Lovell (1995) for a fuller explanation of this suggestion). If we consider control as being derived from either the inner set of values and beliefs held by those charged with the responsibility of producing and delivering an organisation's products or services, or derived from externally imposed performance information systems (such as accounting information systems), it is clear that trust (a key term in business terminology) is evident in only the first of these two forms. The low level of moral reasoning assumed within accounting systems of control of those being controlled (doctors and nurses), does not sit comfortably in a context in which doctors and nurses are required by their respective professional associations to be their patients' advocates. The issue is clearly that hospitals no longer have as their primary and sole objective to provide the very best medical care for patients. This objective remains, but (at best) it vies with a variety of financial objectives. The situation now exists where a major teaching hospital can refuse to undertake anything other than emergency cases for its major purchaser (a District Health Authority) when that health authority has exhausted the contract agreed with that hospital. An example of this was the refusal of the Queen's Medical Centre, Nottingham, in 1996 to accept anything other than emergency cases for a period of over three months from one of its largest purchases a District Health Authority, when that authority exhausted the block contract it had negotiated with the hospital at the start of the year. The power of economic reason literally overrode the power of social justice, social need and social values.

Gorz (1989), quoted in Laughlin (1996), argues that while economic reason may indeed be an appropriate basis for relationships in certain sectors of the economy, the basis of that reasoning sets limits on its more general application. The question, as Gorz poses it, is to determine those activities which can be subordinated to economic reason without negating the meaning in those activities. One might argue that economic reason might indeed be an appropriate basis for managing relationships within say, the motor car industry, or the insurance industry, or the provision of school meals, but can economic reason be allowed to migrate (or be forced) into areas such as healthcare, education and justice? The fact that it has does not negate the question.

Laughlin (1996) analyses the case of The Church of England in terms of principals and agents, with the ultimate principal (God) and the principles upon which a Christian life are based, being used as buffers to resist the encroachment of economic reason into operational decisions.[4] The sacred activities – the higher meaning given to particular examples of human activity such as religion and caring for others – are seen by Gorz to possess meaning which elevates them above and apart from other examples of human activity, where economic rationality can be employed as the sole arbiter of relationships. The latter are referred to as examples of the secular. Staying with this terminology, it is unclear whether the commercialisation and marketisation processes that have been applied in the healthcare sector in the UK over the past twenty years represent an example of the secular coming to dominate the sacred, or whether the principle of economic reason has become the new sacred.

By pricing all aspects of healthcare, one can talk about the commodification of the roles and tasks of healthcare professionals. Alternatively, or as well, one can talk about the rise of one professional ethos, that of the management group and particularly accountants and accounting, over another, that of the healthcare professionals. However, analysis is not that simple (for a thoughtful analysis of the processes leading to whistleblowing acts in healthcare organisations, and the tensions and coping strategies employed, see Anderson 1990).

As mentioned above, within hospital trusts senior management positions are held by doctors and nurses as well as non-medical professionals. If a nurse or doctor who is not in a management position raises concerns about levels of patient care, the professional bodies that represent and/or govern these professionals are faced with a dilemma of their own. The BMA is both a regulatory body and a trade association. In such cases members of the BMA will be on both sides of the argument. Such was the situation in the case of Doctor Helen Zeitlin (Lovell 1992). The trigger for her dismissal appears to have been her opposition at a public meeting to the transfer of the hospital in which she worked to 'Trust' status. Dr Zietlin was one of only two haematology specialists in the hospital, but hospital management (including senior medical staff) judged that following Dr Zeithin's statement at the pubic meeting, her post had become superfluous to requirements. Dr Zietlin was made redundant, but speedily reinstated on appeal. The BMA had members on both sides of this particular case, but the reinstatement of Dr Zietlin avoided the BMA becoming involved.

When we consider nursing, it is the RCN that is the nurses' trade union, while the UKCC is charged with the task of establishing and improving standards of professional conduct. It is also the body that controls the registration of nurses. While the UKCC may be able to remain indifferent to the tensions between different members of the nursing profession arguing over conditions of patient care, the RCN may find itself being asked to support members who are on different sides of an argument. This was the situation in the Graham Pink case. Not only was the RCN supportive of the stand taken by Pink (who was campaigning against what he claimed was the neglect of geriatric patients), but the RCN also represented the Chief Nursing Officer of Stockport Health Authority, who was accused of breaking the Code of Professional Conduct as a result of the Pink case. The situation is a complex one for healthcare professionals, their trade unions and regulatory bodies, but what is the position of accountants in the healthcare sector (or, say, the prison service) and their trade associations and regulatory bodies?

Management in general (and accounting in particular) and the healthcare profession have markedly different philosophical backgrounds. Gorz would certainly see members of the former sector as practitioners of the secular, while the actions of healthcare professionals would be classed as having a meaning beyond the 'value' placed upon them in accounting and financial statements. In other words, healthcare workers are engaged in work of a 'sacred' nature.[5] This has echoes of Seedhouse's term 'dwarfing' (1988), which he used to describe behaviours and actions that have the effect of demeaning or reducing the status of others. The term describes what healthcare is *not* about, but it can be argued that a likely outcome of accounting controls is a degree of dwarfing of the individual, and in this context the individual can be both the controller and controlled.

If one studies the codes of conduct of the professional accountancy bodies it is neither surprising nor a criticism that they recognise the importance of confidentiality of employing organisations' property. This element of the professional codes is both a recognition of legal fact, but also a recognition that even without the legality issues, commercial businesses need protection for their confidential and sensitive practices and property. One of the most crucial assets a business can own is information. However, while protection of information in a commercial sense may have a *soupçon* of legitimacy, can the shield of confidentiality be an acceptable defence for an organisation that is alleged to engage in illegal/immoral practices? Despite the statement by an officer of one of the professional accountancy bodies that the professional bodies could publicly support one of their members should they be victimised for revealing corporate malpractices (Champ 1997), there are no examples of this ever happening. There is evidence, however, of the professional bodies declining to publicly support its members when available evidence suggested that the victimised members had a very strong case of wrongful dismissal and victimisation (Lovell 1992, 1994).

The relationships between the professional accountancy bodies and business interests are strong, both at an individual and an institutional level. The UK auditing profession (still the major force within the UK accountancy profession as a whole despite representing only about 25 per cent of the membership) has experienced very significant problems during the 1980s and 1990s. Many high profile negligence claims have been lodged against large accountancy practices and major concerns have been expressed about the independence of auditors (see, for example, Lovell 1996). The concerns expressed revolve around the closeness of the relationships between auditors and auditees and the very nature of audit itself. It has been suggested that in some cases audit may be approaching the status of a commodity and if so can be treated as a loss leader in order to gain privileged access to non-audit work available from audit clients. With the practices of accounting and audit facing considerable criticism and the accountancy profession's response to these problems itself the subject of critical commentary,[6] it is not without some irony that one acknowledges the apogee of accounting practice in the late 1990s, particularly within public service administration in the UK. With the migration of accounting practices, accounting controls and accounting personnel into the public services, so too migrate the values, the assumptions about human behaviour implicit within accounting models, and the limitations of accounting. The fear exists that what cannot be measured, or what cannot be easily audited, becomes relegated in importance.

While the origins of accounting and audit predate capitalist enterprise, the practice of accounting and accountants in the late 1990s owe their respective status to the expansion of capitalist modes of organisation. The arenas represented by public service organisations, of which healthcare is one of the most identifiable, reflect the values of the secular competing with values of the sacred. It is possible that accountants employed within public service organisations might find themselves more likely to be confronted with ethical dilemmas by the very nature of the organisation's work. However, unlike doctors and, in particular, nurses, there is no requirement for accountants from their trade associations to be advocates of patient care. Indeed, there is no evidence to suggest that any of the professional accountancy bodies would support members who rail against what they consider to be illegal/immoral practices within hospitals, practices which have accounting involvement/implications. As accounting methods of control assume only a 'stage 1' level of moral reasoning on the part of those being monitored/controlled (doctors and nurses), there is an implicit relationship of low trust between the controller (the accountant) and doctors and nurses. The natural orientation of accounting information is directed towards the management of an organisation. In this sense accounting and accountants are an integral part of management. However, to leave the analysis here, implying that management in general and accountants in particular are the evil doers of harm to public services would not be wise.

While the criticisms of accounting's moral base have been argued elsewhere (Lovell 1995), and the reluctance of the professional accountancy bodies to support any of its members when they have taken an ethical stand is a matter of historical fact, to cast all managers and accountants as at best amoral, caring little, if at all, about such matters as the quality of healthcare available to society in general, or the quality of education, would be crass. Watson's (forthcoming) account of managers worrying openly about the ethical base of some of the practices taking place within their organisation is a useful reminder of the dilemmas that managers face, and they way they try to wrestle with them, rather than just tossing them aside as an irritant in an otherwise uncluttered journey towards ever greater levels efficiency and economy.

It is also worth remembering that capital rationing within public services in general and healthcare in particular have not just arisen since 1979. Capital rationing has existed for as long as there have been organisations (public or private) seeking capital. Hard choices have always been made about how much money the healthcare sector should receive as opposed to other sectors such as education, the prison service and social services. Previously decisions were made within central or local government, and there was little quantitative information available to the public by which to judge the defensibility of the decisions. The concern is that little quantitative information was used within the decision-making processes themselves (see Lewis 1997). The notions that considerable inefficiencies existed within public service organisations, that the public interest was too often subordinated to powerful interest groups and that accountability was too often lost in bureaucratic labyrinths, suggest that accounting cannot and should not be targeted as the scapegoat for all the malaise felt in public service organisations. However, the point of this essay is that the encroachment of private sector accounting practices and values into public service organisations raises fundamental questions over the ethical base of the professional groupings involved in the management and operation of these organisations.

CONCLUSIONS

Not only is there the potential for clashes of culture and orientation between those 'delivering' public services (doctors and nurses) and those responsible for managing those organisations. The picture is confused by the appearance of doctors and nurses appearing in both the management and 'workers' camps. However, it is the ethical reasoning to be found both explicitly and implicitly in the codes of conduct of nurses and accountants in particular that gives cause for concern. Putting to one side the issue of whether individual accountants are or are not philosophically committed to the principle of a health service for all, free at the point of delivery, there is the fundamental difference between those professionals whose primary, even sole responsibility, is the protection of patient care, while there are those whose natural orientation is towards 'the organisation'. In practice this means the senior management. All available evidence of the response of professional accountancy bodies towards those of its members who take ethical stands against alleged malpractices by employing organisations, is to provide some limited 'listening' service, but not to become involved in the affairs and not to take any public positions on individual cases. While no professional body (accountancy or otherwise) would support a member who is found guilty of unethical behaviour, neither have the professional accountancy bodies ever publicly supported any of its members who have defended the profession's code of conduct and stood up against alleged illegal practices. If an accountant makes an ethical stand, they are on their own, and as noted earlier, the outcomes normally experienced by whistleblowers are invariably unhappy ones.

While actual relationships might be strong, supportive and positive between individual accountants and nurses and doctors, the assumptions that underpin accounting models of control require low levels of trust to be assumed of doctors and nurses. The natural orientation of accounting information (and accountants) is towards management, if they are not already a part of management. The orientation of the law governing organisational relationships is firmly skewed towards business organisations,[7] and the position of the professional accountancy bodies towards those of its membership who take principled stands against organisational malpractices is to argue that the disagreements are private affairs between employer and employee. For individual healthcare accountants experiencing concerns over patient care, not only has their role within the hospital naturally placed them in the 'camp' which is seen as the source of many of the sectors problems, the accountant's profession has no requirements to take principled stands and will not publicly support that member if they choose to do so.

In the often highly charged and emotionally filled world of public services the accountant possesses a code of conduct and ethical base that owes its legacy to the world of profit-seeking work, in which protection of organisational (and latterly managerial) interests are paramount. Ironically, the professions of doctoring and nursing are facing ethical dilemmas of their own as members representing the management and operator levels vie for professional support in disputes over levels of patient care. The silence of the accountant's code of conduct in terms of wrestling with issues of great social and philosophical import, saves the profession's leaders from engaging in the quicksand of social and political policy choices. Yet accounting information is playing an increasingly important role in shaping public and political perceptions of organisational performance in the field of public services.

NOTES

1   The term 'profession' is itself contentious and has been subject to considerable academic scrutiny and debate. Whether a profession can ever actually exist is a moot point. Many would argue that what is important is understanding the processes that trade associations or other such groupings engage in order to become socially accepted and recognised as a profession. However, the term can only ever be a social construct. To make that construct more real aspiring 'professions' seek to satisfy certain criteria, two of the most important elements being an avowed claim that the association's members will always respect the 'public interest', and the institution and policing of a code of conduct.
2   Most of the UK's professional accountancy bodies provide advice and support systems that are superior to other UK 'professions'. These systems usually include the opportunity for a troubled member to discuss their problems with a fellow member under conditions of strict confidentiality. There may also be an opportunity for the troubled member to have a meeting with a lawyer specialising in employment law, paid for by the professional body. However, these systems can also be interpreted as mechanisms for keeping the troubled member at 'arms length'. The problem always remains that of the member. At no time would a professional accountancy association contemplate publicly supporting the actions of a member who might be fighting the actions of an unscrupulous employer. To debate why this might be so, and to do justice to the professional accountancy bodies and their arguments as to why such involvement is not practical, is beyond the scope of this chapter. The end result is the salient piece of information. As a professional accountant resisting pressure to be involved with something you consider to be immoral or illegal, or both, you are on your own.
3   It is sometimes argued that whistleblowers in sectors such as financial services or manufacturing enjoy low public support because the practices they rail against or the type of products/services provided by their employers are not deemed sufficiently important by the general public (this is sometimes referred to as stimulus ambiguity). However, evidence does not support this line of thinking. Whistleblowers from the health-care sector, whether they be doctors or nurses, have tended to fare no

better than their whistleblowing contemporaries from profit-seeking organisations.

4 Laughlin shows that although the principles of a Christian life represent the philosophical basis of resistance to economic reason within the Church, the way the buffers are operationalised is via the Diocesan committees and the Parochial Parish Councils.

5 With 'sacred' being used in the sense that those who undertake sacred work perform acts with value above that which can be measured in monetary terms (for example, how much would one pay to have the life of a loved one saved?), there are strong echoes of one of the original ideas behind the notion of a 'professional': being paid to work (by society) rather than working to be paid. The former indicates a service or 'output' that is required by society and society is prepared to pay to allow the professional (doctor, lawyer, priest) to practise their science/art/calling. The latter indicates a job of work that an individual undertakes because it is necessary to do so in order to earn a wage. However, the work is not of the kind that elevates it to the status of a social necessity.

6 Not only have commentators such as Mitchell and Sikka been extremely critical of the accountancy profession and its practices, but even one of the professional bodies (the Chartered Institute of Management Accountants) has criticised and divorced itself from proposals to revamp the way the profession is regulated. The proposals have been developed by the professional bodies themselves and in essence the proposals seek to retain self-regulation, but the situation appears to have been reached whereby even some of the professional bodies are openly doubting whether self-regulation can be maintained. It is becoming increasingly acknowledged that many potential conflicts of interest exist and self-regulation, once an inviolate condition of being a profession, is an increasingly problematic issue for the accountancy profession.

7 The basis of this assertion is reflected in the difficulty that principled dissenters in organisations (whistleblowers) have in coping with laws regarding confidentiality and property rights, and the considerable limitations of Industrial Tribunals in terms of the penalties that can be awarded against unprincipled employers and the problems in compensating wrongfully sacked employees for the loss of their employment – which can sometimes last a lifetime.

REFERENCES

Anderson, S.L. (1990) 'Patient advocacy and whistle-blowing in nursing: help for the helpers', *Nursing Forum*, 25 (3): 5–13.

Beaumont, A. (1997) 'Lifting lid on "crisis" prison block', *Evening Post*, 10 October: 6–7.

Butler, P. and Hunter, H. (1994) 'More whistleblowers face sanctions', *Health Service Journal*, 18 August: 6.

Champ, H. (1997) 'Whistle while you work', *Accountancy Age*, 26 June: 14–15.

De George, R.T. (1990) 'Whistleblowing', in W.M. Hoffman and J.M Moore (eds) *Business Ethics*, London: McGraw-Hill, 325–32.

Glazer, M. (1983) 'Ten whistleblowers and how they fared', *The Hasting Center Report*, December: 33–41.

Gorz, A. (1989) *Critique of Economic Reason*, trans. G. Handyside and C. Turner, London: Verso.

Laughlin, R. (1996) 'Principals and higher principals: accounting for accountability in the caring professions, in R. Munro and J. Mouritsen (eds) *Accountability: Power, ethos and the technologies of managing*, London: International Thomson Business Press.

Lewis, D. (1997) *Hidden Agendas: Politics, law and disorder*, London: Hamish Hamilton.

Lovell, A.T.A. (1992) 'Principled Dissent and Accountancy: Ethical dilemmas for individuals, professions and society', unpublished Ph.D. thesis, Nottingham Trent University.

—— (1994) 'Charles Robertson: in the eye of the storm', in G. Vinten (ed.) *Whistleblowing: Subversion or corporate citizenship?*, London: Paul Chapman Publishing Limited, 146–73.

—— (1995) 'Moral reasoning and moral atmosphere in the domain of accounting', *Accounting, Auditing and Accountability Journal*, 8 (3): 60–80.

—— (1996) 'Notions of Accountability and State Audit', *Financial Accountability and Management*, November.

McSweeney, B. (1994) 'Management by Accounting', in A.G. Hopwood and P. Miller (eds) *Accounting as Social and Institutional Practice*, Cambridge: Cambridge University Press.

—— (1996) 'The arrival of an accountability: explaining the imposition of management by accounting', in R. Munro and J. Mouritsen (eds) *Accountability: Power, ethos and the technologies of managing*, London: International Thomson Business Press, 201–24.

Near, J. and Miceli, M. (1986) 'Retaliation against whistleblowers', *Journal of Applied Psychology*, 71, Fall: 137–45.

Royal College of Nursing (1992) *Nurses Speak Out: A report on the work of the RCN whistleblow scheme*, available from the Royal College of Nursing.

Seedhouse, D. (1988) *Ethics: The heart of health care*, New York: John Wiley & Sons.

Soeken, K. and Soeken, D. (1987) *A Survey of Whistleblowers: Their stresses and coping strategies*, Laurel, MD: Association of Mental Health Specialists.

United Kingdom Central Council for Nursing, Midwifery and Health Visiting (1989) *Exercising Accountability: A framework to assist nurses, midwives and health visitors to consider ethical aspects of professional practice*.

Watson T.J. (forthcoming) 'Ethical Codes and Moral Communities: the Gunlaw temptation, the Simon solution and the David dilemma', in M. Parker (ed.) *The Ethics of Organisation*, London: Sage.

Winfield, M. (1990) *Minding Your Own Business: Self-regulation and whistleblowing in British companies*, Social Audit.

5

TAXATION AND ETHICAL ISSUES

Catherine Pilkington

> Taxes are enforced extractions and not voluntary contributions. To demand more in the name of morals is mere cant.
> (Judge Learned Hand, *Commissioner* v. *Newman*, CA – 2, 1947)

INTRODUCTION

On 6 April 1996 a new system for assessing and collecting tax was introduced in the United Kingdom. This system, introduced by the Finance Act of 1994, is called Self Assessment. A similar system of self assessment for limited companies, called Pay and File was introduced in 1993. Self Assessment transfers the legal responsibility for creating a charge to taxation from the Inland Revenue to the taxpayer. This responsibility intensifies ethical decisions for both taxpayers and tax practitioners. A self assessed tax system relies upon individuals filling in tax returns honestly, declaring income and making adjustments for expenses permitted by tax law. Taxpayers who wish to behave ethically must, on the one hand, declare all sources of income and, on the other, not overstate tax deductible expenses. Sometimes tax law requires interpretation to determine the correct amount of income and tax-deductible expenses, in which case a tax practitioner may be needed. A tax practitioner acts as an agent for the taxpayer and, by applying technical knowledge, identifies the limits of the law as it applies to each individual taxpayer (Marshall and Smith 1997: 16). The role of the tax practitioner is to minimise the client's tax liability by ensuring that their affairs are arranged appropriately to secure the lowest possible tax bill. The tax practitioner faces pressures from the client to find loopholes in the legislation to reduce their liabilities. Fear of the loss of a client with consequent loss of fee and status, can lead to aggressive interpretation of the tax laws which might contravene the general public's expectations of professional ethical behaviour.

This chapter addresses two aspects of taxation and ethics: taxpayer ethics and why taxpayers comply with tax laws; and the conflict between the personal and the professional ethics of the tax practitioner.

TAXPAYER ETHICS

Paying tax: deterrence theory?

A generally held belief and one upon which the Self Assessment tax system in the United Kingdom relies for its success, is that the taxpayer's fear of being detected while evading tax, will ensure that they will comply with tax law. The Self Assessment legislation has introduced penalties for the late filing of tax returns and a system of random audit of tax returns. Both these new measures have been heavily publicised in the Inland Revenue's media campaigns. The fear of detection or 'deterrence theory' suggests that taxpayers will maximise their own self interest by performing a cost–benefit analysis, comparing the benefits of evading tax with the penalties of being caught out evading tax (Reckers *et al.* 1994). The penalties of evading may not only be economic in the form of fines but also sociological. Taxpayers consider their own self image and social obligations which would be damaged by being caught evading tax. Currently only between 2.5 per cent and 5 per cent of self-employed taxpayers and 3 per cent of companies are investigated by the Inland Revenue each year. In addition, the new random audit system will only select 8000 tax returns or 0.1 per cent of tax returns for audit. (This actually equates to approximately twenty tax returns per tax district.) Given the comparatively small number of tax investigations and random audits, deterrence theory would suggest that a significant number of taxpayers would evade paying tax. However, evidence from the USA where only 1 per cent of tax returns are selected for tax audit, suggests that compliance rates are as high as 83 per cent (Doucet 1995). Deterrence theory does not therefore provide a wholly satisfactory explanation of why taxpayers comply with tax laws. The question then is this: is there any evidence to suggest that people comply with tax laws because they believe that paying tax is an ethically correct thing to do?

Paying tax: an ethical decision?

There is a significant amount of academic literature which debates why people comply with tax laws when the chances of detection are minimal. Jackson and Milliron (1986) summarise the factors which academic researchers have found to influence taxpayers' compliance with tax laws. Notably, they report that research indicates that older taxpayers and females overestimate the probability of detection and are hence more compliant. People in the middle and high incomes are more compliant than people on lower incomes although factors such as the education level of taxpayers and the source of income are also found to be influential. Self-employed people have a greater opportunity to evade tax than employed taxpayers who pay tax at source under the PAYE scheme. On the influence of ethics on taxpayer compliance, Jackson and Milliron state that 'taxpayer ethics are a nebulous concept to define'. Research by Westat cited by Jackson and Milliron came to the conclusion that 'taxpayers were generally ambivalent about whether tax cheating, especially when small amounts were involved, is morally wrong'.

An attempt to link tax compliance with morality and ethics was made in research carried out by Wallace and Wolfe (1995). In this research, compliance with tax laws was used as a surrogate for ethical behaviour. The empirical research suggested that the threat of a tax audit prompted taxpayers to comply. The level of compliance was even greater when the source of income was perceived to be readily and independently verifiable, for example bank or building society interest. They conclude:

> If obeying tax laws is seen as a desirable attribute of ethical behaviour and such behaviour is enhanced by improved deterrents through audit procedures, then one means of encouraging ethical behaviour is via improved audit procedures.
>
> (1995: 164)

Bailey (1995), in a critique of Wallace and Wolfe's paper, questions whether complying with tax laws is in fact ethical behaviour. Bailey suggests that there is no common ground in the dictionary definitions of the words 'compliance' and 'ethics'. Compliance suggests 'following' whereas ethics suggests 'leading'. He states: 'Cheating on tax is not ethical but does this mean that complying is being ethical?'

Complying with a law which the individual believes to be morally

84

wrong could be in fact behaving in an unethical manner. The wholesale rejection of the poll tax in the United Kingdom is an example of taxpayers' noncompliance with tax legislation which was deemed to be unfair. However, many taxpayers paid their poll tax, and hence complied with tax law. If they believed the poll tax to be unfair, were they behaving unethically?

Reckers *et al.* (1994) recognised that taxpayers do not have a homogeneous viewpoint as regards whether evading tax is a moral issue. They identified that some taxpayers viewed the paying of tax as an ethically correct thing to do, and examined the influence of ethical beliefs on tax compliance decisions. Their research examined the interaction of ethical beliefs in relation to two hypotheses.

The first hypothesis tested whether ethical beliefs interacted with the 'frame' or 'prospect' when taxpayers are arriving at a decision to evade tax. Two frames or scenarios were used. The first scenario considered the taxpayer to be in the position of reclaiming tax and the second presented the taxpayer in the position of having to declare additional income and pay more tax. The second hypothesis tested whether ethical beliefs interacted with high or low tax rates.

Reckers *et al.* found that people who considered tax evasion to be morally wrong were not influenced in their decision to evade by tax rates or by the 'framing' of the situation. Conversely, those who believed that evading tax is morally defensible, did not declare income if it resulted in additional tax being paid but were more inclined to declare income if they were in a tax repayment situation. Their research indicates that not all taxpayers have the same level of morality with regard to tax evasion. Reckers. *et al.* conclude:

> Ethical values effect the decision process by screening or setting bounds on choice possibilities and limiting the means available to achieve desired outcomes. . . . When tax evasion is seen as a moral issue individuals are less likely to evade tax.
>
> (1994: 827)

A rather more radical viewpoint of taxpayers' ethics is expressed by Alm *et al.* (1992) who suggest that individuals demonstrate a wide diversity of ethical beliefs in relation to taxation. 'Compliance does not occur from a belief by subjects that evasion is wrong . . . the results suggest that compliance occurs because some individuals value the public good that their taxpayments finance' (1992: 36).

There is clearly a link between ethical behaviour and efficient running of the economy. Noreen (1988) suggests: 'An individual obeys utilitarian ethical rules in the expectation that others will also obey the rules and that as a consequence systems will function more efficiently and there is more to be consumed by every one' (1988: 360). However, even if ethical norms of behaviour could be established, Noreen warns:

> Behavioural norms or ethical rules are a most fragile enforcement mechanism. The success of behavioural norms in enforcing ethical behaviour crucially depends upon what people think the norms are. If everyone thinks it is normal to cheat and deceive then people will cheat and deceive without feeling guilty.
>
> (1988: 367)

Kaplan *et al.* (1988) consider attribution theory in relation to the topic of tax evasion. Attribution theory assumes that individuals attempt to justify their actions by events that happen in the world round about them. Kaplan *et al.* conclude that if a taxpayer is in financial distress this is seen as a justification for tax evasion. If a taxpayer does not perceive the evasion as a moral issue and can rationalise the evasion with situational needs they are more likely to evade. Their results demonstrate that individuals look to the behaviour of others to justify their own behaviour.

Establishing ethical norms of taxpayer behaviour is further complicated by the belief that the behaviour of people in the public eye is expected to be whiter than white. The recent events surrounding the tax affairs of John Birt, the Controller of the BBC, demonstrate that a higher level of ethical behaviour is demanded of people in high profile positions in public life. John Birt started his career as Director General of the BBC not as an employee but as a subcontractor. His salary and expenses were paid to a company called John Birt Productions Limited, of which Mr and Mrs Birt were the directors and shareholders. This type of arrangement was not uncommon in the entertainment industry and gave a small tax advantage to Mr Birt and his family. There was public outcry in the media and the press when it became known that John Birt was paying less tax as a subcontractor than he would have paid as an employee. Finally, in March 1993, following much public debate, Mr Birt became an employee of the BBC and was paid through the PAYE system. In moral terms John Birt was not treated as an equal.

Brytting (1994: 15–34) relates the story of a similar fate which befell a Swedish banker, Jacob Palmstierna. The banker was forced to resign from SE Banken following a high profile investigation into his tax affairs. Mr Palmstierna was cleared by the Swedish court of tax irregularities on the basis that the use of a luxury villa was needed for Mr Palmstierna's duties at the bank, and its subsequent purchase at a discount, under Swedish tax law, did not constitute a taxable benefit. The discussion which followed in the media highlighted the problems of engaging in public moral discourse. Three basic characteristics of moral behaviour were questioned by the public media debate. First, moral behaviour requires that all individuals be treated equally. This was not the case for Mr Palmstierna since a similar investigation into the affairs of a bank clerk would probably not have led to resignation. Second, Mr Palmstierna was denied autonomy. He was forced to resign to save the reputation of the bank and was not permitted to follow his own conscience. Third, there was no consistency in the treatment of Mr Palmstierna since other top managers received similar benefits and were not forced to resign. Brytting concludes that, given the modern mass media, arriving at a moral consensus of ethical behaviour is not possible because the participators are not following the same rules. Therefore the issue of what is and is not taxpaying ethical behaviour is clouded by different and higher expectations by the media and the public, of persons in positions of authority.

In summary, following the introduction of Self Assessment, the Inland Revenue has attempted to establish a culture of compliance by advertising the penalties for late filing of tax returns and the prospect of a random audit. Academic research supports the view that the threat of detection is most effective with taxpayers who misapprehend the risks of detection. Taxpayers consider the morality of evading tax but are influenced by both their own situational needs and the situational needs of others. The establishment of norms of ethical taxpaying behaviour is hindered by the media and the public who demand a higher level of ethical behaviour from people in public life.

TAX PRACTITIONER ETHICS

Tax avoidance and tax evasion: the conflict of professional ethics and personal ethics

Every man is entitled if he can to arrange his affairs so that the tax attaching under the appropriate Acts is less than it

could be. If he succeeds in ordering them so as to secure
that result, then however unappreciative the Commissioners
of Inland Revenue or his fellow taxpayers may be of his
ingenuity he cannot be compelled to pay an increased tax.

(*Lord Tomlin IRC* v. *Duke of Westminster, 1936*)

The tax practitioner, acting as an agent of a client, has a professional ethical duty to that client to minimise the client's tax liability
by legal means. Pressure to exploit the law and find loopholes
comes from the client, and fear of losing the client will intensify the
personal moral dilemma of the tax practitioner. In a wider sense,
the constant cat and mouse game of the so-called tax avoidance
industry (in which the tax professionals find a loophole which is
then plugged by legislation leaving the tax professionals to find
another hole which in turn will be filled by more legislation), under-
mines the integrity of the tax system.

The personal moral dilemma of the tax practitioner is further
intensified by the courts, who permit within certain parameters a
grey area called tax avoidance. The above quotation taken from the
cornerstone tax avoidance case, *Lord Tomlin IRC* v. *Duke of
Westminster* (1936), demonstrates the dividing line between tax
evasion and tax avoidance. Tax evasion is a criminal offence and
involves deliberate falsification of information and deceit, whereas
tax avoidance involves arranging events and transactions in a
certain timescale to secure a tax advantage. There is no general anti-
avoidance legislation in the UK that would enable the courts to
cancel a transaction because it is motivated by tax avoidance. The
courts must apply the facts of each individual case to the legislation. Case law has moved on from the *Duke of Westminster* case,
and the tax authorities and the courts now see a distinction between
artificial arrangements to avoid tax which they will reject, and
arrangements of a taxpayer's affairs or selection of a commercial
option in order to minimise tax liabilities. The courts will reject a
wholly false scenario and will view the stages in a series of transactions as one, as in the tax cases *Furniss* v. *Dawson* (1984) and
Ramsay v. *IRC* (1981). However, if a commercial motivation is
evident, the courts are likely to permit a transaction even if tax
avoidance was a primary reason for the events; this was the position
taken in *Craven* v. *White* (1988). A more recent case, *Pigott* v.
Staines Investment Co. Ltd (1995), involved a company which
obtained a tax advantage from transferring profits within the group.
The courts decided that the method of transferring profits was both

normal and commercial, and the fact that the motivation for the transactions was to secure a tax advantage was incidental. In *IRC* v. *McGuckian* (1997), it is clear that the court did not view tax avoidance as a moral issue. The counsel for the taxpayer admitted that the complex series of transactions involved in the case, motivated by tax avoidance, had no ethical merit. Lord Browne Wilkinson commented that this was irrelevant and that 'statutory construction' was more important than 'moral approval'. The case was decided against the taxpayer not on the morality of the tax avoidance scheme but on the grounds that the series of transactions, following the principle established in the *Ramsay* case, had no commercial motivation. Flint (1997) comments that criticism in the professional press of the scheme in the *McGuckian* case, centred on the scheme being 'flawed' and 'unsubtle' rather than the morality of attempting to avoid tax. The tax profession has not yet fully addressed the issue of whether they accept the ethical view that a tax avoidance scheme which is within the letter of the law but not the spirit, is acceptable. In other words, is there such a thing as unethical tax avoidance?

Hansen *et al.* (1992) illustrate the conflict between professional tax ethics and personal ethics by way of a case study. The example of transfer pricing is used to demonstrate that a legitimate tax avoidance scheme can have consequences beyond the corporate objective of minimising tax liabilities. Transfer pricing is the practice of setting a price between divisions or groups of companies. Sometimes groups and divisions operate in different countries with different tax regimes. There is potential for obtaining a tax advantage by fixing transfer prices. Therefore, to eliminate unfairness legislation exists to establish acceptable methods of transfer pricing. The scenario set by Hansen *et al.* is of a manufacturing company making losses in the USA while its European marketing divisions are making profits. An increase in the transfer price between the US company and its divisions secures a tax advantage by absorbing US losses and reducing the local taxes paid in Europe. The adjustment to the transfer prices is within the US tax laws, which state that providing the transactions are at arm's length there will be no intervention by the tax authorities (IRC s.482). A similar provision exists in UK tax law (ICTA 1988 s.770) which allows various methods of calculating transfer prices in order to demonstrate that a transaction is at arm's length. In the case outlined by Hansen *et al.*, the company is using one such method based on the ultimate resale price less the divisions costs. Normally, transfer prices were negotiated by the divisions who were appraised and remunerated on the basis of the divisions' profits. The points to consider were these:

1   From the viewpoint of tax avoidance, the law permits a choice in method of calculating the transfer price and the taxpayer is allowed to select the method which minimises their tax liability. The scheme used by the company in the case study would satisfy both the US and the UK courts in that it is both commercial and not preordained in the sense that the outcome is uncertain. A tax professional would not, in advising this scheme and minimising the tax liability, be in breach of professional ethical requirements.

2   However from a personal ethical standpoint the application of the transfer price increase creates other problems. The motivation and remuneration policies for the divisional managers are affected by removing the responsibility for negotiating transfer prices. Other commercial decisions may be made regarding plant closures and the curtailing and expansion of operations dependent upon the profits made by the divisions.

Hansen *et al.* conclude as follows:

> Tax professionals should be more concerned with what is right than with technical compliance with the law. [...] Ethical standards and conduct should be above the self serving actions taken by those with a vested interest in the outcome of a particular event. [...] The human issue must be a component of an ethical code of conduct.
>
> (1992: 685–6)

In relation to taxation, is it possible to resolve the conflict between professional tax ethics and personal ethics by incorporating the consideration of the outcome of a tax avoidance scheme, into an ethical code of conduct for tax practitioners?

Establishing a code of ethical behaviour for tax practitioners is already complicated by the diverse structure of the tax profession. In the UK there is no system of approval or regulation of tax practitioners and the services they offer, either by the Inland Revenue, the government, or the 'tax profession' itself. The tax profession comprises largely members of the Chartered Institute of Taxation (CIOT), the Institute of Chartered Accountants of England and Wales (ICAEW), the Institute of Chartered Accountants of Scotland (ICAS), and the Chartered Institute of Certified Accountants (ACCA). However, taxation services are also offered to the general public by members of other accounting bodies and by unqualified accountants. Self assessment introduced for the tax year 1996–7 has widened further the market for tax services to include banks and tax shops who offer tax return completion services. As a consequence of the diversity of participants in the tax profession, there is no one code of ethics to which tax practitioners must adhere. The professional accountancy bodies issue ethical codes independently and these include guidance in relation to taxation. However two of the major players in the tax profession, the CIOT and the ICAEW, have issued ethical rules in relation to taxation jointly and their members must comply with these rules or face disciplinary actions by their professional bodies. These ethical rules and some of the practical ethical conflicts they attempt to resolve are discussed in the following section.

Practitioners' ethics: 'Ethical rules and practice guidelines on professional conduct in relation to taxation'

The 'Ethical rules and practice guidelines on professional conduct in relation to taxation' were issued jointly by the CIOT and the ICAEW on 6 November 1995. This set of rules and practice guidelines brings together existing advice published by the CIOT and the ICAEW. In the following passages, references to sections of the 'Ethical rules and practice guidelines' are given in brackets. The ethical conflicts faced by tax practitioners can be grouped into four areas: the grey area governing tax avoidance and tax evasion; the discovery of an error made by the tax authorities which results in an under-collection of tax or an over-repayment of tax; and the discovery of an irregularity perpetrated by a client; extent, manner and timing of disclosure.

Tax avoidance

The 'Ethical rules and practice guidelines' do not specifically rule out avoidance schemes but asks members to consider the 'merits of arrangements that are within the letter but not the spirit of the law' (2.11). The practice of avoidance is not therefore dismissed entirely by the 'Ethical rules and practice guidelines'.

The discovery of an error made by the tax authorities

An error made by the tax authorities can result in an under-collection of tax or an over-repayment of tax. Both the taxpayer and the tax practitioner are liable to prosecution under the Theft Act 1968 if they fail to inform the tax authorities of their mistake. The 'Ethical rules and practice guidelines' advise strongly that permission is obtained from the client to inform the tax authorities of the error. If permission to disclose is not granted, the practitioner should consider whether there are any 'special circumstances' why this permission should be withheld. The 'Ethical rules and practice guidelines' do not give any examples of such 'special circumstances' and the Inland Revenue do not see how 'special circumstances' could exist (5) although in practice, trivial amounts need not be disclosed. However, there is no guidance on the level of error that is considered trivial. Ultimately the practitioner is advised to cease acting for the client and to consider telling the tax authorities without the client's permission in order to be protected from prosecution.

The discovery of irregularities perpetrated by a client

An ethical dilemma encountered in practice concerns the discovery by the tax practitioner of an 'irregularity' in a client's tax affairs. Where the irregularity amounts to deliberate fraud, the 'Ethical rules and practice guidelines' are quite clear that a 'member must do nothing to assist a client to commit a criminal offence' (4.1). An irregularity can be defined as a deliberate under-declaration of income or the claiming of an expense which is not allowable for tax relief. The 'Ethical rules and practice guidelines' give the following recommendations with regards to the discovery of tax irregularities in a client's affairs.

If the irregularity is considered to be material and by implication this includes examples of deliberate fraud, the 'Ethical rules and practice guidelines' require that the practitioner must cease to act for the client in all matters not just those relating to direct tax, and also inform the tax authorities that he no longer acts for the client. The tax practitioner has no whistleblowing duty in law to report the circumstances of the irregularity to the tax authorities except in the case of suspicions regarding money laundering. However 'if the matter in question affect the accounts or statements which carry a report signed by the member as to their accuracy' the member must 'inform the Revenue that he has information indicating that the accounts or statements cannot be relied upon' (4.22). The tax authorities are then in a position to instigate their own investigation into the client's affairs. If the irregularity is not considered material by the member, the member need not cease to act for the client (4.21). There is no guidance given regarding the definition of materiality and according to the 'Ethical rules and practice guidelines' and this is left to the practitioners' 'judgement'. Materiality is a multi-faceted concept and can relate to both the size and the significance of an item. A relatively small item, for example the omission of the disclosure of some of a director's emoluments, is likely to be material for its significance rather than its size. Materiality is not accepted by the tax authorities as a concept; they believe that simply because an error is small does not mean it can be overlooked (2.21). The dilemma is further compounded by the situation that often occurs in practice where the tax agent also acts as the auditor of a limited company.

An auditor defines materiality according to the Statement of Auditing Standard 220 (SAS 220) as 'an expression of the relative significance or importance of a particular matter in the context of financial statements as a whole'. A matter is judged material by an auditor if its omission would 'reasonably influence the addressees of the auditor's report' (SAS 220). An audit opinion giving a true and fair view can be given on financial statements which contain a tax irregularity provided it is not material by the definition in SAS 220 and does not influence the addressees of the auditor's report who are the shareholders and not the tax authorities. For example, a company may pay a supplier in kind at cost and therefore omit the gross profit on this transaction from the accounts by understating turnover. The transaction is not significant to the addressees of the audit report, the shareholders, providing its size does not distort the picture presented by the accounts and affect the level of dividend distribution. In the case of a proprietary company where the directors are the shareholders, the size of the transaction would be even less of an issue because the directors are in the position to influence the dividend policy regardless of the level of profit. However such a transaction would be material for tax purposes for two reasons. First, the government is defrauded of its share of the profit on the transaction. Second, if the tax authorities had knowledge of the transaction, the credibility and honesty of the directors would be undermined. The tax authorities, unlike the auditor, are unable to assess the risk of this transaction being an isolated incident and therefore they could be influenced in their decision to investigate the company. The problem for the tax practitioner is to determine which definition of materiality is applicable. Clearly if the practitioner judges that the tax authorities would consider the non-disclosure of this irregularity as material then, under the guidance given in the 'Ethical rules and practice guidelines', the practitioner should resign both as auditor and as agent for the client and suffer the consequential loss of fee income.

The extent, manner and timing of disclosure of information to the tax authorities.

The 'Ethical rules and practice guidelines' advises tax practitioners to assist the client to make 'full disclosure' of the 'relevant' facts but recognises that the tax practitioner is bound by client confidentiality, and that sometimes the client will not cooperate. 'Full disclosure' and 'relevant' are open to interpretation and even negotiation. The Inland Revenue penalty system allows for mitigation of penalties based on the timeliness of disclosure and also, the extent of disclosure. Empirical research by McBarnet (1991) indicated that practitioners adopt a minimalist approach to disclosure to the tax authorities. One respondent commented, 'ask and it shall be disclosed but not otherwise'. An Inland Revenue officer quoted by McBarnet defined the grey area between avoidance and evasion as follows: 'It is not evasion if they (tax practitioners) don't tell us, but it is overstepping the boundary if they lie when we ask' (1991: 329).

Practitioners were presented with the case of a client claiming a deduction for wages paid to his mother. It was accepted that the client would overpay his mother. The tax practitioners suggested that the probable approach of the UK profession would be to 'put it forward as a deduction and let the Revenue argue if they thought it fit'. How much to disclose regarding the background of the deduction, the age of the mother, nature of her duties, and state of her health, would clearly influence the Inland Revenue in initiating questions. In practice, if any disclosure of the background were made to the tax authorities, the words would be carefully chosen to give the facts without exciting questions from the Inspector. It is clear from this example that professional ethics, the minimisation of the client's tax liability, overrides any personal ethical considerations of the tax practitioners.

Resolving the professional ethic conflict?

The 'Ethical rules and practice guidelines' do not resolve the conflict between professional ethics and personal ethics. Indeed, they could be seen to provide a means of circumventing ethical conflict (Hansen *et al.* 1992). Their function is primarily an exercise in establishing mutual trust between the tax authorities and the tax practitioner. Mutual trust can save unnecessary tax investigations and therefore clients' fees and tax authorities' costs. The 'Ethical rules and practice guidelines' were reviewed by the Inland Revenue and by Customs and Excise and although they did not agree with 'every view expressed', they accept that the 'Ethical rules and practice guidelines' are a 'basis for dealings with members and the Departments'. To some extent, the 'Ethical rules and practice guidelines' are sold as a marketing tool and can be viewed as a public relations exercise (Mitchell *et al.* 1994). Tax returns and computations submitted by a qualified tax practitioner, who is also bound by ethical rules are possibly perceived by the Inland Revenue as more reliable and hence provide an insurance for the client against an Inland Revenue investigation. One of the important reasons for the issuing of the 'Ethical rules and practice guidelines' is as a defence against the regulation of the tax profession by an outside body such as the Government or the Inland Revenue. At present the market for providing tax services is completely open. The 'Ethical rules and practice guidelines' issued by the CIOT and the ICAEW are binding only on the members of those professional bodies and therefore do not ensure exclusive jurisdiction over the practice of taxation (Jamal and Bowie 1995). Mitchell *et al.* (1994) express the view that issuing codes of ethics is a means of securing members' sectional interest and in this respect, the 'Ethical rules and practice guidelines' are a means of ensuring that the two professional bodies, the CIOT and the ICAEW, are in the forefront of any moves by the Government towards regulation of the tax profession. The CIOT are clearly in favour of regulation which is viewed by one past president of the CIOT as a means of providing protection to the public from 'the unclean, the unwashed, the unqualified practitioner with no professional standards' (Luder 1994). The issuing of these joint ethical rules by the CIOT and the ICAEW are an exercise in demonstrating a united front and a willingness to put their own houses in order should regulation of the tax profession happen in the future.

CONCLUSION

Regulation of the tax profession may not solve the conflict which exists between the tax practitioner's duty to minimise the client's tax liability and a wider duty to consider the consequences of tax avoidance schemes. Australia is the only country which requires formal registration of tax return preparers. However of the 28,000 registered agents only 50 per cent are members of professional accounting bodies and hence bound by a code of ethics (Marshall and Smith 1997: 16). Even if there was a way of unifying the many facets of the tax profession in the UK, professional ethics or minimising a client's tax position will remain the overriding motivation of tax practitioners, as can be seen by the example of the 'Ethical rules and practice guidelines' of the CIOT and the ICAEW. The question raised earlier in this chapter was: is it possible to resolve the conflict between professional tax ethics and personal ethics? Another question may be more relevant. Is it necessary to resolve the conflict at all? Taxation is imposed by a higher authority. Ethics forms part of decision process (Reckers *et al.* 1994); however, to do more or pay more for the sake of a consequential ideal could be viewed as excessive. To return to the opening quotation of this chapter:

> Taxes are enforced extractions and not voluntary contributions. To demand more in the name of morals is mere cant.
> (Judge Learned Hand, *Commissioner* v. *Newman*, CA – 2, 1947)

TAX CASES

Commissioner v. *Newman* (CA – 2, 1947) 159 F 2d 848
Craven v. *White* [1988] STC476
Furniss v. *Dawson* [1984] STC 153
IRC v. *McGuckian* [1997] STI 741
Lord Tomlin IRC v. *Duke of Westminster* [1936] AC 1,19 TC 490
Pigott v. *Staines Investment Co. Ltd* [1995] STC 114
Ramsay v. *IRC* [1981] STC 174

REFERENCES

Alm, J., McClelland, G.H. and Schulze, W.D. (1992) 'Why do people pay taxes?', *Journal of Public Economics*, 48: 21–38.
Bailey, A.D. (1995) 'Commentary on the ethics of compliance with tax laws and regulations', *Research on Accounting Ethics*, 1: 177–86.

Brytting, T. (1994) 'The victimised banker. On the moralising discourse about Jacob Palmstierna', in Harvey, van Luijk and Steimann (eds), *European Casebook on Business Ethics*, Prentice Hall.

Butterworths UK Tax Guide (1995–6): 10–29.

CIOT and ICAEW *Ethical Rules and Practice Guidelines Professional Conduct in Relation to Taxation*, November 1995.

Doucet, M.S. (1995) 'Comments on "Do expected audit procedures prompt ethical behaviour? Evidence on tax compliance rates" ', *Research on Accounting Ethics*, 1: 169–76.

Flint, A. (1997) 'Editorial', *Taxation Practitioner*, 8: 3.

Hansen, D.R., Crosser, R.L. and Laufer, D. (1992) 'Moral ethics v. tax ethics. The case of transfer pricing among multinational corporations', *Journal of Business Ethics*, 11: 679–86.

Jackson, B.R. and Milliron, V.C. (1986) 'Tax compliance research problems and prospects', *Journal of Accounting Literature*, 5: 125–61.

Jamal, K. and Bowie, N.E. (1995) 'Theoretical considerations for a meaningful code of professional ethics', *Journal of Business Ethics*, 14: 703–14.

Kaplan, S.E., Reckers, P.M.J. and Roark, S.J. (1988) 'An attribution theory analysis of tax evasion related judgements', *Accounting Organizations and Society*, 13 (4): 371–9.

Lagerberg, F. (1995) 'Chartered bodies unite over ethics', *Taxation*, 16 November: 150.

Luder, I. (1994) *Taxation Practitioner*, June: 33.

Marshall, R. and Smith, M. (1997) 'The taxation lottery', *Accountancy Age*, 10 July 1997.

McBarnet, D. (1991) 'Whiter than white collar and crime: tax, fraud, insurance and the management of stigma', *British Journal of Sociology*, 42 (3).

Mitchell, A., Puxty, T., Sikka, P. and Willmott, H. (1994) 'Ethical statements as smokescreens for sectional interests: a case of the UK accountancy profession', *Journal of Business Ethics*, 13: 39–51.

Noreen, E. (1988) 'The economics of ethics: a new perspective on agency theory', *Accounting Organizations and Society*, 13 (4): 359–69.

Reckers, P.M.J., Sanders, D.L. and Roark, S.J. (1994) 'The influence of ethical attitudes on taxpayer compliance', *National Tax Journal*, 4: 825–36.

Wallace, C. and Wolfe, C. (1995) 'Do expected audit procedures prompt more ethical behaviour?', *Research on Accounting Ethics*, 1: 145–67

6

THE PROFESSIONAL ACCOUNTING BODIES AS THE GUARDIANS OF ACCOUNTING AND AUDITING ETHICS

John Blake and Ray Gardiner

INTRODUCTION

In recent years a formidable group of four campaigners has argued that the professional accounting bodies have failed in their duty as guardians of accounting and auditing ethics. The group comprises one politician, Dr Austin Mitchell, the Labour MP for Great Grimsby, and three academics, the late Professor Tony Puxty, Professor Prem Sikka, and Professor Hugh Willmott. The tone of their argument is captured in an article by the three academic members of the group:

> Accountancy professes to be a profession distinguished by its claim to serve the public. It also claims to report independently of the management. This is not evident from the ethical guidelines, auditing practices or the lobbying practices of the accountancy bodies. The accountancy bodies urge their members to avoid conflicts of interest but they themselves routinely compromise their own ethical position.
>
> (Sikka *et al.* 1994: 29)

The choice of Professor Sikka as 'Personality of the Year' by *Accountancy Age* readers in 1995 indicates the strong influence of this group.

THE RADICAL CRITICS' CASE

The term 'radical critics' is one that we have devised to cover the group of four campaigners. Their case is that the UK accounting profession is currently failing society at what we term both the 'micro' and the 'macro' level.

At the 'micro' level failure by audit firms on specific assignments is evidenced by corporate collapses within weeks of receiving clean audit reports and by DTI investigations which highlight audit deficiencies. These firms also connive at 'creative accounting' both with their own clients and with other firms' clients, through the practice of 'opinion shopping'.

At the 'macro' level the professional accounting bodies are dominated by the large accounting firms. They act against the public interest by:

1 Operating a disciplinary system that is considered to be unduly tolerant, particularly in relation to the big accounting firms.
2 Failing to tighten up on accounting standards in such a way as to eliminate 'creative accounting' abuse.
3 Formulating auditing standards designed to restrict auditors to a 'passive' rather than an 'active' role.
4 Lobbying government to restrict accountability and auditor responsibility.

A key element in this critique is the 'auditor expectations gap'. Sikka *et al.* refer to numerous studies which 'have shown that there are considerable differences between what the public expects from an audit and what the auditing profession understands the audit objectives to be' (1992: 1). They conclude that 'the gap can be managed or reduced only by embracing socially desirable audit objectives and reforming the institutions of auditing' (1992: 30). We explore the view that the existence of an 'expectations gap' can and should be solved by matching audit performance to user expectations below.

We see two elements to the radical critics case against existing audit and accounting practices:

1 That these fail to meet needs for information about the financial standing of companies. Thus Sikka and Armstrong argue 'the ultimate concern is to provide protection for shareholders' (1995: 30). Taking a broader view, Sikka *et al.* criticise auditors whose 'silence has resulted in investors, creditors, pension scheme

members, insurance policy holders, bank depositors and employees losing savings and jobs' (1994: 29).

2 The radical critics are among those who argue that, apart from information on a company's own financial standing, there is an implicit duty on a company to report to a much wider range of 'stakeholders'. Examples of issues include employee and environmental information. The professional bodies are particularly criticised for not pursuing the ideas for a broadening of 'accountability' put forward in the *The Corporate Report* (Accounting Standards Steering Committee 1975).

An extensive range of remedies are put forward. A brief summary of those in Mitchell *et al.* is:

1 Accounting and auditing should be regulated by a single body. 'These functions are best performed by independent agencies reflecting a plurality of interests. An independent and democratic body with a statutory base is needed. It should be composed of representatives from all interested parties' (Mitchell *et al.* 1991: 17).

2 Specifically accounting should:
   - Include systematic information on corporate objectives.
   - Contain future-oriented information.
   - Be filed within ninety days.
   - Show cash flow data.
   - Analyse 'the expected maturity of current items'.
   - Include an audited chairman's report.
   - Restrict the definition of extraordinary items.
   - Give extensive detail on research and development.
   - Drop the 'true and fair view' override.
   - Drop interest capitalisation.
   - In addition, audit committees should be compulsory for large plcs.

3 Auditing reforms include:
   - Auditors should not be allowed to provide other services.
   - Appointed auditors should be changed every five years.
   - Regulations on internal control, similar to those for building societies, should apply to all plcs.
   - Each audit report should state the matters for which auditors acknowledge responsibility.
   - Auditors' responsibilities should be clarified by statute. Mitchell

et al. argue that 'audits are a meaningless and expensive burden unless auditors owe a duty of care to all the corporate stakeholders' (1991: 19).

- Auditors should be subject to tighter disciplinary sanctions.
- Accountancy firms should be required to file, for public information, a financial report.
- There should be a monitoring system for audit firms independent of the accounting profession.
- Key information on the audit firm's relationship with the company, such as the letter of engagement and the letter of representation, should be on public record.

Finally, an extensive list of social disclosures is called for on:

1 Environmental issues.
2 Energy consumption.
3 Health and safety.
4 Employee training.
5 Employment of the disabled.
6 Low pay.

To summarise, the radical critics see a history of incompetent and unethical behaviour by a range of audit firms. The professional accounting bodies are seen as acting as a trade association, protecting the interests of their members and particularly the large firms, while not acting effectively in their role of 'self-regulation'. The remedy is seen as being to introduce a broad based, accountable, independent body to regulate accounting and auditing and to pursue an extensive range of reforms to auditing and accounting regulation that will considerably extend the responsibility of the accounting profession.

EVIDENCE FOR THE CASE

The range and extent of the evidence mustered by the radical critics to support their case is at first sight impressive. Indeed, we would accept that there is a case for reform and explore below the response of the accounting profession to that case, contrasting it with the solutions put forward by the radical critics. At the same time we feel that the case has been overstated in a number of respects. To illustrate our argument we now turn to three aspects of the evidence put forward:

1 Criticism of the auditors in DTI reports.
2 Claims that the profession has a history of obstructing progress.
3 The expectations gap.

Criticism of the auditors in DTI reports

A theme that runs repeatedly through the criticism of auditors' work is that investigations authorised by the UK Department of Trade and Industry (DTI) into companies have, on occasion, been critical of the role of auditors. An impression is given that the larger firms are particularly culpable. For example: 'Over the years, Department of Trade and Industry inspectors have criticised several of the major accounting firms for the inadequacies in their work' (Willmott *et al.* 1990: 15).

A particularly thorough examination of DTI reports is provided by Sikka and Willmott (1995). Their analysis of eighty-two DTI reports over the period from 1971 to 1993 is summarised in Table 6.1:

Thus in only half these cases of company difficulty was any blame attached to the auditors. In these cases sometimes more than one auditor firm is criticised. Splitting these by audit firm size we find that of a total of fifty-two, thirteen were 'Big Six' (formerly 'Big Eight'), the remaining thirty-nine being accounted for by other firms.

Mitchell *et al.* advise us that: 'Around six firms audit two-thirds of all quoted companies' (1991: 27). In view of this, to attract only 25 per cent of critical comment in DTI reports might appear a creditable performance. Nevertheless, it appears that when any client of an audit firm, which may have over a hundred partners, appears in this list then the profession's radical critics would subject all those partners to an extensive blacklist. It can only be on this basis that they:

1 Complain that a partner from Price Waterhouse was a member of a Joint Disciplinary Scheme committee when the firm had been subject to criticism in two DTI reports (Cousins *et al.* 1993: 312).

Table 6.1 DTI audit reports, 1971–93

Interim reports	4
Final report – no audit firm criticised	39
Final report – criticism of audit firm	39
Total	82

Source: Based on Sikka and Willmott (1995: 351–4)

2 Complain that the government 'has awarded lucrative privatisa-
   tion contracts to the same firms' and that 'partners from firms
   criticised by the DTI inspectors, and even by the disciplinary
   panels of the profession, have been given knighthoods' (Mitchell
   et al. 1991: 26).

Apparently, this draconian penalty for attracting criticism in a DTI
report is to apply to the whole firm however mild the comment.
Thus one of the reports held against all the partners of Price
Waterhouse states:

> The principal responsibility . . . must rest with the earlier of
> the two sets of non executive directors. . . . After the directors
> the next line of defence should have been the auditors: they
> had a more limited role but must share some responsibility.
>
> (DTI, 1983: 393, para. 20.04)

An example of rather selective citation of DTI reports can be
found in Mitchell *et al*., where it is observed: 'The Department of
Trade and Industry (DTI) inspectors' report on Burnholme and
Forder was critical of audit work and once again felt that auditor
independence was compromised by the provision of non-auditing
services to audit clients' (1994: 15). They support this assertion with
a quotation from a 1979 DTI report:

> In our view the principle of the auditor first compiling and
> then reporting upon a profit forecast is not considered to be a
> good practice for it may impair their ability to view the forecast
> objectively and must endanger the degree of independence
> essential to this work.
>
> (DTI, 1979: 97, para. 221)

This quotation is selective in two respects. First, it fails to cite the
mitigating circumstance identified by the inspectors later in the
same paragraph:

> We can quite imagine that given the circumstances of some
> companies where there is no particular expertise in producing
> forecasts, the auditors may well think that unless they lend a
> hand the company might never be able to produce a forecast
> and would then be at a disadvantage when it came either to
> the making of or the defending of a bid.

Second, the previous paragraph reports:

On the question of auditors it is perhaps appropriate at this time to say that in connection with the annual accounts it seemed evident to us, certainly as time progressed, that all three firms of auditors, JLB, Coopers and Fuller Jenks (now Mann Judd) did their best to cope with a difficult situation. During the period of the material delay in the production of accounts JLB, in particular, consistently reported the delay to the Department of Trade and regrettably there was nothing more that an auditor could do.

To summarise, this particular piece of evidence cited by Mitchell *et al.* to demonstrate the dangers to auditor independence of other work for the same client:

1 Involves a case where the normal process of auditing the annual accounts was explicitly found to be satisfactory.
2 Arose from giving support to a client with problems in their level of experience of a special accounting need.

Obstructing progress

In opposing the concept of 'self-regulation' the profession's radical critics claim that there is a long history of the accounting profession obstructing reform. The examples cited do not always stand close scrutiny. Thus, referring to the Institute of Chartered Accountants in England and Wales (ICAEW) Mitchell *et al.* argue:

It has always lagged behind the need for reform. In the 1930s, there was the infamous Royal Mail scandal. The company had created secret reserves in good years to flatter profits in bad. The then President of the ICAEW defended the practice.

(1991: 14)

Mitchell *et al.* repeat this claim: 'In the infamous Royal Mail case of the 1930s, the ICAEW President defended the practice of "secret reserves" (Hastings, 1962)' (1993: 5). The Royal Mail case involved the then legal and common practice of using secret reserves. In 1926 the Royal Mail Steam Packet Company turned a trading loss of some £300,000 into a declared profit of some £400,000 by utilising £750,000 of secret reserves. The auditor, Mr Morland, had noted against the declared profit the words 'including adjustment of taxation reserves'. The UK treasury took the view that the accounts were fraudulent, and accordingly criminal proceedings were taken against the company chairman, Lord Kylsant, and the auditor, Mr Morland. Mr Morland's counsel, Sir Patrick Hastings, explains the defence:

> The whole defence must necessarily turn upon the one question, whether or not the works used by Mr Morland were well recognised in accountancy circles, and were sufficient to give notice of the manner in which the trading loss had been turned into an apparent profit. . . . Whether or not this accountancy practice was to be commended was, in our view, wholly immaterial.
>
> (Quoted in Baxter and Davidson 1977: 341)

The account of the trial makes it clear that Sir Patrick was at pains to direct questions to the accountant witnesses on whether the approach taken by his client was in line with established practice, and to avoid raising questions about the desirability of that practice. He was successful in this and tells us: 'What was of equal importance to us was that the Attorney-General asked no questions in re-examination of Lord Plender to minimise the effect of the evidence he had given' (1977: 344–5). Thus leading accountant witnesses in the case testified, quite truthfully, that the use of secret reserves in the Royal Mail case was in line with general practice. This explicitly did *not* involve 'defence' of that practice.

Mitchell *et al.* offer a more recent example:

> When the poverty of accounting/auditing practices was revealed by the mid-1970s secondary banking crash and the property banking collapse, the profession's response was to rush out *The Corporate Report* (Accounting Standards Steering Committee 1975) in the hope that this would pre-empt sustained criticism and help the profession in presenting a reforming image (Stamp, 1985). However, once the critics were appeased and the profession's powers preserved, the report was quietly shelved. To this day it has not even been ratified by any of the UK's six accounting bodies.
>
> (1993: 2)

The Corporate Report was a discussion paper published by the Accounting Standards Steering Committee which put the case for accountability by companies to a wide range of user groups. A series of specific proposals to implement that accountability were made. The two allegations made by Mitchell *et al.* are as follows: first, that the professional bodies 'rushed' *The Corporate Report* as a smoke screen to cover failures of accounting and auditing practice. In the reference cited to support this Stamp reports:

> In the case of *The Corporate Report*, the Accounting Standards Steering Committee was motivated by two principal considerations: the first was a wish to placate the growing number of people who were arguing in favour of a conceptual, as distinct from an ad hoc approach, to the development of accounting standards in Britain. Second, it hoped that the working party would favour a replacement cost inflation accounting system and, by reporting ahead of the Sandilands Committee, pre-empt whatever conclusions Sandilands might be able to reach.
>
> (1985: 118)

Neither of these considerations supports the motive alleged by Mitchell *et al.*; overall the tone of Stamp's article is positive about his experience of working with the UK profession to produce *The Corporate Report*, as compared to the negative impression claimed by the radical critics.

The second allegation is that the accounting profession 'quietly shelved' and failed to 'ratify' *The Corporate Report*. The Law Society's standing committee on company law made representations to the ASSC:

> If their wider philosophy were to be adopted it would, in our judgment, diminish the present legal rights of shareholders and creditors. While those rights are doubtless not immutable, any changes should be made by deliberate alteration of the law.
>
> (unpublished)

Many of the ideas of *The Corporate Report* were taken up in a Government Green Paper in 1977 (see Mathews and Perera 1991: 81–2). It was the decision of the government, following the election in 1979, that led to the idea being dropped.

Far from being 'quietly shelved' by the profession, therefore, *The Corporate Report* could not be progressed because of lack of support in the legislature. In putting forward *The Corporate Report* the profession, or at least influential elements of it, showed itself willing to put itself at the disposal of a radical agenda. Even from a radical perspective, to hold this against the UK accounting profession seems perverse.

The expectations gap

On the audit expectations gap the radical critics take a trenchant line in attributing responsibility to the audit profession. Thus Sikka *et al.* argue: 'The expectations gap can only be reduced when the auditing industry embraces the responsibilities which the public associates with auditors' (1992: 10). Similarly Sikka *et al.* call on the government to: 'ensure that auditors reduce the "expectations gap" by ensuring that they perform the tasks that are widely expected of them' (1993: 23).

Porter argues:

The gap has two major components:

1 A gap between what the public expects auditors to achieve and what they can reasonably be expected to accomplish (designated the 'reasonableness gap').

2 A gap between what the public can reasonably expect auditors to accomplish and what they are perceived to achieve (designated the 'performance gap'). This component may be further subdivided into:

  (i) a gap between what can reasonably be expected of auditors and auditor's existing duties as defined by the law and professional promulgations ('deficient standards'); and

  (ii) a gap between the expected standard of performance of auditors' perceived performance, as expected and perceived by the public – ('deficient performance').

(1991: 4)

Sikka *et al.* effectively challenge the validity of the 'reasonableness gap'. They argue: 'In our view, the expectations gap can only be reduced when the profession is required to accept the 'common sense' objectives expected by the wider public' (1992: 29).

Garcia Benau *et al.* discuss two surveys of attitudes to the expectations gap, one in the UK and one in Spain. One of their questions was whether the auditors' role should be to ensure that 'the balance sheet provides a fair valuation of the company'. They report:

In Britain, the responses to this statement generated the second largest across-group difference of the survey, with 71 per cent of auditors disagreeing with the statement and 58 per cent of financial directors and 81 per cent of users agreeing with it.

(1993: 288)

It is interesting to compare this particular aspect of the 'expectations gap' with the observation by Mitchell *et al.* that: 'Conceptually, a balance sheet cannot show the market value of a business because following the practice of eighteenth-century financiers, accountants focus on individual assets rather than their collective value' (1991: 20). In this case Mitchell *et al.* call for the disclosure of market values of fixed assets to reduce the gap, but implicitly acknowledge that it cannot be closed.

A clear explanation of the impossibility of achieving a balance sheet that places a fair valuation on a business has been put forward by Edey: 'Accrual accounting is in fact an uneasy compromise between a wholly objective record of past cash receipts and payments, and a wholly subjective assessment of the current value of the enterprise, based on peering into the future' (1971: 441). In 1993 the Institute of Chartered Accountants in England and Wales persuaded Professor Edey to develop these thoughts, with a view to closing the 'reasonableness gap'. He observes: 'financial statements are a working compromise, far from perfect and capable of improvement, but not to be blamed for failing to do what they were not developed to do and indeed could not do' (1993: 8).

To summarise, we by no means reject all aspects of the case put forward by the radical critics. To take the three aspects we have considered:

1 DTI reports do indeed indicate failures in the audit process. We feel that the radical critics overstate their case, particularly in relation to the 'Big Six'.
2 While the accounting profession may well learn from history the need to be adaptable, some instances of obstruction of progress cited by the radical critics here are not sustained as in the cases of 'Royal Mail' and *The Corporate Report*.
3 While the audit expectations gap needs to be addressed, the radical critics fail to give due weight to the 'reasonableness gap'.

THE CRITICS' PROPOSALS AND THE PROFESSION'S RESPONSES

We now turn to consider the radical critics' proposals in more depth:

1 We explore two key aspects, the call for a more 'democratic' regulatory structure and the issue of cost.

2 We consider the response of the accounting profession to two specific areas of criticism: the conflict of interest that arises when an auditor provides non-audit services and the extent to which auditors should be 'active' rather than 'passive' in investigating a client's going concern status.

Democratic structures

We have seen that Mitchell *et al*. (1991) propose 'an independent and democratic body with a statutory base' to regulate accounting and auditing. While the workings of this body are explored in some detail the process by which it should emerge is not. We are told that it 'should be composed of representatives of all interested parties' (Mitchell *et al*.: 17). Allusions to democracy occur throughout the work of the radical critics. For example: 'the institutions and practices of accounting are found to be collusive and undemocratic' (Mitchell and Sikka 1993: 29), and 'reforms that will bring the auditing industry under democratic control' (Sikka and Armstrong 1995: 30).

A reference to 'major accounting firms' observing that 'the partners from such firms, without ever being elected, make audit policy' (Willmott *et al*. 1990: 15), suggests that the radical critics would like to see some form of electoral process involved in appointing the regulatory body; this might prove challenging, given the wide range of 'stakeholder' groups to whom they claim the process should be accountable.

There is also a call for more 'democratic' processes within the accounting profession. Referring to the Chartered Association of Certified Accountants Sikka reasons:

> The leadership argues that the members cannot be asked to directly elect presidents because they will not know enough about the candidates. This is an insult to accountants who make complex decisions and routinely elect people in national, local and other elections.
>
> (1995: 15)

If we examine the comparison between the professional associations and the UK political process, we see that in fact both run on the same principles. Electors vote for members of the council of their professional body in the same way as they elect members of parliament and local councillors. They do not directly elect presidents of their professional associations any more than they directly elect prime ministers or mayors. In this sense the professional accounting bodies work firmly within the UK tradition of 'democracy'.

Given the focus on 'democracy' in the arguments of the radical critics, it would be helpful if they were to spell out both how they interpret the term and how they would apply it in practice. Gray *et al.* (1996: 36–8) offer a useful example of such a discussion in the context of making a case for accounting reform.

Costs

The radical critics' proposals clearly involves substantial costs, both at the 'macro' level in financing the elaborate proposed regulatory system and at the 'micro' level in producing a wide range of new disclosures to be audited to a standard that meets the claims of all stakeholders. At the 'macro' level the question of financing the regulatory structure is explicitly addressed:

> Costs of the standard setting bodies can be met from the licensing fees levied from auditors which currently go to the professional bodies plus a modest increase in the fees associated with filing accounts at Companies House which recently announced an operating surplus of some £11 million. Some of this should be available for strengthening auditing and accounting regulation. Further revenue can also be generated through the sale of literature relating to accounting and auditing standards.
>
> (Mitchell *et al.* 1991: 18)

The reliance on the allocation of tax revenues for the main part of finance would render the new 'independent' regulatory body strongly dependent on government, while publications as a source of income may create a 'bias for action' stimulating the regulatory body to publish amended rules to generate income (Sunder 1988).

However, in relation to implementing their proposals at the 'macro' level at least the radical critics do address the issue of cost in a way that we can evaluate. At the 'micro' level, by contrast, they dismiss the issue of cost with casual asides. When it suits their argument they have no difficulty in identifying where such costs fall. Thus in referring to the costs of the profession's Joint Monitoring Unit they observe: 'The cost of these monitoring rituals is likely to be borne by the public through audit fees passed on in the prices of goods and services' (Puxty *et al.* 1992: 33).

By contrast no such awareness informs their discussion of the costs of their own proposals. Thus in relation to the additional audit work need to face up to a greatly increased auditor liability for much expanded financial statements to a range of stakeholders, they assert: 'there is no question of giving additional fees to auditors for what they already should be doing' (Mitchell *et al.* 1993: 26).

We are not told of any mechanism whereby auditors would be induced or compelled to undertake a substantially increased workload with no corresponding increase in remuneration. Costs to companies of greatly expanded disclosure requirements are dismissed on an equally casual basis:

> No doubt the suggestion of publishing future oriented data would be opposed by many on the grounds of cost and confidentiality. As far as costs are concerned, there are unlikely to be any significant additional factors, as most companies would already have budgets and forecasts.
>
> (Sikka 1986: 31)

The argument ignores the cost of adapting systems to produce forecasts that are both sufficiently reliable to justify publication and so well documented as to provide an audit trail.

THE PROFESSION'S RESPONSE

We now turn to the profession's response to two specific areas of criticism, comparing the critics' assessment of the challenge confronted by the profession with the analysis of the profession's position in a recent auditing text (Porter *et al.* 1996). The first area is the threat to auditor independence when other services are provided to clients. On this Mitchell *et al.* argue: 'Auditors should act exclusively as auditors. They should not be allowed to sell non-auditing services to the companies they audit' (1991: 23).

Sikka *et al.* (1994: 29) explore the then ethical guidelines issued by the profession. They give some credit for change: 'the new rules will prevent auditing firms reporting on balance sheets that contain asset valuations carried out by the same firm.' They see some ongoing problems: 'Although welcome, such recommendations do not deal with any of the fundamental relationships that give rise to conflicts of interest.' 'The guidelines offer no justification why some activities are frowned upon while others are unchecked.'

An independent evaluation in this case supports them: Porter *et al.* (1996), in their evaluation of the subsequent Guide to Professional Ethics Statement (GPES) 1, issued by the ICAEW in 1996, see a continuing weakness here, observing: 'the profession's ethical guidance is quite permissive in this regard' (1996: 72).

In this first area, then, the criticism seems to be valid. By contrast, in a second area the profession appears to have responded to criticism. The second issue, that of the extent to which auditors should investigate the going concern status of a client, has been investigated in particular depth by Sikka (1992). He argues that the then Auditing Practices Committee (APC) 'supported a "passive" rather than an "active" approach to going concern' (383). Sikka sees the APC taking this line 'presumably on the grounds that it best served the economic interests of major firms'. Subsequently Statement of Auditing Standards 130 was issued in 1995.

The statement takes a strong 'active' position on the auditor's role in probing the going concern position. Porter *et al.* conclude:

> By helping to ensure that uncertainties regarding the going concern assumption are detected, adequately disclosed in the financial statements and, where appropriate, referred to in the audit report, application of SAS 130 should enable users of the financial statements to assess for themselves the impact of any major uncertainties and the consequent risk to the viability of the entity. It should also ensure that auditors meet, far more closely than previously, society's expectation of their 'flagging' doubts about the ability of an entity to continue in existence, and thus should reduce the criticisms previously levelled against auditors for failing to perform this duty adequately.
>
> (1996: 257)

To summarise, in key areas the radical critics offer proposals, in relation to both 'democracy' and costs, which are poorly developed and unconvincing. Equally some of their specific proposals have a demonstrable validity and have been taken up, in whole or in part, by the profession.

THE PROBLEM OF PARTISANSHIP

A recurring theme in the work of the radical critics is the belittling of those who take an alternative approach to achieving reform of accounting and auditing either by the attribution of unworthy motives or straightforward misinterpretation. To give two examples:

Example 1   Sikka and Willmott (1995) respond to one of their critics with the observation: 'Vociferous support of the status quo and the profession's claims was also forthcoming . . . from academics with close connections to the profession' (for example, Fearnley 1992: 571).

Now Fearnley is indeed critical of Mitchell *et al.* (1991), observing:

> The authors of the Fabian Society paper have sacrificed what could have been a first class proposal for reform by failure to recognise the real underlying problems and by using the paper as a means of directing destructive criticism at our profession, rather than seeking positive solutions.
>
> (1992: 26)

And: 'Bearing in mind that there is not an experienced listed company auditor among them, the arrogance is outstanding' (1992: 26). However, Fearnley summarises her own proposal thus:

> We also need to find a means whereby, in the event of reck-lessness on the part of directors and auditors, shareholders have an identifiable means of recourse. The absence of such a route at the moment is one of the causes of public frustration when companies collapse. Could we perhaps have criminal negligence subject to massive fines in the worst cases, followed by automatic compensation for investors? It would certainly focus a few minds.
>
> (1992: 26)

Neither the tone nor the content of this statement justify the description 'vociferous support of the status quo' put forward by Sikka and Willmott.

Example 2   Sikka *et al.* (1995) review the career of the late Professor Edward Stamp of Lancaster University. Having listed, fairly, a selection of Stamp's achievements, including his successful campaign to launch a UK accounting standards programme and his contribution to *The Corporate Report* they then turn to a dispute in the early 1980s as to whether the accounting practices followed by the National Coal Board (NCB) in deciding on pit closures were justified. They report that Stamp was a member of a group invited by the NCB to review the accounting issue. They claim the ensuing report:

> Excused NCB accounting practices – without raising any substantial questions about the chosen basis of calculations – an outcome which, sadly, places in some doubt Mumford's claim that Stamp was 'committed to making power open and accountable' (Mumford 1994: 290) by strongly held moral principles.
>
> (Sikka *et al.* 1995: 126)

This is a remarkably strong rejection of the work of a particularly distinguished academic, based on his taking a view on a matter of professional judgement that failed to match the political preferences of the radical critics.

The radical critics work within a framework that is explicitly political, and indeed party political. One of their main publications has been a Fabian Society discussion paper (Mitchell *et al.* 1991), and Professor Sikka has acted as an adviser to the Labour party (see Cousins and Sikka 1993: 70). The combination of political and academic insights has been a powerful one, with publications flowing in academic, practitioner, and trade journals as well as the business press. However, the combination lends a strongly partisan approach, as we have seen in the judgements passed on those who take an alternative view. The strong political approach also leads to a combination of proposals to reform the abuses identified by academic research and proposals to advance the critics' own agenda. As an example of the latter, Cousins and Sikka (1993) discuss amendments unsuccessfully tabled by the Labour party to the 1989 Companies Bill requiring disclosures of details on low pay in company accounts, supporting the Labour Party's target of a minimum wage. Their rhetorical question, 'Can accounts which are silent on such issues really be true and fair?' (Cousins and Sikka 1993: 59), seeks to invoke the basic accounting concept of the EU Fourth Directive in support of an issue that lies firmly in the domain of party politics. A similar case on low pay disclosure is made in Mitchell *et al.* (1991: 31).

The term 'true and fair' has a wide range of interpretations (see Higson and Blake 1993). To invoke it to support an assertion that accountants have a duty to make disclosures that advance one political party's belief in the minimum wage stretches the term beyond the point of credibility.

114

CONCLUSION

The accounting profession's radical critics have constructed an elaborate case against the ethical standards of the accounting profession both at the 'macro' level, in the administration of self-regulation, and at the 'micro level', as individual company auditors. Our view is that:

1 The evidence on which the case is built is overstated, and indeed at times seriously misrepresented.

2 The critic's own proposals for an alternative framework for accounting and auditing regulation are cumbersome and costly.

3 Legitimate issues raised by the critics have been partially, but by no means completely, addressed by the accounting profession.

4 The highly partisan approach taken by the radical critics has led them to misrepresent those who advocate reform from a different perspective.

5 The radical critics, in putting forward proposals to remedy the abuses they have identified, have tagged on a series of unrelated disclosure requirements for the advancement of their own political agenda.

In driving the accounting profession towards a more rigorous formulation and enforcement of ethical standards the radical critics have played, and continue to play, a valuable role. However, we are not convinced of the validity of their case for taking away the accounting profession's responsibility for maintaining and enhancing ethical standards.

REFERENCES

Accounting Standards Steering Committee (1975) *The Corporate Report*, London: Accounting Standards Steering Committee.

Cousins, J. and Sikka, P. (1993) 'Accounting for change: facilitating power and accountability', *Critical Perspectives on Accounting*, 4: 53–72.

Cousins, J., Mitchell, A. and Sikka, P. (1993) 'Secret government and privileged interests', *Political Quarterly*, July/September: 306–15.

Department of Trade and Industry (1979) *Burnholme and Forder Limited* [in liquidation], London: HMSO.

—— (1983) *Ramor Investments Limited*, London: HMSO.

Edey, H. (1971) 'The true and fair view', *Accountancy*, August: 440–1.

—— (1993) *Understanding Financial Reporting*, London: Institute of Chartered Accountants in England and Wales.

Fearnley, S. (1992) 'Outsiders' view obscures the real problems', *Accountancy*, February: 26.

Garcia Benau, M.A., Humphrey, C., Moizer, P. and Turley, S. (1993) 'Auditing expectations and performance in Spain and Britain: a comparative analysis', *International Journal of Accounting*, 28: 281–307.

Gray, R., Owen, D. and Adams, C. (1996) *Accounting and Accountability: Charges and challenges in corporate social and environmental reporting*, London: Prentice Hall.

Hastings, P. (1977) 'The case of the Royal Mail', in W.T. Baxter and S. Davidson (eds) *Studies in Accounting*, London: Institute of Chartered Accountants in England and Wales: 339–46.

Higson, A. and Blake, J. (1993) 'The true and fair view concept: a formula for international disharmony: some empirical evidence', *International Journal of Accounting*, 28: 104–15.

Institute of Chartered Accountants in England and Wales (ICAEW) (1996) *Guide to Professional Ethics*, London: ICAEW.

Mathews, M.R. and Perera, M.H.B. (1991) *Accounting Theory and Development*, South Melbourne: Thomas Nelson.

Mitchell, A. and Sikka, P. (1993) 'Accounting for change: the institutions of accountancy', *Critical Perspectives on Accounting*, 4: 29–52.

Mitchell, A., Puxty, T., Sikka, P. and Willmott, H. (1991) *Accounting for Change: Proposals for reform of audit and accounting*, London: Fabian Society.

—— (1994) *The Auditor Liability Charade*, London: University of East London Press.

—— (1993) *A Better Future for Auditing*, London: University of East London Press.

Porter, B.A. (1991) 'Narrowing the audit expectation–performance gap: a contemporary approach', *Pacific Accounting Review*, June: 9–36.

Porter, B., Simon, J. and Hatherley, D. (1996) *Principles of External Auditing*, Chichester: John Wiley & Sons.

Puxty, T., Sikka, P. and Willmott, H. (1992) 'Watchdogs must be forced to bark', *The Times*, 19 March: 33.

Sikka, P. (1986) 'Distributable profiles and creditor protection', *Management Accounting*, November: 30–31.

—— (1992) 'Audit policy making in the UK: the case of "the auditor's consideration in respect of going concern"', *European Accounting Review*, 1: 349–92.

—— (1995) 'Certified fail to board the democracy express', *Accountancy Age*, 9 February: 12.

Sikka, P. and Armstrong, P. (1995) 'Silence on the agenda', *The Times*, 15 June: 30.

Sikka, P., Puxty, T., Cooper, C. and Willmott, H. (1992) 'Audit reforms are not enough', *The Times*, 25 June: 27.

Sikka, P., Puxty, T. and Willmott, H. (1993) 'After Maxwell and BCCI, the auditors must be audited', *Guardian*, 21 June: 12.

—— (1994) 'A gaping hole in auditing practice – professional bodies must lead the way in promoting ethics', *Independent*, 19 April: 29.

Sikka, P., Puxty, T., Willmott, H. and Cooper, C. (1992) *Eliminating the Expectations Gap?*, London: Chartered Association of Certified Accountants.

Sikka, P. and Willmott, H. (1995) 'Illuminating the state-profession rela-tionship: accountants acting as Department of Trade and Industry inspectors', *Critical Perspectives on Accounting*, 6: 341–69.

Sikka, P., Willmott, H. and Puxty, T. (1995) 'The mountains are still there: accounting academics and the bearings of intellectuals', *Accounting, Auditing and Accountability Journal*, 8 (3): 113–40.

Stamp, E. (1985) 'The politics of professional accounting research: some reflections', *Accounting, Organizations and Society*, 10: 111–23.

Sunder, S. (1988) 'Political economy of accounting standards', *Journal of Accounting Literature*, 7: 31–41.

Willmott, H., Puxty, T. and Sikka, P. (1990) 'While the DTI still baulks at bringing auditors to book', *Guardian*, 3 December: 15.

7

THE PARTISANSHIP OF THE ACCOUNTANCY BODIES: SOME OBSERVATIONS

Prem Sikka

Acknowledgements

I am grateful to Abimbola Adedeji and Hugh Willmott for their comments on an earlier draft.

INTRODUCTION

Headline episodes such as the Bank of Credit and Commerce International (BCCI), Maxwell, Polly Peck, Barlow Clowes, Levitt, Wickes, MTM, Resort Hotels, Wallace Smith, Barings, NatWest Markets and others show that accounting and auditing practices are implicated in the loss of pensions, savings, investments, bank deposits and jobs. The 'visible hand' of accountancy has blighted the lives of many people (Tinker 1985; Lehman 1992). The recurring failures of accounting and auditing call for a critique of conventional 'accounting-think', the institutions of accountancy and the social privileges enjoyed by professionally qualified accountants.[1] Many accounting scholars have responded to such calls and a voluminous literature showing the disabling (and enabling) influence of accounting in shaping social relations can be found in 'critical' journals[2] and a number of books (see, for example, Tinker 1985; Cooper and Hopper 1990; Lehman 1992; Hopwood and Miller 1994).

Within the above context, a major disappointment is that the contribution by John Blake and Ray Gardiner[3] (hereafter B&G)

makes no attempt to critique either accounting practices or my work (some published alone, some in conjunction with others), which has sought to problematise contemporary practices and the power wielded by the institutions of accountancy. (Hereafter the use of 'our work' will refer to the work I have produced jointly with my colleagues.) They offer no reflections upon the politics and ethics of the auditing industry. Instead, in their eagerness to defend the status quo, B&G have drawn up a potpourri of some random points that are grounded neither in any social theory nor in any ethical or educational principle. Words and concepts, such as 'radical', 'partisan', 'political', 'credibility', 'ethics', 'unworkable' and so on are thrown about as though they were unproblematic and self-evident. They provide no clue as to how these concepts are deployed.

Before dealing with the seemingly random criticisms that B&G raise, it is appropriate to reject totally the charge that the quotations cited in my work are in any sense pejorative. On the contrary, B&G themselves are engaged in the very activity of which they accuse others: producing selective quotes. Inevitably, all writing is constrained by the availability of space and all quotations produced within it are selective. Readers are invited to refer to the original papers cited by B&G and consider whether the claims made by B&G have any validity.

It appears that most of the points raised by B&G relate to issues about partisanship, democracy, politics of accounting regulation, the profession's resistance to change and possible regulatory alternatives. To help the reader to follow various arguments, this chapter is, therefore, organised in three further sections. The first section deals with a theme running through the B&G contribution, that my work is partisan and political. Such claims require an engagement with B&G's unreflective notion of politics and democracy. The second section responds to B&G's points about the regulation of auditing practices. The third section briefly summarises the arguments. As this paper is a contribution to a book on accounting ethics, the final section also offers some reflections on ethics of accounting teachings and ethical challenges to educators.

THE POLITICS OF ACCOUNTING

Partisanship

B&G's contribution is the claim that our work is 'political', 'biased' and 'partisan'.[4] They offer no clues as to what this means, or what methodology enables them to make or ground such claims. Neither is there any reflection on whether their own support for the *status quo* and opposition to reforms is deserving of the labels (partisan, political and so on) which they so eagerly attach to others.

In a world with numerous inequalities, maldistribution of wealth, homelessness and hunger, they even castigate us for supporting calls for decent wages [p. 114 above] for people who have been systematically disadvantaged.[5] Seemingly, they believe that mobilising accounting/auditing practices in support of markets and finance capital (held by shareholders, for instance) is ethically acceptable, but mobilising accounting to give visibility to poverty and institutionalised exploitation is somehow unethical. Yet they fail to provide any ethical arguments to support their stance.

B&G remain silent about the way accountancy trade associations and firms frustrate and stifle public debates by hiring Members of Parliament, lobbyists, public relations experts and others to stifle public debate and oppose reforms (Robinson 1989: 1; Sikka *et al.* 1992). These bodies use in-house magazines, PR departments, press releases and their massive economic resources to influence news stories and mobilise support for their preferred policies. The same organised interests routinely urge governments to shift tax burdens and change laws (see, for example, *Certified Accountant*, June 1997: 9) without reference to those who might be economically and socially disadvantaged as a result. At the time of writing (July 1997), the accountancy bodies are engaged in an orchestrated press campaign to secure liability concessions for auditors, but their campaign remains silent on the plight of bank depositors, investors, pension scheme members and others who have been affected by accounting and auditing failures.

B&G's silence seems to imply that the interventions in the policy arena by professional bodies and big business are acceptable, but interventions by others (including academics) are not. They seem to suggest that showing compassion and support for the disadvantaged is partisan and political while silence on these issues is not. It is for the reader to decide which is the more desirable ethical position: silence on the institutionalised inequalities, with academics hiding behind some prim (and idealised) notions of writing, or commenting on worldly affairs in their capacities as human beings which gives full recognition to their social existence and responsibilities as mothers, fathers, brothers, sisters, neighbours and citizens.

B&G's comments about partisanship seem to imply that human beings can somehow take refuge in a world which is untouched by politics. They do not indicate how one can find or take up residence in such a place. B&G do not seem to appreciate that 'politics' is about choices, preferred values and social relations. In a world already marked by inequalities in the distribution of income, wealth, power, influence, class and imperialism, value-free positions are, to say the least, difficult to find and defend (Gramsci 1971). The only access to our identities and the social world is through language (oral, written, visual, electronics), but language is not a value-free medium of communication. Everyday words, such as 'assets', 'liabilities', 'markets', 'efficiency','freedom','personal','black','feminine','democracy', are pregnant with already articulated histories and social struggles. From this perspective, there is nothing that anyone can think, speak, write or imagine which is beyond the realm of politics (Foucault 1980; Connelly 1987; Taylor 1987).

There is no escape from politics. All talks, lectures, classroom notes, academic papers and articles, prioritise or negate some values and seek to position social subjects in a particular way. They consciously or unconsciously advocate some things to be desirable and others to be undesirable. Accounting practices and accounting academics are political in that they inevitably prioritise some concerns and values and negate others. This is evident from the way accounting and auditing practices remain preoccupied with prioritising capital over labour (as in the profit and loss account) and property rights (as in the balance sheet). Most accounting books, especially those recommended by the professional bodies, have little to say about social justice or the rights of employees (see Puxty *et al.* 1994).

An underlying narrative in the B&G contribution appears to be that activities such as writing, researching and teaching should be restricted to some 'facts' (whose facts and why?) and be 'balanced' (whose balance?). Such beliefs presuppose that there exists some value-free standard against which 'facts' can be measured and interpreted and that balanced writing, research and teaching does not 'misrepresent an unbalanced state of affairs' (Simons 1994: 141). B&G fail to provide any explicit clues to their epistemological position.

Democracy

B&G reveal little awareness of the discourse of democracy. A variety of institutionalised democratic arrangements are possible, and changes have frequently been advanced by the tensions between the liberalist and radical conceptions of democracy (see Held 1993, 1996 for a discussion). Within the contradictory discourses of modernity, democracy is broadly conceived of as an ensemble of institutional and other arrangements which are emancipatory, render power visible, call the powerful to account and encourage concerns for humanity, freedom from oppression, exploitation, poverty and injustice.[6] Democracy does not have a fixed meaning. Its meaning is always subject to struggle and negotiations. In recent years, new social movements relating to feminism, gay liberation, disability, black civil rights, animals protection, ecology and other areas have problematised the prevailing institutional structures and ideological climate to argue that life can be lived in a different way. In defending the *status quo*, B&G do not seem to be aware that the rights which we enjoy today are only there because someone in the past argued differently and sought to challenge the established understandings of governance.

Despite the history of 'democracy' struggles, B&G object to the idea [pp. 109–10] that the leadership of a professional body, or the composition of its major committees, might be directly elected through contested elections by ordinary members. Their objections are grounded neither in any theory of democracy nor in contemporary social practices. Contrary to B&G's claims, the leadership of numerous organisations is directly elected. For example, the leadership of most UK trade unions and the Labour Party is directly elected by ordinary members through contested elections. The Prime Minister, Tony Blair, was elected to be the leader of the Labour Party by ordinary members of the Party. The President of the Law Society is also directly elected by the ordinary members. After the 1997 general election, the incoming Labour administration has proposed that the mayors of major cities, including London, should be directly elected as well.

Contrary to B&G's claims [pp. 109–10], there is an enormous difference between the way elections are conducted for the councils of the UK accountancy bodies, local authorities and Parliament. For example, the Institute of Chartered Accountants in England and Wales (ICAEW) co-opts (that is, does not elect) around 20 per cent of its Council members, a practice not permitted for local councils or the House of Commons. The Association of Chartered Certified Accountants (ACCA) operates a delegated proxy voting system which has routinely enabled its self-appointed leadership to cast more than 20 per cent of the total vote, thus ensuring that reformers are not elected to its Council. Such a voting system is illegal for trade unions and local authorities. No leader of any political party in the Western world is able to cast hundreds of votes. The proceedings of the UK courts, the House of Commons and local authorities are open (unless specifically closed for some stated reason) to the public. Among the UK accountancy bodies, the ICAEW admits the public to parts of its Council meetings. From July 1997, the Chartered Institute of Management Accountants (CIMA) admits its members to Council meetings. The Institute of Chartered Accountants of Scotland has announced proposals to appoint lay observers to its Council. The ACCA is currently (May 1998) the only major UK accountancy body which does not admit its members or representatives of the public to its Council meetings. Order papers of the courts, local authorities and the House of Commons are available to the public, as are the transcripts of judgements and debates. In contrast, the same information is not made available by the professional bodies (such as the ACCA). The fact that the Vice President of a major accountancy body (Ray Gardiner) should oppose even modest reforms is a testimony to the irresponsiveness of the accountancy bodies.

B&G's favourable citation of a quote from Fearnley [p. 113][7] seems to imply that somehow only certified experts have the right to comment on worldly affairs.[8] Such an approach to democracy would render the vast majority of the public silent, as the public sphere would be governed by technocrats who are notorious for their narrowness of vision. Readers would be aware that it is ordinary individuals (working through organisations such as Greenpeace and Friends of the Earth) rather than the certified experts who routinely alert the public to environmental dangers. How many auditors have alerted the public to audit failures? While professionally qualified accountants may help to massage, cook and even roast the accounts, how often have they warned the public of any impending collapse?

Technical experts may have a role to play, but the public policy sphere cannot be entirely conceded to them. As technical experts, nuclear scientists, no doubt, have a role to play in debates about nuclear power, but theirs is one voice among many. Whether a nation should have nuclear weapons, power stations, nuclear waste and so on requires consideration of wider social issues, especially as the consequences of nuclear energy affect a wide variety of citizens.

Similarly, as the consequences of auditing and accounting affect many, accounting/auditing policy decisions should not be under the control of an occupational elite.

The cult of personalities

B&G [pp. 113–14] object to our (re)evaluation of Professor Stamp's interventions in the coal miners' dispute in the mid-1980s (Sikka *et al.* 1995). Contemporary commentators were critical of the National Coal Board's (NCB) accounting and questioned its relevance to making economic and social decisions. Some felt that the NCB accounts 'fail to form an adequate basis for informed management decisions' (Berry *et al.* 1985a: 10) while others argued that a range of political choices could be justified from the NCB accounting data (Cooper and Hopper 1988; Berry *et al.* 1985b). Professor Stamp's approval of the NCB accounting practices played a part in the coalmine closure programme which eventually decimated many people's lives and destroyed whole communities. B&G make no attempt to locate or compare alternative interpretations of the NCB accounting with those endorsed by Stamp. Unlike B&G, many would question whether professional judgements which take no account of the consequences can ever be described as ethical.

B&G's objections to our (re)evaluation of Stamp's interventions are at odds with democratic practices. In liberal democracies, (re)evaluation of various intellectual endeavours is an on-going tradition. Thus the works of thinkers are re-read and constantly re-interpreted. From this process of re-evaluation, social and scientific ideas are transformed (Kuhn 1970). There is no justification whatsoever to exempt the interventions of an accounting academic, no matter how respected or revered that individual may be.

REFORMING ACCOUNTING AND AUDITING

Politics of soothing reports

B&G show no appreciation of the way the UK accountancy bodies have sought to defend and expand their jurisdictions (see Sikka and Willmott 1995b for some details). One of the strategies developed by them has been to disarm critics by issuing soothing reports. It is in this context that *The Corporate Report* (Accounting Standards Steering Committee 1975) was issued [see pp. 100 and 105–6]. Our reading of the evidence and timing is that it was issued to pre-empt any government intervention, a concern which was compounded by the prevailing public visibility of audit failures (see Sikka *et al.* 1989 for some evidence). The rise of the 'New Right' Conservative administration in 1979 and the abandonment of consensus politics influenced shelving of the report. But B&G fail to explain why, to this day, none of the UK professional bodies has ratified the report. The profession could have applied its strictures to auditing firms. For example, *The Corporate Report* stated that

> there is an implicit responsibility to report publicly (whether or not required by law or regulation) incumbent on every economic entity whose size or format renders it significant. By economic entity we mean every sort of organisation in modern society, whether department of central government, a local authority, . . . an unincorporated firm. . . . By significant we mean that the organisation commands human and material resources on such a scale that the results of its activities have significant economic implications for the community as a whole.
>
> (Accounting Standards Steering Committee 1975: 15)

Following the above edicts, the professional bodies could have mounted a public campaign to ensure that auditing firms embrace public accountability by publishing some meaningful information about their affairs. They did not. The silence further supports our thesis that the profession has a tendency to issue soothing reports to disarm critics and then quietly shelve the reports.

Opposing change

The accountancy profession has a long history of resisting change. At one time or another, it has opposed the publication of income statement, balance sheet, group accounts, turnover, replacement costs, and fees paid to auditors for non-audit work, to name just a few (Puxty *et al.* 1994). It has also opposed the need for large companies to have elected audit committees. The UK professional bodies have mobilised their economic and political resources to oppose any need for auditors to detect/report material fraud to the regulators (Sikka *et al.* 1992). In the aftermath of the BCCI scandal, the ICAEW in its evidence to Lord Justice Bingham urged that auditors should not have a statutory 'duty' to detect/report material fraud to the regulators (Bingham 1992). Lord Justice

Bingham disagreed with the ICAEW view and recommended that financial sector auditors should have a 'duty' to report material fraud and irregularities to the regulators and this duty was duly enacted by Parliament (*Hansard* 15 February 1994: 852–75). Change had to be introduced in the teeth of opposition from the accounting establishment. In their readings of various episodes, B&G offer no ethical reflections on the ingrained opposition to this extension of public accountability. Their reflections upon the Royal Mail case [pp. 104–5] seem to suggest that as long as something is 'in line with general practice' [p. 105], it is acceptable. They never problematise the notion of 'general practice'. On the basis that something 'was in line with general practice', holocausts, slavery, colonialism, ethnic cleansing, exploitation and environmental destruction would not be challenged.

The pursuit of sectional interest shows no signs of abating. Despite being public regulators, major accountancy bodies are currently spearheading an organised political campaign to secure liability concessions for auditors (Sikka 1996). Their submissions to the Department of Trade and Industry show no concern for the plight of pension scheme members, employees, bank depositors, savers and investors who have suffered from poor audits. All readers of this chapter acquire consumer rights when purchasing the most mundane of products, such as a packet of sweets or crisps. These include a right of redress against producers who are also obliged to withdraw faulty goods. No equivalent rights exist for audit consumers. Readers would be hard pushed to find instances where the professional bodies have ever led a campaign to secure rights for audit stakeholders. Can anybody really have any confidence in these bodies' claims of being guardians of ethical behaviour?

To resist change, the professional bodies have disseminated misleading information. For example, for a considerable time, some have argued that the provision of non-auditing services by auditors to their audit clients compromises auditor independence. Any ban on such services has the capacity to constrain lucrative consultancy income enjoyed by major firms. In this context, the ICAEW developed an argument that 'There is no evidence – for example, in DTI inspectors' reports – that auditors' objectivity is compromised by provision of other services' (press release dated 4 March 1993). In response to these claims, we (Mitchell *et al.* 1993) excavated a number of DTI inspectors' reports and drew attention to instances where the inspectors stated that 'We do not accept that there can be the requisite degree of watchfulness where a man is checking either his own figures or those of a colleague . . . for these reasons we do not believe that [auditors] ever achieved the standard of independence necessary for a wholly objective audit' (Department of Trade 1976: paras 249 and 250) and that 'the principle of the auditor first compiling and then reporting upon a profit forecast is not considered to be a good practice for it may impair their ability to view forecast objectively and must endanger the degree of independence essential to his work' (Department of Trade and Industry 1979: 271). The observations by B&G [pp. 103–4] do not dilute the inspectors' conclusions. They offer no comments on the profession's modes of resistance.

B&G claim that even our fairly modest proposals for reforms will 'extend the responsibility of the accounting profession' [p. 101]. They are also concerned about additional financial rewards for auditors [p. 111]. In their analysis, change seems to be conditional upon giving more and more concessions to accountants. Such a view is not encountered in other markets. For example, producers of consumer products go some way towards meeting the consumer expectations. They do not easily dismiss consumer expectations by saying that they are unreasonable [pp. 107–8]. Seemingly, the monopolies enjoyed by accountants have resulted in prioritisation of their self-interest. B&G show no appreciation of the way an occupational group has to renegotiate continuously its jurisdictions and territories (Abbott 1988; Sikka and Willmott 1995b). Any occupational group which continually seeks to frustrate public expectations jeopardises its legitimacy and ultimately its survival. As Lowe and Tinker put it:

> if the management of a business enterprise relied almost exclusively on advising customers that the product did not do what they wanted, the company would soon become popular business school case material on 'marketing myopia'. It is quite usual to regard business enterprises as expendable social artefacts because their responsiveness to human needs is a precondition of their survival. The accounting profession in the longer run is unlikely to be exempt from such social evolutionary processes.
>
> (1977: 273)

In opposing modest proposals for reform, B&G shelter behind

primitive neo-classical dogma and an appeal to 'costs' [pp. 110–11]. However, they do not recognise that the absence of information and regulation also has social costs: ask anyone suffering from the headline scandals involving accounting and auditing such as the collapse of BCCI and the Maxwell pensions fiasco. Some accountants may oppose change, but they cannot stifle the pressures for change. In a market economy, it is likely that a number of alternative occupational groups and institutional mechanisms can emerge to meet the challenges. One possibility is that changing social scenarios may also produce new modes of accountability (Power 1994). Thus there is no reason why the disclosures and practices suggested in our writings have to be under the control of accountants. It is not unreasonable to envisage institutional arrangements (laws, works councils, two-tier boards) which would help to secure a minimum wage, a cleaner environment and so on.

In opposing change, B&G are clutching at straws. They oppose the idea of companies publishing future-oriented data [p. 111], yet fail to notice that under the London Stock Exchange's rules, profit forecasts have to be included in all prospectuses published by companies seeking a listing. Such forecasts are also reported on by accountants. In the event of a contested takeover bid, profit forecasts are published. It seems that having induced investors to buy shares, companies are unwilling to make the same information available to them. At the same time, institutional investors and major creditors are in a position to secure future-oriented information through the appointment of directors, debenture trust deed covenants and lunchtable meetings. It seems that only the ordinary and relatively powerless people are denied information. B&G offer no reflections upon contemporary practices, or their ethics. Seemingly, they consider conventional published company accounts to be adequate even though most of the information contained in them is more than a year old.[9] How many self-respecting directors make an investment decision by relying solely upon past data?

B&G [p. 112] show no understanding of the politics of auditing standard-setting where auditing standards have been used to dilute auditor responsibility (Sikka 1992), especially as in the event of litigation the courts might attach some importance to professional pronouncements. Thus to advance the economic interest of the auditing industry, the UK profession recommended a 'passive' approach to auditor's evaluation of going concern (Charlesworth 1985). There was no consideration of the impact of such inward-looking pronouncements on stakeholders. Only scandals (such as Polly Peck), public disquiet and pressures from the DTI[10] resulted in a revised standard. In a similar vein, B&G [p. 111–12] fail to note that so-called 'ethical statements' are produced to disarm critics. Some hardly touch large auditing firms. For example, consider a contemporary suggestion (enshrined in the ethical guidelines issued by the accountancy trade associations) that auditing firms should not derive more than 10 per cent of their fees from one public client. Firms such as Coopers & Lybrand have an annual estimated income of some £600 million. It is unlikely that they derive £60 million per annum from any one client. The ethical statements do little to expose the firms to external scrutiny or disturb the internal working arrangements of auditing firms where trainees are encouraged to appease clients rather than give any consideration to social aspects (Hanlon 1994). B&G [p. 111] offer no reflections on why auditors and accountants continue to find themselves in relationships which exacerbate conflicts of interests.

Self-regulation

In mounting their defence of the status quo, B&G [pp. 102–4] engage in a feeble manipulation of our analysis of the Department of Trade and Industry (DTI) inspectors' reports (Sikka and Willmott 1995a). They unashamedly claim that 'to attract only 25 per cent of critical comment in DTI reports might appear a creditable performance' [p. 102] even though most of the quoted companies are audited by the firms criticised in the DTI reports. Their comments show no appreciation of the circumstances and consequences of real/alleged audit failures. First, poor auditing work is brought to public attention by a scandal and fraud rather than by any vigilance on the part of the present regulators or as a result of revelations by the firms concerned. If an audit client continues to survive by hook or by crook, poor auditing practices remain covered. Following the implementation of the Companies Act in 1989, the accountancy bodies (in their capacity as recognised supervisory bodies) are now required to monitor auditor's work, but this only involves checking mechanical compliance with auditing standards (Sikka 1997). These standards and processes ignore the issues relating to audit quality. As the ACCA puts it, 'the main purpose of practice monitoring is to monitor compliance with auditing standards, rather than to obtain statistical information about the quality of work being done' (p.25 of the ACCA's 1992 annual report on Audit Regulation). Second, the DTI inspectors are not invited to probe specific institutional aspects of auditing. Third, the state has very limited resources to investigate failures. Fourth, as our research shows (Sikka and Willmott 1995a), a large number of the DTI inspectors' reports, possibly due to heavy lobbying by the auditing industry, remain unpublished. Fifth, B&G totally ignore the impact of audit failures on jobs, savings, investments and bank deposits of ordinary people. Consider just three examples: the closure of Polly Peck resulted in the loss of 17,227 jobs (Mitchell *et al.* 1991); the demise of Sound Diffusion resulted in losses to 11,000 shareholders (Department of Trade and Industry 1991); at the time of the BCCI closure, it had 14,000 employees and some one million bank depositors with deposits of $1.85 billion (Kerry and Brown 1992: 75). B&G show no appreciation of the impact of any real/alleged audit failure on people.

B&G also mount a defence for the partners from firms implicated in major scandals. B&G seem to suggest that their right to sit on disciplinary hearings for others and enjoy lucrative government (or public) contracts should not be disrupted [pp. 102–3]. One might respond by arguing that arsonists are not invited to write fire regulations, BCCI executives are not invited to draft banking legislation and neither the companies implicated in pensions mis-selling[11] nor any of their staff are now being invited to draft financial regulations. Why should the representatives of the accounting industry be treated any differently? If audit partners of the firms implicated in major scandals are really so knowledgeable, let them begin by reforming their own businesses first. If audit partners do not know what goes on within their businesses, why are they so willing to share the financial spoils, but are so reluctant to deal with the negative consequences?

The disciplinary processes of the profession have shown a marked inability to deal with major firms. As a result of my earlier work with Willmott (1995a), on more than one occasion, the Minister for Corporate Affairs was obliged to inform Parliament that no auditor criticised in any of the DTI inspectors' reports has been disqualified from public practice. Little has changed since then, though some token gestures have been made. None of the professional bodies has investigated the overall standards of any of the firms implicated in major scandals or criticised in any of the DTI reports. Since the implementation of the Companies Act in

1989, the professional bodies have been required to investigate real/alleged cases of audit failures. What has been their performance? Some seven years after the collapse of BCCI, we are still waiting for a report on the BCCI audits. There have been no reports on the real/alleged audit failures in the cases of Maxwell, Levitt, Polly Peck, London United Investments, Homes Assured and Wallace Smith, to name but a few.

The feather duster effect of professional regulation has encouraged accountancy firms to openly engage in antisocial and predatory pursuits. For example, the 1990 High Court case of *AGIP (Africa) Limited* v *Jackson & Others* [1990] 1 Ch 265 showed that accountancy firms are engaged in money laundering activities (Mitchell *et al.* 1996). In his judgment, Mr Justice Millett stated that '[Accountants] obviously knew they were laundering money. [. . .] It must have been obvious to them that their clients could not afford their activities to see the light of the day.' Despite the high profile High Court judgment, the ICAEW took no action. There was no public statement or public report to explain its silence. When pressed, it would only say that 'there is insufficient evidence available to the Institute to justify the bringing of a disciplinary case against any of its members' (letter dated 9 May 1994). How and why the ICAEW considered its powers and judgement superior to that of the High Court is not known. In their efforts to defend the status quo, B&G fail to examine, probe or comment on the profession's propensity to sweep things under its dust-laden carpets.

Independent regulation

In all regulatory matters, there is a constant danger that the regulatory processes, values, vocabularies and agendas will be (or are) 'captured' by those who are to be regulated. In self-regulation, this has been the starting point and government ministers have described self-regulation as 'a cumbersome and expensive fiction' (*The Times*, 26 June 1997: 28). In May 1997, the government announced its intention to replace self-regulation in the financial sector (banks, financial services and so on) with a statute-based independent regulatory system. Needless to say this does not in any way diminish the problem of 'capture', but it nevertheless provides a mechanism for giving transparency and some resistance to 'capture'.

The issue of 'capture' is highly relevant to auditing, where the whole regulatory process is 'captured' by the very industry which is to be regulated. Accountants and their patrons have colonised the auditing standard-setting, regulatory and disciplinary matters. Despite the rhetoric of 'serving the public interest', the accountancy trade associations have continued to advance the interests of the auditing industry. It is difficult to recall any campaign of substance under which they have sought to advance the interests of stakeholders. In a world of global businesses, can accountancy trade associations really regulate giant multinational auditing firms? Their history and contemporary practices do not inspire much confidence.

The spokespersons for the auditing industry have recognised the need for some kind of an independent regulation, or at the very least, an independent oversight of the powers of the accountancy bodies (Swinson 1995, 1996). The UK government has indicated its intention to introduce a system of independent regulation for auditors (*Hansard*, 17 June 1997: 218–26) though the shape of these arrangements is as yet unclear. In theory, a number of possibilities would seem to exist which are all enabled and constrained by contemporary discourses. Our proposals have been explained in a number of places (for example, Mitchell *et al.* 1991, 1993; Mitchell and Sikka 1996). Among these is the view that all the regulatory powers of the accountancy bodies should be transferred to a body independent of the profession and the DTI. The composition of such a body can be decided by the government according to publicly declared criteria. Bearing in mind the concerns about 'capture' of regulators, ministers should not be the final appointers. Each nomination should be the subject of a public scrutiny by the DTI Select Committee (and the related press publicity). This independent body should have a plurality of representations, but none from any organised interests. Thus accountants would be present on such a body, but only in their capacity as 'accountants' rather than as representatives of any accountancy trade association. The body would not be dominated by any sectional interest, thus ensuring that discussions and concerns of a wide variety of stakeholders would inform decisions. To ensure transparency, all the meetings of the regulatory body would be in the 'open' with the public able to attend and record the proceedings. All the minutes and agenda papers of the body would be publicly available. It would be an offence for any member of the regulatory body to collude with another and reach decisions behind closed doors. The independent body, which we envisage, would be a statutory body and would thus owe a 'duty of care' to all stakeholders. It would be responsible for licensing, monitoring and disciplining auditors. Its main concern would be to recognise and advance the interests of a plurality of stakeholders.

SUMMARY AND DISCUSSION

The recurring failures of accounting and auditing make daily head-lines in newspapers. Since much of accounting/auditing is under the control of the professional accountancy bodies, the same headlines are also reminders of the narrowness of their visions and concerns. In this context, one might have expected B&G to examine contemporary practices or engage with an expanding body of literature which problematises the role of accounting and its institutions. Sadly, B&G show no awareness of this literature and only a dim awareness of the social, political and ethical context of accounting. In their eagerness to defend the accounting establishment, they show no ethical concerns for those suffering from poorly regulated accounting and auditing practices.

B&G's defence of the *status quo* is ahistorical. They show no appreciation of accounting/auditing as a political technology which is implicated in the legitimisation of social inequalities. B&G's defence of the auditing industry shows no awareness of the impact of accounting/auditing practices on the lives of ordinary people. They have shown little awareness of the politics of accounting regulation. B&G fail to explain any methodology which enables them to claim that apolitical and non-partisan writing is possible. They provide no evidence to show that the accountancy trade associations and/or their spokespersons have operated in a non-partisan manner.

As this chapter is a contribution to a book on accounting ethics, it is appropriate to conclude with some reflections on ethics. The deeply ingrained conservatism (as exhibited by the B&G contribution) invites a range of ethical questions about the role of accounting academics and intellectuals. In the hope of securing grants, fellowships, titles, awards and high office, they may side with the powerful institutions and firms to legitimise some self-serving 'conventional-think'. Or, in a world marked by inequalities between the powers of accountancy trade associations, major firms, corporations and the relative powerlessness of many individuals and groups, they may prefer to represent change by becoming 'opposi-tional figures' and give visibility to things, people and arguments which are marginalised and ignored. Through the latter role, scholarly interventions have a capacity to unfreeze potentialities for change by persuading people that their lives are not governed by some 'invisible hand' of fate, but by the more 'visible hand' of social arrangements, including accounting practices, which can be changed. It is for this reason that a number of scholars have sought to problematise accountancy practices, education and regulation.

The recurring failures of accounting and auditing also invite questions about the appropriateness of accounting education, especially professional education. Aspiring accountants are inculcated into ideologies, practices and techniques whose failures are headline news. The knowledge which has already failed forms a major element of the professional curriculum. Students are encouraged to learn the technical aspects through legalistic and pedantic means. They are expected to become greyhounds in book-keeping and accounting/auditing standards. There is little concern about the impact of accounting and its institutions on the lives of people. Most of the accounting/auditing books recommended by professional bodies make no reference to audit failures or to the role of accounting in disadvantaging people, far less undertake an analysis. Students are asked to live a schizophrenic existence where the technical, sanitised, censored world of accounting promoted by the accountancy bodies and encountered in books bears little relationship to the world of practices and the events reported in the media. Lived human experiences have been purged from accounting education and the considerations of the accountancy bodies. Their claims of developing ethical accounting practices and reflective accountants are difficult to sustain.

The potentialities for change, even the supporters of the *status quo* might acknowledge, are enormous. Such potentialities can enable accountants to become better and reflective citizens and managers. But in-built conservatism deflects professional bodies and their spokespersons from moving beyond ritualistic resistance. On numerous occasions the accountancy bodies have been urged to examine their policies and practices, but show little sign of doing so. The contribution by Blake and Gardiner further shows that the spokespersons for the profession are preoccupied with narrow technical and sectional interests. They show little awareness of the social context of accounting, its ethical significance, or its consequences.

NOTES

1 Professionally qualified accountants enjoy a statutory monopoly of insolvency and external auditing.
2 This material will be found in journals such as *Accounting, Organizations and Society*; *Critical Perspectives on Accounting*; *Accounting, Auditing & Accountability Journal*; *Advances in Public Interest Accounting* and others. This is also paralleled by specific sections in the American Accounting Association and the British Accounting Association.
3 Ray Gardiner is the 1997/98 Vice-President of the Association of Chartered Certified Accountants (ACCA) and will in due course become the President.
4 At a more practical level, my/our work has been accessible to individuals from the 'left' and the 'right' of the political spectrum (see Sikka and Willmott 1997: 162).
5 Some of our calls to use accounting to enable the disabled and the poorly paid people to secure greater visibility will be found in Sikka, Lowe and Willmott 1989; Cousins and Sikka 1993, and Cousins *et al.* 1997.
6 Needless to say that the discourse of democracy may also be deployed to disadvantage some groups and individuals and may thus have negative consequences.
7 After her article, Ms Fearnley was invited to engage in a dialogue through a scholarly journal, but for a variety of reasons has not done so.
8 As B&G seem to object to our claim that there is/was a 'vociferous support of the *status quo* . . . from academics with close connections to the profession', interested readers are invited to pursue references in works (for example, Sikka and Willmott 1995a, 1995b; Sikka *et al.* 1995) and draw their own conclusions.
9 In the UK, public limited companies need to publish information within seven months of the year end.
10 Copies of Sikka 1992 and its earlier versions were distributed to government ministers. Subsequently they were asked to explain their oversight of the profession.
11 For some background to the scandal see *Financial Times*, 25 June 1997: 29.

REFERENCES

Abbott, A. (1988) *The System of Professions: An essay on the division of expert labour*, Chicago, IL: University of Chicago Press.

Accounting Standards Steering Committee (1975) *The Corporate Report*, London: Accounting Standards Steering Committee.

Berry, A., Capps, T., Cooper, D., Hopper, T. and Lowe, E.A. (1985a) 'NCB Accounts – a mine of misinformation', *Accountancy*, January: 10–12.

Berry, A., Capps, T., Cooper, D., Ferguson, P., Hopper, T. and Lowe, E.A.

(1985b) 'Management control in an area of the NCB: rationales of accounting practices in a public enterprise', *Accounting, Organizations and Society*, 10 (1): 3–28.

Lord Justice Bingham, J (1992) *Inquiry into the Supervision of the Bank of Credit and Commerce International*, London: HMSO.

Charlesworth, R. (1985) 'Less room for doubt on the going-concern tack', *Accountancy Age*, 29 August: 13.

Connelly, W. (1987) 'Appearance and reality in politics', in M.T. Gibbons (ed.) *Interpreting Politics*, Oxford: Blackwell.

Cooper, D. and Hopper, T. (1988) *Debating Coal Closures*, Cambridge: Cambridge University Press.

—— (1990) *Critical Accounts*, London: Macmillan.

Cousins, J. and Sikka, P. (1993) 'Accounting for change: facilitating power and accountability', *Critical Perspectives on Accounting*, March: 53–72.

Cousins, J., Mitchell, A., Sikka, P. and Willmott, H. (1997) 'Accounting for a minimum wage', *The New Review*, May/June 1997: 9–11.

Department of Trade (1976) *Roadships Limited*, London: HMSO.

Department of Trade and Industry (1979) *Burnholme and Forder Limited*, London: HMSO.

—— (1991) *Sound Diffusion plc*, London: HMSO.

Foucault, M. (1980) *Power/Knowledge*, Brighton: Harvester Wheatsheaf.

Gramsci, A. (1971) *Selections From the Prison Notebooks*, London: Lawrence & Wishart.

Hanlon, G. (1994) *The Commercialisation of Accountancy: Flexible accumulation and the transformation of the service class*, London: Macmillan.

Held, D. (1993) *Prospects for Democracy*, Cambridge: Polity Press.

—— (1996) *Models of Democracy*, Cambridge: Polity Press.

Hopwood, A.G. and Miller, P. (1994) *Accounting and Social and Institutional Practice*, Cambridge: Cambridge University Press.

Kerry, J. and Brown, H. (1992) *The BCCI Affair*, vol. 1, September, Washington DC: US Government Printing Office.

Kuhn, T.S. (1970) *The Structure of Scientific Revolutions*, Chicago, IL: University of Chicago Press.

Lehman, C.R. (1992) *Accounting's Changing Role in Social Conflict*, New York: Markus Wiener.

Lowe, E.A. and Tinker, A.M. (1977) 'Siting the accounting problematic: towards an intellectual emancipation of accounting', *Journal of Business Finance and Accounting*, 4 (3): 263–76.

Mitchell, A. and Sikka, P. (1996) *Corporate Governance Matters*, Discussion Paper 24, London: Fabian Society.

Mitchell, A., Puxty, T., Sikka, P and Willmott, H. (1991) *Accounting for Change: Proposals for reform of audit and accounting*, Discussion Paper 7, London: Fabian Society.

—— (1993) *A Better Future for Auditing*, London: University of East London.

Mitchell, A., Sikka, P. and Willmott, H. (1996) 'Sweeping it under the carpet: the role of accountancy firms in moneylaundering', a paper presented at the Fourth Critical Perspectives on Accounting Symposium, Baruch College, The City University of New York.

Power, M. (1994) *The Audit Explosion*, London: Demos.

Puxty, T., Sikka, P. and Willmott, H. (1994) '(Re)Forming the circle: education, ethics and accountancy practices', *Accounting Education*, 3 (1) 1994: 77–92.

Robinson, D. (1989) 'Certifieds accused by MP of "stifling small audit debate" ', *Accountancy Age*, 18 May: 1.

Sikka, P. (1992) 'Audit policy-making in the UK: the case of "The auditor's considerations in respect of going concern" ', *European Accounting Review*, December: 349–92.

—— (1996) 'Auditors' rocky road to Jersey', *The Times*, 4 July: 30.

—— (1997) 'Regulating the UK Auditing Profession', in M. Sherer and S. Turley (eds) *Current Issues in Auditing*, London: Paul Chapman.

Sikka, P. and Willmott, H. (1995a) 'Illuminating the state-profession relationship: accountants acting as Department of Trade and Industry investigators', *Critical Perspectives on Accounting*, 6 (4): 341–69.

—— (1995b) 'The power of 'independence': defending and extending the jurisdiction of accounting in the UK', *Accounting, Organizations and Society*, 20 (6): 547–81.

—— (1997) 'Practising Critical Accounting', *Critical Perspectives on Accounting*, 8 (1–2): 149–65.

Sikka, P., Lowe, T. and Willmott, H. (1989) 'Accounting for the Low Paid', *Low Pay Review*, Autumn: 22–4.

Sikka, P., Puxty, T., Willmott, H. and Cooper, C. (1992) *Eliminating the Expectations Gap?*, Certified Research Report 28, London: Chartered Association of Certified Accountants.

Sikka, P, Willmott, H. and Lowe, T. (1989) 'Guardians of knowledge and public interest: evidence and issues of accountability in the UK accountancy profession', *Accounting, Auditing & Accountability Journal*, 2 (2): 47–71.

Sikka, P., Willmott, H. and Puxty, T. (1995) 'The mountains are still there: accounting academics and the bearings of intellectuals', *Accounting, Auditing & Accountability Journal*, 8 (3): 113–40.

Simons, H.W. (1994) 'Teaching the pedagogies: a dialectical approach to an ideological dilemma', in H.W. Simons and M. Billing (eds) *After Postmodernism: Reconstructing ideology critique*, London: Sage.

Swinson, C. (1995) *Interim Report of the Regulation Review Working Party*, London: ICAEW.

—— (1996) *Regulation – the way forward*, London, ICAEW.

Taylor, C. (1987) 'Language and human nature', in M.T. Gibbons (ed.) *Interpreting Politics*, Oxford: Blackwell.

Tinker, A.M. (1985) *Paper Prophets: A social critique of accounting*, New York: Praeger.

8

ETHICAL ISSUES AND THE AUDITOR

Catherine Gowthorpe

Audits are virtually meaningless because they are paid opinions. Many companies go under after a clean audit report. I did several audits in my training where I thought there was no way in which we could give the company a clean audit. One of the pillars of capitalism is the audit system, but you cannot rely on it or on the auditing firm's reputation.

(Professional auditor, quoted by Goodwin, 1996: 5)

INTRODUCTION

In this chapter some of the ethical issues which face the auditor are examined, with particular reference to relevant empirical research evidence. First, the problem of professionalism is discussed, with reference to the demands, which may often conflict, of self-interest and public interest. Then, research evidence is cited which provides support for the view that 'irregular auditing' practices are widespread throughout the profession. Subsequently, Kohlberg's model of moral development is described and discussed in some detail, as it is the foundation of most of the empirical work on accounting (and especially auditing) ethics. The application of Kohlberg's model in some empirical studies of members of the auditing profession and students is then described. Finally, the role of education as a plausible solution to the problem of insufficiently developed auditor ethics is debated.

THE PROBLEM OF PROFESSIONALISM

In recent times auditors of companies in the private sector have been criticised in trenchant terms. The criticisms levelled against them include their alleged inability to achieve a decent quality of work, their firms' willing acceptance of consultancy work from audit clients, their reluctance to face responsibility for detecting and reporting fraud, their lack of accountability, independence and integrity and their unreasonable insistence upon self-regulation. The radical critics of modern auditing have been vociferous in their accusations of conduct unbecoming to people who hold themselves out to be professionals. For examples see, among many possible references, Parker (1994), Hooks (1991), Mitchell and Sikka (1993) and Mitchell et al. (1994).

The crux of the matter resides in the notion of professionalism. Included among the common characteristics of a profession are an ethos of public service, a body of knowledge attainable only as a result of a long period of study, and a set of ethical principles. These and other functional characteristics distinguish a profession from a mere occupation, and despite the fact that professional status is claimed by people involved in an ever increasing diversity of human activities, the distinctions retain some authority and conviction. The power of the description is evidenced, if by no other means, by the frequency and ferocity of the attacks of the critics on accountancy as a professional activity. The public service ethos is an especially significant focus of attack, as it lies at the heart of the expressly stated objectives of the accountancy profession. Lest we suppose that the compromise of the public service ethos of accounting is a phenomenon of the iconoclastic late twentieth century, Lee (1995) gives a detailed account of the rise of the profession in the UK during the nineteenth century, and how its beginnings were firmly rooted in self-interest: 'The most obvious feature of early UK professionalization is the pursuit by accountants and their institutions of economic self-interest in the name of a public interest' (Lee 1995: 53). Those who are inclined, then, to deplore the recent transformation of the accounting profession from public servant into self-interested businesses, are perhaps referring to a 'golden age' of professional rectitude which may always have been compromised.

Expressly and officially, the accountancy profession regards itself as operating principally in the public interest; however, the dichotomy of interests is neatly captured by the story of the mission statement of the Institute of Chartered Accountants in England and Wales (ICAEW). The ICAEW, in common with many other organisations, decided to formulate a mission statement during the early 1990s. Its initial draft, issued in 1992, encapsulated the single mission of working in the public interest. However, following heated objections from many of its members the ICAEW was obliged to incorporate members' interests into the mission statement. It was left in little doubt that a substantial proportion of its members consider that its primary purpose is to represent their own sectional interests; Irvine quotes a practitioner on this point: ' . . . as a membership, we've always thought we were a trade association' (1993: 32). The revised statement reads: 'The Institute's mission is to promote high standards of objectivity, integrity and technical competence, thereby serving the interests of both the public and its members and enhancing the value of the qualification chartered accountant' (ICAEW 1993). The ICAEW attempted to smooth over the conflict of interest by adopting the comforting notion that 'over the longer term there is a natural convergence between the public interest and members' interest' (Plaistowe – then president of the ICAEW – 1993: 7), a nostrum which failed to convince many of the critics both within and outside the profession.

There is a high level of agreement among professional bodies as to the qualities of the professional auditor, and the principles which should govern their working life. Key qualities which appear in the codes of ethics of professional bodies include independence, integrity, objectivity, competence and judgement. For example, the ICAEW's introduction to its 'Guide to Professional Ethics' (ICAEW 1997: 178) includes a list of five fundamental principles which either expressly mentions or clearly implies all of these qualities, along with other related qualities such as honesty, fair-dealing, truthfulness, courtesy, skill and diligence.

However, there is no avoiding the fact that in the UK, the USA and other significant world economies, auditing is a business, and its practitioners operate the business with a view to profit. The ethical problems that face accountants generally may be particularly acute for the auditing subdivision of the profession, as noted by Waples and Schaub (1991: 387), because of the possibly conflicting demands made upon auditors' loyalty by the public and by their clients. The laws which establish private sector auditing and thus, incidentally, guarantee a flow of income-producing activity for audit practitioners, were enacted to ensure a flow of reliable and verified information from companies to the financial markets. On the other hand, the contractual relationship lies between the auditor and the company, and the bill for services is paid out of company resources, with a consequent reduction of profits available for retention or distribution. The potential conflict of loyalties is a rich source of actual ethical dilemmas for the auditor: included among the major ethical dilemmas facing American CPAs which were identified by the enquiries of Finn *et al.* (1988: 609–10) are problems of conflict of interest and independence and proposals by clients to alter financial statements. Gunz and McCutcheon (1991) focus upon three issues relating to confidentiality, conflict of interest and conflict of duty which will pose tricky ethical dilemmas for auditors. Goodwin's interviews with auditing staff at a major firm in the UK (1996: 5), revealed conflicts relating to confidentiality, conflicting loyalties to shareholders and directors, and disclosure issues.

There is a wide range of behaviour by auditors at all levels which prejudices the successful application of the ethical principles recognised by their professional bodies. Self-interested egoistical behaviour will place the interests of the individual ahead of any other considerations: examples of such behaviour would include bowing to pressure from management to accept a strictly indefensible interpretation of accounting rules, issuing a false audit report in order to retain the client's audit and other work, not searching for evidence as exhaustively as possible, and under-reporting time spent on an audit.

EVIDENCE OF UNPROFESSIONAL BEHAVIOUR

Evidence of the incidence of prejudicial behaviours may be difficult or, in some cases, impossible to find. Any auditor who signs a false audit report in order to retain an assignment occupies, by definition, a senior position in their firm and is highly unlikely to admit that they have done so. Also, very often complex auditing and accounting issues genuinely demand the exercise of judgement and it may be possible for individuals to rationalise their conduct as 'taking a view' or 'a close call'.

But there is research evidence that some transgressions, referred to by Willett and Page (1996) as 'irregular auditing', may be widespread. Pressure upon auditors to meet time budgets appears to have grown, because of reduced audit fees resulting from keen competition in the audit market. Otley and Pierce (1996), in a study of audit seniors in three of the 'Big Six' firms in Ireland, found that time budgets were perceived by almost half of their respondents to be 'very tight, practically unattainable or impossible to achieve'. They found a high level of dysfunctional behaviour; for example, only 25 per cent of their respondents could say that they had never accepted weak client explanations. Many admitted to deliberately reducing the quality of their audit work and/or under-reporting time. The principal reason for resorting to dysfunctional behaviour appears to be self-interest; those auditors who manage to complete their work, by whatever means, within the budget allocation of time are much more likely to receive favourable personal performance evaluations, and therefore in due course to be promoted. Respondents in Willett and Page's (1996) survey identified a range of irregular behaviours which they had known colleagues adopt. These include rejecting awkward-looking items from a sample, not testing all sample items and accepting doubtful evidence.[1]

What impetus is there towards ethical behaviour by auditors? A set of motives can be identified which range between the more or less noble and the disinterested. At the most basic level is perhaps the fear of being found out in an unethical act, the consequences of which might be loss of reputation and disciplinary action; the motive may be ignoble and negative, and it would be impossible to identify its prevalence among the population of auditors, but it may be responsible for an extensive degree of compliance. Moizer (1997: 59) has identified this type of behaviour among auditors as consequential egoism; that is, it takes into account the consequences of action but only as it affects the auditor. At a higher level of moral reasoning a more conscientious auditor may choose to adopt a wider consequentialist view of their own actions by assessing the likely consequences for other individuals, or for the more general concept of the public interest.

Alternatively, auditors may reason that any citizen, but especially a professional person, should obey laws and rules; the very existence of a set of rules would be sufficient to ensure compliance by many individuals. A more refined and thoughtful deontological approach might involve the application of not only the ethical and other rules of a professional body, but also of a more general moral code which has been internalised by the individual. There is, then, a hierarchy of motivations and actions; a few of the possibilities have been identified above.

KOHLBERG'S MODEL OF MORAL DEVELOPMENT

A frequently cited model of progressive moral reasoning was developed by Kohlberg, who demonstrated that there are age-related stages in moral, as in cognitive, development: 'universal and regular age trends of moral development may be found in moral judgement, and these have a formal-cognitive basis' (1969: 375). Kohlberg's classification is shown in Table 8.1. Not all individuals will reach the final stage of the model; moral development may cease at Stage 4 or 5 or even sooner, but it is argued that the stages are sequential so that in order to reach Stage 6 an individual would have to have progressed through all of the other stages in order. It is important to the student of auditing ethics to work through and understand the implications of Kohlberg's model, because it has been used as the basis of most of the empirical work which has been carried out on the moral development of auditors and accountants.[2]

Kohlberg's model offers a helpful, concise and very persuasive view of moral development, although it may be argued that the model, like most models, is too reductive. Several criticisms have been made of it. An important and fundamental criticism is offered by Gilligan (1982: 18); the empirical work on the development of moral judgement upon which Kohlberg bases his six stages was based upon a group of boys. If female moral reasoning is qualitatively different from that of males, and Gilligan argues that it is, then the Kohlberg model explains the moral development of only one half of humankind.

Thomas (1993: 469), among a range of serious criticisms, claims that Kohlberg is mistaken in his ordering of Stages 5 and 6, as it implies that deontological moral reasoning, which is implied by Stage 6 is superior to, and more sophisticated than, the utilitarian moral reasoning expressed by Stage 5. Further, he observes that Stages 1 to 4 do not entail a substantial moral content at all; it is only at the post-conventional level that the essential components of a critical outlook and moral courage enter the picture. He also suggests that those of us (that is, most of us) who do not achieve the sixth stage of moral reasoning, probably do not achieve it because leading a moral life is not the primary source of our self-esteem; our careers are much more likely to provide that. Perhaps the most telling criticism of all in view of widely held beliefs (which will be discussed later) that moral reasoning can be taught, is that Kohlberg's work does not ascribe much importance at all to the role of training in moral development.

Thomas's and Gilligan's criticisms are substantial, although they can be at least partially challenged. The empirical work which has

Table 8.1 Kohlberg's classification of levels of moral development

Level	Basis of moral judgement	Stages of development
I	*PRE-CONVENTIONAL* Moral value residing in external quasi-physical happenings, in bad acts, or in quasi-physical needs rather than in persons and standards	Stage 1: Obedience and punishment orientation. Egocentric deference to power or prestige. Trouble-avoiding. Objective responsibility. Stage 2: Naively egoistic orientation. Right action is that which instrumentally satisfies the needs of self and occasionally of others.
II	*CONVENTIONAL* Moral value resides in performing good or right roles, in maintaining the conventional order and the expectancies of others	Stage 3: Orientation to approval of others, to pleasing and helping others. Conformity to stereotypical images of majority or natural role behaviour, and judgement by intentions. Stage 4: Authority and social-order maintaining orientation. Orientation towards doing duty and showing respect for authority and maintaining the given social order for its own sake. Regard for earned expectations of others.
III	*POST-CONVENTIONAL* Moral value resides in conformity by the self to shared or shareable standards, rights or duties.	Stage 5: Contractual legalistic orientation. Recognition of an arbitrary element or starting point in rules or expectations for the sake of agreement. Duty defined in terms of contract, general avoidance of violation of the will or rights of others, and majority will or welfare. Stage 6: Conscience or principle orientation. Orientation not only to actually ordained social rules but to principles of choice involving appeal to logical universality and consistency. Orientation to conscience as a directing agent and to mutual respect and trust.

Source: Adapted from Kohlberg (1969: 376)

been done on gender differentiation in moral reasoning has not definitively concluded whether or not there are distinct gender-based differences; some studies conclude that significant differences exist, others reach the opposite conclusion. In response to Thomas's criticism of the ordering of the stages, there are those who would argue strongly that utilitarianism is indeed an inferior form of moral reasoning and so Stage 5 is properly inferior to Stage 6; to take a notable example, Bernard Williams (Smart and Williams 1973) presents a convincing series of arguments against utilitarianism. Also, it should be noted that Kohlberg himself points out: 'it is not at all clear that stages 5 and 6 should be used to define developmental end points in morality . . . stage 4 is the dominant stage of most adults' (1969: 384). Finally, in response to the criticism that Kohlberg's work ascribes little importance to training it should be noted that Rest (1979: 12) identifies Kohlberg as a great champion of moral education.

APPLICATION OF KOHLBERG'S MODEL TO AUDITORS

Kohlberg's model has been dealt with at some length because of its importance to the methodologies of many of the empirical studies which have been carried out in recent years. A body of research evidence is building up which aims to deliver a conclusive verdict on the extent to which auditors do act ethically.

Rest (1979) has developed the Defining Issues Test (DIT) to test an individual's level of moral development; this gives a score, known as the 'P' score (P standing for 'principled reasoning'), expressed as a percentage, which estimates the proportion of an individual's thinking which takes place at the post-conventional level identified by Kohlberg. The work of Kohlberg and Rest is very closely associated, and is often used by researchers into the ethical reasoning of auditors and accountants.

Lampe and Finn (1992) studied the responses of auditing students and auditing practitioners to the DIT and to a series of seven ethical dilemma vignettes. The results of the DIT showed a relatively low level of post-conventional reasoning. Audit managers showed the highest level of the groups tested with mean P scores of 41.9, but this is below the moral reasoning level of college graduates which is used as a comparator in the study; further analysis of this result showed that auditors had higher Stage 4 but lower Stage 6 measures than college graduates. The authors of the study interpret this result as reflecting 'an orientation to internalised compliance with GAAP, GAAS, codes of ethics and other rules of social order', and this leads them to question the imposition of an 'artificial barrier' of rules, which may inhibit auditors' development towards post-conventional reasoning.

Sweeney and Roberts (1997) applied a similar methodology to that used by Lampe and Finn to a respondent group of just over three hundred auditing professionals, and found that the DIT tests yielded a mean P score of 42.8, consistent with earlier studies, and confirming earlier findings that auditors mostly operate at conventional levels of moral reasoning. They observed that, 'consistent with moral development theory, the higher an auditor's level of development, the less likely he or she is to resolve an independence dilemma by referring solely to technical standards' (1997: 348). Sweeney (1995), again using the Kohlberg/Rest methodology, found, as had some earlier studies, that the P scores for women in his sample were significantly higher than for men, that the P scores for auditors with 'a liberal political orientation' were significantly higher than for political conservatives, and that P scores decreased significantly at progressively higher levels in the firm, partners obtaining the lowest score of any group. He concluded that the most significant differentiating factor in moral reasoning among his sample of auditors is political orientation, followed by gender. He explains the decline in moral reasoning discernible in the progression through the hierarchy of firms by the fact that few women achieve high status in the auditing profession.

The research evidence, then, appears to support the view that auditors on the whole have no higher level of moral reasoning than the population at large. In terms of Kohlberg's model they are at the conventional level of moral development, at a stage where they would respond to ethical difficulties by reference to rules, motivated by a desire to maintain the social order, and by a respect for authority. This characterisation of auditors is supported, to some extent at least, by Granleese and Barrett's study of the personality characteristics of male chartered accountants in the UK (1993: 197). While observing that the typical male chartered accountant 'places great value on ethical standards' they describe him as a 'socially conforming, stable introvert'. The desire for social conformity may indicate that the level of moral reasoning of the average auditor is unlikely to breach the bounds of the conventional in most instances.

If auditors do not possess integrity and are not independent then an audit is a pointless exercise. The descriptions of the qualities required of auditors (for example those qualities described in guides to professional ethics) imply that an auditor should have the capacity for moral reasoning at a high level; research evidence indicates that they do not on the whole possess such a capacity, and further, that social and occupational factors mean that those at the highest levels of the profession who are, it is safe to assume, resolving the really difficult ethical dilemmas are even less likely to reason at post-conventional levels.

The exercise of true integrity may be uncomfortable for all concerned; post-conventional moral reasoning requires the moral courage to make difficult and often personally compromising decisions. In an audit context, examples of the exercise of moral courage would include issuing an adverse audit report in the face of pressure and the threat of auditor change from clients, refusing to bow to pressure to under-report time spent on an audit, even at the expense of personal advancement, and acting against personal instinct and feeling by refusing to be drawn into close relationships with client staff. Putting public before personal interest at all times demands uncommon moral qualities.

Is there a problem here at all? Why should auditors function at a higher level of moral reasoning than the public at large? Auditors might argue for a continuance of the status quo on the grounds that, while most members of the profession are perhaps not possessed of great moral courage, conscientious adherence to a set of rules provides an acceptable surrogate, leading in the end to more or less the same result. Moreover, an audit firm staffed only by highly principled, politically liberal and preferably female (according to the evidence of Sweeney (1995)) moral mavericks represents a somewhat unlikely vision. Nevertheless, the foundation of audit lies in disinterested ethical behaviour so there is a moral imperative to ensure that ethical standards are as high as possible. Furthermore, there is a significant, urgent problem with public perceptions of audit, which is unlikely to disappear without radical change.

THE ROLE OF EDUCATION

How, then, could this problem, assuming that there is a problem, be tackled? The auditing profession has successfully resisted alterations to its self-regulatory status, but perhaps only substantial regulatory intervention is likely to change the climate in which audit is conducted. At the other extreme from those who would seek to preserve the current self-regulatory position, would be those who argue that audit as a profit-making activity cannot be independent, and so it should be brought under governmental control. An alternative approach to additional regulation is to try to tackle the problem through education.

Gaa, in an examination of the issue of moral expertise, identifies moral cognition as a skilled activity and asserts that this 'expert skill is acquired rather than innate' (1995: 259). Mintz suggests: 'Moral virtue . . . is formed by habit. . . . [It] is not inborn but results from training' (1996: 829). The obvious implication for auditors (and others) is that the level of moral cognition can be improved through an educational process. The typical auditor in the UK goes through an educational process comprising several years of basic schooling followed by a university degree, not necessarily in accounting or related areas, followed by rigorous and intensive professional training with a heavy emphasis on examinations which appear to be intended as much to exclude from as to admit to the profession. At none of these stages is the embryonic professional likely to be exposed to much education in moral reasoning. And yet, as Lovell points out: 'accountants are assumed to understand the ethical behaviour expected of them during their practising careers' (1995: 68).

There are dangers, however, in proposing the introduction of ethics into the education of auditors. First, the activity might be undertaken in a spirit of cynicism, as a means of avoiding regulatory interference; this would, quite rightly, attract opprobrium. Second, much would depend upon the objectives of the educational process; there is a danger that it would be undertaken in a mechanistic way, serving only to reinforce students' beliefs that in order to be a good, ethical auditor it is necessary only to follow the rulebook. Third, if education in ethics were to be introduced only into undergraduate and qualifying professional syllabuses, it would, even if effective, take a very long time to permeate the profession. Fourth, there is the problem that, although it is relatively easy to teach students to recognise ethical problems, and even to identify right action in the particular circumstances, encouraging them to take the right action is much more challenging. Indeed, empirical research carried out by Fulmer and Carlile (1987: 216) suggests that accounting students perceive ethical issues more clearly than general business students, but that they are not more likely to act 'more ethically'. Finally, there is the profound problem identified by Lovell (1995): the accounting profession, in the form of the professional accounting bodies, imposes an institutional inhibitor to the development of moral 'atmosphere'; the systems of the professional bodies

> can be interpreted as a Stage 1 level of moral reasoning and behaviour, i.e. a behaviour borne out of fear of antagonizing its (the profession's) two masters – the State, which grants its royal charters, and the business community, which payrolls its own and its members activities.
>
> (Lovell 1995: 74)

If these objections were not enough, education in business ethics is itself fraught with danger. Macdonald and Beck-Dudley (1994) warn against an approach to business ethics education which has become a standard in the USA, that is, the presentation of utilitarianism and deontology as polarised alternative approaches to moral thought: '[Students'] brief exposure to moral philosophy often leaves them worse off than they were before' (1994: 616). Mintz (1995: 261) identifies a further problem in ethics education: the focus on the act, rather than upon the agent. Macdonald and Beck-Dudley (1994) and Mintz (1995, 1996) all advocate approaches to ethical education based upon an appreciation of virtue ethics. The key question to be answered in order to be able to recognise and deal with ethical dilemmas is not 'What should I do?' but rather 'What should I be?' Ethical educators can encourage their students to develop their moral characters and this approach holds out a better chance of developing the requisite moral courage in professional people to take unpalatable and unpopular decisions.

If ethical education were to provide an answer to the problem of insufficient levels of moral development among auditors, then it would need to be handled carefully in order to avoid the dangers discussed above. It ought not be used as a short-term palliative to get the profession off the hook of adverse criticism and to fend off regulatory interference. It would need to be undertaken thoroughly and to permeate all levels of professional development. It would have to be comprehensive and rigorous in its approach, so as to avoid confusing students whose previous acquaintance with the recognition and discussion of ethical issues is likely to be superficial at best.

CONCLUSION

The evidence cited in this chapter does not flatter members of the auditing profession. Various types of dysfunctional and self-interested behaviour are coming to light in the course of empirical studies on auditing practice, and the application of Kohlberg's model of moral development shows no very high level of moral reasoning among members of the profession. Demands for ethical education for auditors in the USA have been frequent and vociferous in recent years, and a supply has arisen to meet the demand; however there is little evidence as yet to indicate whether or not the initiatives taken in this area have been effective. The crisis of confidence in the UK auditing profession may result in similar demands in years to come, especially if the profession is successful in maintaining self-regulation, and it is likely that we stand at the beginning of an era of increased consciousness of the importance of professional ethics in the auditing profession.

NOTES

1   The level and incidence of 'irregular auditing' appears, on the evidence, to be such that 'unethical' hardly captures the flavour of the misdemeanours. One might question whether or not in the circumstances there is some element of breach of the contract between the auditor and the company, given that the product offered is in so many cases apparently sub-standard.

2   The predominance of the psychological approach to the study of accountants' ethics, based upon the work of Kohlberg, has been criticised by Fogarty (1995) who contends that psychological insights derived from the application of a model based upon individual differences cannot be used to explain the behaviour of the profession as a group.

REFERENCES

Finn, D.W., Chonko, L.B. and Hunt, S.D. (1988) 'Ethical problems in public accounting: the view from the top', *Journal of Business Ethics*, 7: 605–15.

Fogarty, T.J. (1995) 'Accountant ethics: a brief examination of neglected sociological dimensions', *Journal of Business Ethics*, 14: 103–15.

Fulmer, W.E. and Carlile, B.R. (1987) 'Ethical perceptions of accounting students: does exposure to a code of professional ethics help?', *Issues in Accounting Education*, Fall, 2 (2): 207–17.

Gaa, J.C. 'Moral judgement and moral cognition: a comment', *Research on Accounting Ethics*, 1: 253–65.

Gilligan, C. (1982) *In a Different Voice: Psychological theory and women's development*, Cambridge, MA: Harvard University Press.

Goodwin, B. (1996) 'Ethics and responsibility in a large accountancy firm', Henley Working Paper Series, HWP 9601, Henley-on-Thames, Henley Management College.

Granleese, J. and Barrett, T.F. (1993) 'Job satisfaction, and the social, occupational and personality characteristics of male chartered accountants from three professional bodies', *British Accounting Review*, 25: 177–200.

Gunz, S. and McCutcheon, J. (1991) 'Some unresolved ethical issues in auditing', *Journal of Business Ethics*, 10: 777–85.

Hooks, K.L. (1991) 'Professionalism and self-interest: a critical view of the expectations gap', *Critical Perspectives on Accounting*, 3: 109–36.

ICAEW (1993) 'Objectives, priorities and progress: a summary' in *Accountancy*, April: 113–14.

—— (1997) 'Guide to Professional Ethics', in *Members' Handbook*.

Irvine, J. (1993) 'Keeping the membership happy', *Accountancy*, April: 32.

Kohlberg, L. (1969) 'Stage and sequence: the cognitive-developmental approach to socialization', in D.A. Goslin (ed.) *Handbook of Socialization Theory and Research*, Chicago, IL: Rand McNally College Publishing Co.

Lampe, J.C. and Finn, D.W. (1992) 'A model of auditors' ethical decision processes', *Auditing: a Journal of Practice and Theory*, supplement to vol. 11: 33–59.

Lee, T.A. (1995) 'The professionalization of accountancy: a history of protecting the public in a self-interested way', *Accounting, Auditing & Accountability Journal*, 8 (4): 48–69.

Lovell, A. (1995) 'Moral reasoning and moral atmosphere in the domain of accounting', *Accounting, Auditing & Accountability Journal*, 8 (3): 60–80.

Macdonald, J.E. and Beck-Dudley, C.L. (1994) 'Are deontology and teleology mutually exclusive?', *Journal of Business Ethics*, 13: 615–23.

Mintz, S.M. (1995) 'Virtue ethics and accounting education', *Issues in Accounting Education*, Fall, 10 (2): 247–67.

—— (1996) 'Aristotelian virtue and business ethics education', *Journal of Business Ethics*, 15: 827–38.

Mitchell, A. and Sikka, P. (1993) 'Accounting for change: the institutions of accountancy', *Critical Perspectives on Accounting*, 4: 29–52.

Mitchell, A., Puxty, T., Sikka, P. and Willmott, H. (1994) 'Ethical statements as smokescreens for sectional interests: the case of the UK accountancy profession', *Journal of Business Ethics*, 13: 39–51.

Moizer, P. (1997) 'Independence', in M. Sherer and S. Turley (eds) *Current Issues in Auditing*, London: Paul Chapman Publishing.

Otley, D.T. and Pierce, B.J. (1996) 'Auditor time budget pressure: consequences and antecedents', *Accounting, Auditing & Accountability Journal*, 9 (1): 31–58.

Parker, L.D. (1994) 'Professional body accounting ethics: in search of the private interest', *Accounting, Organizations and Society*, 19 (6): 507–25.

Plaistowe, I. (1993) 'Objectives, priorities and progress', *Accountancy*, March: 7.

Rest, J.R. (1979) *Development in Judging Moral Issues*, Minneapolis, MN: University of Minnesota Press.

Smart, J.J.C and Williams, B. (1973) *Utilitarianism – For and Against*, Cambridge: University Press.

Sweeney, J.T. (1995) 'The moral expertise of auditors: an exploratory analysis', *Research on Accounting Ethics*, 1: 213–34.

Sweeney, J.T. and Roberts, R.W. (1997) 'Cognitive moral development and auditor independence', *Accounting, Organizations and Society*, 22 (3/4): 337–52.

Thomas, L. (1993) 'Morality and psychological development', in P. Singer (ed.) *A Companion to Ethics*, Oxford: Blackwell.

Waples, E, and Schaub, M.K. (1991) 'Establishing an ethic of accounting: a response to Westra's call for government employment of auditors', *Journal of Business Ethics*, 10: 385–93.

Willett, C. and Page, M. (1996) 'A survey of time budget pressure and irregular auditing practices among newly qualified UK chartered accountants', *British Accounting Review*, 28: 101–20.

9

A MODEL FOR ETHICAL EDUCATION IN ACCOUNTING

Ray Carroll

The nature of an accountant's work puts them in a special position of trust. The accountant is commonly thought of as a public watchdog. This phrase captures the essence of the very critical role that accountants play in society. Accountants are expected to adhere to rules of confidentiality, objectivity and independence. As the conscience of business, professional accountants often find themselves facing competing obligations. Accountants have obligations to shareholders, creditors, employees, suppliers, the government, the accounting profession and the public at large. In other words, their obligations go beyond their immediate client. Behaving ethically is an essential and expected trait. The daily work of the accountant involves dealing with confidential files about the personal and business affairs of countless individuals. Decisions made on information provided by accountants can materially affect the lives or any or all of these stakeholders.

Trust is an ethical concept that obligates the accountant to exercise his function responsibly. Integrity is expected of all professionals but 'Of all the groups of professions which are closely allied with business, there is none in which the practitioner is under a greater ethical obligation to persons who are not his immediate clients' (May, quoted in Sack 1985: 125). However, because of reports of unethical behaviour in the business community, the accounting profession has come under increasing criticism, and public confidence in the profession is in doubt. Lost confidence is a threat to the economic system. 'For capital markets to work efficiently in allocating resources among business enterprises, the investing public must have confidence in financial information and in the accountants who help to prepare and audit it' (Stanga and Turpen 1991).

Users of accounting information generally do not share accounting expertise and are consequently not in a position to access the work of accountants. This information asymmetry puts members of the accounting profession in a special position of power. Accountants have power due to their special expertise and power due to their access to confidential information. To be worthy of user confidence that this power will not be abused requires a high standard of ethical conduct.

Ethics is important to accountants and those who rely on information provided by accountants because ethical behaviour entails taking the moral point of view. That is, the effect that one's actions will have on others is taken into account. The seriousness of ethical behaviour in business is no trivial matter. Many still remember the case of the Ford Pinto automobile in the late 1970s as a reminder of how costing can be misused. The Pinto had a defective gas tank about which Ford failed to warn the public. The company used statistical analysis to do a cost–benefit analysis of steps required to correct the problem. It worked out that the cost of lawsuits from burn deaths, burn injuries and burned vehicles was less then the cost of making the improvement; so Ford decided to stay with the original design. (See Dowie 1977: 28 and Velasquez 1991: 110–14.) Surely questions of harm to the life and health of others are not merely economic or scientific questions. From an ethical perspective one can condemn Ford for failing to consider the interest of all affected parties and for treating individuals as mere variables in a cost–benefit equation rather than as human beings who deserve to be treated as ends in themselves and not as means only. Other famous cases such as Hooker Chemical's waste disposal at Love Canal (*New York Times*, 5 August 1979: 1 and 39), Nestlé's powdered milk scandal, A.H. Robins's marketing of the Dalkon Shield (Mintz 1985; Grant 1992), Dow Corning's experience with silicone breast implants and many others accent the serious impact that business decisions can have on human lives and on the environment in which we live.

Scandals such as those mentioned in the preceding paragraph as well as others involving insider trading, bribery and the passing on of negative externalities[1] to third parties have made ethics a critical issue for the accounting profession. The attainment of high ethical standards is a central problem for the accounting profession and for those responsible for the education of accounting professionals. Ethical problems have been costly for the profession. Ernst & Young, for example, had agreed to pay $400 million to the Resolution Trust Corporation and the Federal Deposit Insurance Corporation to settle charges that Ernst & Young had improperly audited federally insured banks and savings institutions that later failed (*New York Times*, 26 January 1994: C3).

ETHICS IN TERMS OF PROFESSIONAL CODES OF CONDUCT

One approach to countering the perception of ethical deterioration in the accounting profession and business community in general has been through the use of professional codes of ethics. Accountants enjoy special rights and privileges that are not available to other members of society. The state grants autonomy, including the exclusive right to determine who can legitimately do the work and how it should be done (Gaa 1986). In return for the autonomy granted to it, the accounting profession has a special public interest responsibility to society to carry on its business competently and ethically. One role of a code of ethics is to convince the state and those with whom the profession will do business that it is deserving of the confidence, respect, and financial benefits accruing to its members. A code of ethics may be used to persuade others that the professional is trustworthy and will not take advantage of his access to privileged information. To quote Friedson:

> A code of ethics can be seen as a formal method of declaring to all that the occupation can be trusted, and so of persuading society to grant the special status of autonomy. The very existence of such a code implies that individual members of the occupation have the personal qualities of professionalism, the importance of which is also useful in obtaining autonomy. Thus most of the commonly cited attributes of professions may be seen as consequences of autonomy or as conditions useful for persuading the public and the body politic to grant such autonomy.
>
> (Friedson 1986)

All major Western accounting bodies have a code of professional conduct in place. Such codes provide a set of standards that its members are to regard as the minimal level of professional conduct. The intent is to provide assurance to the public that the profession is monitoring itself, and that it has set high standards and has a disciplinary procedure in place to deal with violations of these standards. Professional codes are high-sounding. They use words like 'due care', 'integrity', 'responsibility', 'public interest', 'objectivity', and 'independence'. In the United States the Anderson Committee, appointed by the American Institute of Certified Public Accountants, undertook the role to 'evaluate the relevance of present ethical standards to professionalism, integrity, and commitment to both quality service and the public interest' (AICPA 1986). In restructuring the Code of Professional Ethics, the Committee revised the rules and standards to meet the above stated goal:

> The restructured Code will shift the emphasis from compliance with specific rules to an emphasis on achieving positively stated goals. Professionalism requires much more than compliance with specific rules. It requires a pattern of conduct – indeed a pattern of thinking – that results in the performance of all professional activities with competence, objectivity, and integrity. Specific rules by themselves cannot be comprehensive and flexible enough to provide members with the incentive to achieve that level of performance.
>
> (AICPA 1986: 22–3)

However, of even more importance than the restructuring of the Code is the influence that a professional code of conduct exerts on practising accountants. Beets (1992) conducted a study to determine practitioner familiarity with the Code. The approach used was a set of hypothetical cases where a public accountant performed in an ethically questionable manner. Each respondent was required to comment on whether the accountant had behaved in a manner prescribed by the Code. The outcome demonstrated that the respondents were not familiar with rules which had changed since 1977, as evidenced by the fact that they evaluated only 52 per cent of the cases dealing with these issues correctly (compared with 88 per cent of the other cases). Thus, this indicates that perhaps a code of ethics is not the best way to improve ethical behaviour. Those respondents who had taken continuing professional education (CPE) courses in ethics did much better in the study. Beets suggests that 'While allowing practitioners to retain much of their current freedom in selecting CPE courses, the AICPA could mandate that some of the required hours be devoted to certain topics, such as accounting ethics' (1992: 32). Likewise, Scribner and Dillaway note that codes of ethics 'are viewed as having limited deterrent value and are considered to serve at most an informational role' (1989: 50).

While the informational role is important, codes of ethics have some rather serious limitations. It is not possible to foresee all of the potential ethical problems that a professional accountant will encounter. To attempt to do so would result in an unmanageable maze. A code may be effective in dealing with blatantly unethical conduct. In such cases it is not uncommon for a discipline committee, for example, to require a member who has been found to violate the code to actually take an ethics course before being permitted to continue using his or her designation. But what about borderline cases? Here codes are not likely to be of much use. They are often subject to broad interpretation due to sometimes vague and general wording. For example Rule 222 of the Certified General Accountants' Association of Ontario says: 'A member shall safeguard the interest of the recipient of the service(s) and the general public'. This code also says: 'This section would not be contravened when an accountant sacrificed the interest of his client or his employer for the common good of the general public, notwithstanding any other sections of this code.' Note that the auditor does not have a specific duty to act in the interest of either the client or the third party but has only a general fiduciary duty to act in the interest of others.

Ethical codes can also be used by the profession to limit the supply of members or restrict competition (Larson 1977). Ethical codes can be used by individuals to hide behind rules as an excuse to avoid making appropriate decisions (Heyne 1968: 47). What is required is moral character and ethical reasoning ability and no code can provide this. According to MacIntyre (1981: 47) when rules become the central focus of morality character is interpreted as the ability and desire to follow the rules and sight of fundamental qualities is lost. Codes cannot serve as the final moral authority. To do so would eliminate the possibility of criticising the rules from a broader moral framework and would effectively silence debate. One may agree with MacIntyre that ethical codes make rules, rather than moral character, the focus of morality. An ethical code by itself is not sufficient:

But codes of ethics function all too often as shields; their abstraction allows many to adhere to them while continuing their ordinary practices. In businesses as well as in those professions that have already developed codes, much more is needed. The codes must be but the starting point for a broad inquiry into the ethical quandaries encountered at work. Lay persons, and especially those affected by professional practices, such as customers . . . must be included in these efforts, and must sit on regulatory commissions. Methods of disciplining those who infringe the guidelines must be given teeth and enforced.

(Bok 1978: 260)

Ethics, however, goes well beyond enforcement. The essence of ethics is in that behaviour which is unenforceable and must be entrusted to self-regulated conduct. Ethical behaviour implies taking the right actions out of free choice. Codes may help improve the ethical dimensions of practice by helping people develop the habit of doing the right thing and by providing a framework for ethical practice. Clearly, however, codes of ethical conduct are not sufficient. Without a firm commitment to do what is right, the desire for money, power and position may take precedence over codes in the absence of effective enforcement.

COMMITMENT TO MORALITY

We need to move beyond codes to an organising principle that will serve to guide accounting practice. One such principle is that of integrity. Literally, integrity means a wholeness, possessing a coherent and consistent set of principles and acting in accordance with these principles. In referring to the wholeness of human life, integrity has a moral quality and is an ideal that can never be fully achieved by everyone one hundred per cent of the time. Alasdair MacIntyre has said that integrity cannot be specified at all except with reference to the wholeness of human life (1981: 189). Taylor (1981) is convincing in his argument that wholeness of character cannot be achieved without the individual possessing a firm grounding of moral values. These would include, among others, values such as tolerance, altruism, trust, respect, empathy, fairness and justice. According to Pincoffs (1986) virtues are dispositional properties that provide grounds for preference of persons. The list could be potentially long and varied but Pincoffs argues that one can choose virtues by categorising them based on 'the aptness or appropriateness of the person for the accomplishment or achievement of goals or objectives' (1986: 83–4). It is arguable that, for the accountant, integrity is essential to properly carrying out the duties of the profession and that the accountant must possess a solid foundation of moral virtues in order to maintain integrity.

Unfortunately the professional view of integrity is a very narrow rules-oriented conception. Integrity is usually thought of in the context of identifying fraudulent financial reporting, auditing the reasonableness of uncertainties, applying analytical procedures, examining internal control, and communicating matters relating to the nature and scope of the audit. Integrity however is a broader concept that gives special attention to the development of others (Srivastva 1988) and doing what is best under conditions of adversity. Once can agree with Halfon (1989) that integrity requires that one has the intention to do what is best and takes actions consistent with this perceived intention. This suggests that one can possess integrity but still make incorrect judgements. Integrity, however, would require that one be reflective and willing to change actions when the evidence warrants.

Integrity strongly implies the virtues of honesty and truthfulness – virtues widely regarded as essential to the accountant. Reaching the truth is the goal of open-mindedness (see Hare 1981, 1985). It appears that open-mindedness is an essential ingredient of integrity. For the accountant this means being open to the reporting needs of various interest groups and not just the needs of those with economic power. Integrity means much more than just uncovering fraud or the fudging of figures; it means finding and reporting true costs and benefits to society as a whole. To accomplish this, accountants must acquire a genuine concern for others – the moral point of view. Accounting education can be geared towards reaching this ideal by addressing the issue of values and helping accounting students develop the habits of critical and reflective thinking and taking the moral point of view.

Developing an ethical curriculum implies a programme of studies which helps students to reach their intellectual potential while building qualities of tolerance, altruism, trust, respect, empathy, fairness, justice, and open-mindedness which are central to constructing integrity. The challenge is to develop an accounting curriculum that is consistent with the idea of the educated person and the role of the university as with integrity as the organising principle. There is probably not much one can do to change the behaviour of someone who is truly evil. The premise here is that it is possible to develop a curriculum that encourages the morally weak and strengthens the morally strong by sensitising students to moral issues with the aim of building integrity. The essential theme in the ideal ethical curriculum presented in this paper is that individuals must be educated to deal with explicit ethical issues such as code of ethics violations, be sensitive to implicit ethical issues such as the use of accounting controls that favour the interests of capital providers over other interests, and also develop the professional technical and moral expertise to begin their careers.

Research has shown that students can improve their ethical reasoning ability through exposure and practice (Rest 1986). Research from the Kohlbergian tradition has shown that ethical reasoning ability can be raised if students are exposed to ethical reasoning which is one stage higher than their current stage (Kohlberg 1969; Rest 1979a and b, 1986, 1988). Students in any one class are likely to encompass several of these stages. By encouraging debate within the classroom, students have an opportunity to be exposed to the stage of reasoning that is needed for improvement. Those who are already at the higher stages can also gain by increasing their exposure to ethical issues and reinforcing the habit of ethical thinking. It is one thing to have ethical reasoning ability, but it is quite another to have developed the habit of bringing this ability into action. In highly specialised areas like accounting it is arguable that even people at the higher levels of ethical reasoning need formal exposure to the ethical issues of their profession. While greater ethical reasoning ability may not translate into moral action, it is reasonable to assume that a person with this ability is better able to address complex moral problems.[2]

Whenever people interact or decisions are made that affect other people, there are ethical implications. Therefore, in most subjects it is possible to integrate problems and issues that nurture ethical reasoning ability and foster the habit of thinking about ethical and moral consequences. Values of a democratic society which promote deliberation and concern for others are important to building an ethical culture. Students, however, must be educated as perceptive and wise critics of their discipline and of society. This idea of being a reflective person who can think carefully and critically about one's discipline and the role of that discipline in society is a form of moral education for which the university is well adapted. In the accounting curriculum there is plenty of opportunity for bringing students into the arena of ethical choice and value judgement.

The ethical curriculum is one that helps students develop a moral point of view. It taps the students' capacities for logical thinking, critical analysis and inquiry that are essential for ethical reasoning. Since Aristotle it has been widely believed that these capacities grow out of experience, encouragement and habit of use. This curriculum should aim at improving literacy skills of writing, reading, speaking and listening. Such skills potentially improve thinking and increase the life chances of students in the competitive world of business. These skills can be partially met through a combination of specific accounting and non-accounting courses.

An ethical accounting curriculum is one which aims at developing a truly educative programme that will help to prepare students for their life experiences, designed with the goal of maximising students' chances of living full, productive and ethical lives. Students must be prepared to meet the technical and ethical responsibilities of the profession. This demands a curriculum that balances training and education and focuses on both the moral and intellectual development of students.

The recommendations of the Accounting Education Change Commission (AECC)[3] calling for a profile of capabilities for accounting graduates that includes general knowledge, intellectual skills, interpersonal skills, communication skills, organisation and business knowledge, accounting knowledge, accounting skills, and personal capacities and attitudes are a positive step forward. The AECC appears to promote students' development of a sense of history, broad knowledge and an interdisciplinary focus. One could make the case that abilities developed in these areas would better equip one to recognise ethical issues and defend one's judgements regarding ethical matters.

The AECC has stated that the development of intellectual skills is an essential for accounting graduates, including 'capacities of inquiry, abstract logical thinking, inductive and deductive reasoning and critical analysis'. The AECC sees the 'ability to identify ethical issues and apply a value-based reasoning system to ethical questions' as an essential intellectual skill. However there is only scattered reference to the importance of values, ethics and aesthetic development. The AECC also falls short by not promulgating the importance of critical inquiry. Critical inquiry is challenging because it forces one to look inward and perhaps question the very purpose of the accounting profession, and can lead to controversy. It is likely that this interpretation is not what the AECC has in mind when it uses the phrase 'critical analysis'. According to Fay (1977, 1987; also see Carr and Kemmis 1986) educational institutions take social structures for granted and play a 'transmitter' role of uncritically reproducing the social, political and economic relations of the status quo. Higher education institutions have a responsibility to encourage serious deliberation on such issues and to help inculcate in their students the habits of critical inquiry. For accounting students this may result in a greater understanding of the need to report cost and revenue information that takes into account more than the narrow interests of shareholders. A greater appreciation of aesthetic values, more awareness of environmental impact of business decisions, and a stronger sensitivity to human costs and political expediencies are new challenges to the accounting profession. These issues have strong ethical content.

In compiling cost data which will influence decisions, for example, accountants have an ethical responsibility to disclose the full cost, including social costs which may not be borne directly by the firm. In some cases this additional disclosure could potentially reverse an otherwise sound decision. This is a view of accounting that may create an ethical dilemma for the accountant in instances where one has to make a choice between loyalty to the firm or loyalty to society. As a member of a profession, the accountant has a particularly strong obligation to society, which has granted the profession special privileges. The dilemma can be very serious for the accountant who is is an employee of a firm rather than an external auditor: integrity will be required in taking a stand and doing what is ethically right.

The critical component of education aims at exposing students to multiple and conflicting perspectives on themselves and their society in order to test and challenge their previously unexamined assumptions (see Habermas 1970). Critical education strives to create a setting that facilitates intellectual, moral and emotional growth, so that students may mould their skills in a more mature, humane and compassionate setting of values. Critical education purposely tries to stimulate students to reformulate their goals, their cognitive map of the world, the way they think and their view of the accountant's role in society (Keniston and Gerzon 1972: 53). When the student enters the world of work, this ability to reflect on conflicting perspectives puts the accountant in a position of greater social responsibility. The ability to recognise when change is needed and to take the decisions to implement necessary changes after considering the interests of those affected is an ethical responsibility of the professional accountant. In cases where the individual does not actually have the authority to make these decisions, a concerted effort should be taken to make one's views known to those who are in the position to make decisions.

At times it takes a person of strong moral character and conviction to challenge the status quo or to recommend actions which may be politically unpopular but are morally right. It may not be possible to act with integrity without having developed the ability to take manifold perspectives into account. One cannot guarantee that individuals in practice will always act with integrity. Providing them with a strong educational foundation at least equips them with the ability to consider different points of view, and seems to be a reasonable goal of accounting education. Accountants typically work with the interest of investors and creditors in mind, even though the health and wellbeing of the organisation depends on contributions from employees, customers, managers, and others who have a deep stake in the enterprise. Any serious model of accounting education must explicitly address this very fundamental element of accounting education.

EDUCATING FOR INTEGRITY

Because accounting is built on a moral base of trust it is imperative that ethics be an explicit part of the accounting curriculum. Ethics is already an implicit component. As put by Etzioni:

> There is no ethically neutral teaching. Everything in the classroom communicates an ethical position. The only difference between business ethics courses and all others is truth in advertising: ethics courses state explicitly when value positions are communicated; the regular curriculum embodies hidden assumptions of which even the professor may be unaware.
>
> (Etzioni 1989: 18–19)

Explicit recognition of ethical issues in business and accounting should be offered early in the programme. One possibility is to devote one half of the introduction to business course to ethics. This indicates to students that ethics is a subject that is integral to business studies. This, however, implies a trade-off. Students may lack the technical competence and business and accounting skills to apply concepts as much as they would if the course were offered later in the curriculum. There will, however, be an adequate supply of business issues with ethical implications that are within the grasp of their understanding. This fact, combined with the very positive signal that business ethics is a foundation course, outweighs the disadvantage.

In addition, every course should include an ethical dimension, so that students will not compartmentalise their thinking such that ethics becomes important only in ethics classes.

THE CAPSTONE

A final recommendation is to develop a capstone course. Teaching will have its greatest impact if ethical issues are raised continuously throughout the entire accounting programme. This, of course, is an empirical question, but it certainly makes intuitive sense. Four years of exposure to ethical issues in business and accounting would help to develop a habit of thinking about ethical issues and help to stamp out moral ignorance. Exposure may not change the morally corrupt, but it should help to strengthen ethical sensitivity and improve ethical reasoning.

From an ethical perspective, the traditional model of accounting is constraining. The emphasis is on stewardship to investors and creditors. While it is known that others have legitimate interest in an enterprise's performance, fairness is usually thought of in the context of meeting the information needs of these two groups as specified by generally accepted accounting principles (GAAP). This conception of fairness can be criticised as being too narrow. It fails to recognise the extensive interdependencies which exist among business persons and others in society. To help free students from this moral ignorance, an accounting course can be structured to explicitly take these interests into consideration. Social responsibility accounting (SRA) attempts to do this. Mathews (1995) argues that the most persuasive moral argument in favour of increased social and environmental disclosures in annual reports lies with the social contract between business and society.

Much was written about SRA in the 1970s and it was quite popular in England and Germany. Unfortunately it has received less attention in North America,[4] although there has been pressure from environmental groups for more 'green' reporting. Widespread media coverage of events such as the Exxon Valdez oil spill has added to the urgency of the problem. The costs of rectifying past environmental damage, including legal costs, make environmental practices and disclosure of these practices a priority. Pressure also comes from insurance companies which demand that firms seeking coverage must fulfil certain environmental requirements. A sound environmental reporting system facilitates compliance with such demands (see O'Kane 1994). There are also a growing number of equity funds[5] which will invest only in environmentally responsible businesses. In spite of the fact that environmental auditing is not yet required by statute, existing federal and provincial environmental legislation in Canada and elsewhere is putting pressure on accountants to at least recognise the potential obligations that firms are increasingly facing. According to Rubenstein (1991) companies are spending more money on the environment, as well as more time in the boardroom, discussing what they are doing to the environment and what the environment will be doing to the bottom line.

Business plays a key role in issues involving the environment, but also with issues concerning civil rights, employment equity, product safety, consumer satisfaction, gender issues and many others. To structure accounting reports to serve the interest primarily of investors and creditors, as is the current practice, underestimates the impact business actually has on society. One can agree with Lehman (1988) that accountants are implicated in social issues whenever they set disclosure rules. Rules such as those for restructuring debt, for funding pension plans, or for keeping externalities off the balance sheet favour some interest groups over others. The moral point of view is that an accounting is owed to all interest groups. It is this argument that provides the rationale for social responsibility accounting as the capstone course. SRA is the integration of ethics into the curriculum in the sense that the issue of fairness becomes a primary concern for the accounting student. Students are plunked right into the middle of issues involving respect and concern for others. Attention is directed at serving society's information needs regarding the relations between the business enterprise and its constituents. The business enterprise is an institution created by society to serve society. It is society that gives production and distribution rights to business. Business relies on society's educational system to provide it with employees, on society's maintenance and transportation system, on a stable social and political setting in which to conduct business, and on a legal system to settle disputes. In return for special rights, privileges and protection, a duty is owed to all of society. The corporation incurs private costs and accrues private benefits from the role society has permitted it to play. The traditional accounting model captures these private costs and benefits. Social costs, such as environmental pollution, are usually not reported. Similarly, social benefits, such as aesthetic buildings and grounds, hiring of minorities, and so forth, are not disclosed.

As agents concerned with the rights of those who receive accounting reports, accountants can be educated not only to provide measures of net income but also to report measures of corporate contribution to the environment, to quality products or services, and to the community internal and external to the organisation. Due to cost and competitive concerns, businesses may resist such extensive disclosure. Educating accountants, however, to their full professional responsibilities to society is an essential step to achieving fair reporting and promoting integrity and ethics in business.

In summary, the model for integrating ethics into the accounting curriculum presented in this chapter is as follows:

- Devote half a semester of the Introduction to Business course to general business ethics.
- Integrate ethics into each and every accounting course throughout the curriculum.
- Develop a capstone course at the senior level that deals with complex issues of business social responsibility and professional responsibility.

This approach to ethics integration provides the student with both broad and specific exposure to business and accounting ethics. Society will benefit from educated individuals with high ethical reasoning ability who are sensitised to ethical issues and who have developed the habit of careful reflection. This combination of ethical reasoning, sensitisation and reflective thought are the seeds for building integrity, the central organisation principle of ethical behaviour.

NOTES

1   If, for example, the smoke from a factory makes a neighbour's house dirty and the air unpleasant to breathe, without the neighbour being

able to charge the factory owner for the damage suffered, then there exists an 'external' relation. Externalities can be positive or negative. The market does not allocate the effects of externalities.

2   The relationships among moral judgement, moral education and moral conduct are extremely complex. There are many unresolved problems associated with the developmental approach to moral development (see Gilligan 1982; Kurtines and Greif 1974; and Peters 1975). This line of research, however, should not be abandoned unless and until alternatives are available.

3   The AECC is a task force appointed by the American Accounting Association in 1989 to serve as a catalyst for improving accounting education. The recommendations of this task force are well known and will not be reviewed here.

4   Several researchers, however, such as Abraham Briloff (1972, 1976, 1981, 1990) and Tony Tinker (1985, 1991 [with Okcabol], 1991 [with Lehman and Neimark]) have actively promoted social responsibility accounting.

5   There are fifteen ethical funds in Canada managed by five mutual fund companies. Source: http:www.web.net/ethmoney/perform.htm

REFERENCES

American Institute of Certified Public Accountants (AICPA) (1986) *Restructuring Professional Standards to Achieve Professional Excellence in a Changing Environment*, Report to the Special Committee on Standards of Professional Conduct for Certified Public Accountants, New York: AICPA.

Beets, S. D. (1992) 'The revised AICPA code of professional conduct: current considerations', *The CPA Journal*, April: 26–32.

Bok, S. (1978) *Lying: Moral choice in public and private life*, New York: Pantheon Books.

Briloff, A. (1972) *Unaccountable Accounting*, New York: Harper & Row.

—— (1976) *More Debits than Credits*, New York: Harper & Row.

—— (1981) *The Truth About Corporate Accounting*, New York: Harper & Row.

—— (1990) 'Accountancy and society: a covenant desecrated', *Critical Perspectives on Accounting*, 1 (1): 5–30.

Carr, W., and Kemmis, S. (1986) *Becoming Critical: Education, knowledge and action research*, Philadelphia, PA: The Falmer Press.

Dowie, M. (1977) 'Pinto madness', *Mother Jones*, September/October: 28.

Etzioni, A. (1989) 'Are business schools brainwashing their MBA's?', *Business and Society Review*, 70: 18–19.

Fay, B. (1977) *Social Theory and Political Practice*, London: Allen & Unwin.

—— (1987) *Critical Social Science: Liberalism and its limits*, Ithaca, NY: Cornell University Press.

Friedson, E. (1986) *Professional Powers*, Chicago, IL: University of Chicago Press.

Gaa, J. (1986) 'User primacy in financial reporting rulemaking: a social contract approach', *The Accounting Review*, 435–54.

Gilligan, C. (1982) *In a Different Voice: Psychological theory and women's development*, Cambridge, MA: Harvard University Press.

Grant, N. (1992) *The Selling of Contraception: The Dalkon Shield case, sexuality, and women's autonomy*, Columbus, OH: Ohio State University Press.

Habermas, J. (1970) 'Towards a theory of communicative competence', *Inquiry*, 30.

Hare, W. (1981) *Open-mindedness and Education*, Montreal, Que.: McGill-Queen's University Press.

—— (1985) *In Defence of Open-mindedness*, Montreal, Que.: McGill-Queen's University Press.

Halfon, M. (1989) *Integrity: a philosophical inquiry*, Philadelphia, PA: Temple University Press.

Heyne, P. (1968)*Private Keepers of the Public Interest*, New York: McGraw-Hill.

Keniston, D. and Gerzon, M. (1972) 'Human and social benefits', in L. Wilson and O. Mills (eds) *Universal Higher Education*, Washington, DC: American Council on Education.

Kohlberg, L. (1969) 'Stages and sequences: the cognitive developmental approach to socialization', in D. Goslin (ed.) *Handbook of Socialization Theory and Research*, Chicago, IL: Rand McNally College Publishing Co.

Kurtines, W. and Greif, E. (1974) 'The development of moral thought, review and evaluation of Kohlberg's approach', *Psychological Bulletin*: 453–70.

Larson, M. (1977) *The Rise of Professionalism*, Berkeley, CA: University of California Press.

Lehman, C. (1988) 'Accounting ethics: surviving survival of the fittest', *Advances in Public Interest Accounting*, 2: 71–82.

MacIntyre, A. (1981) *After Virtue*, Notre Dame, IN: University of Notre Dame Press.

Mathews, M. (1995) 'Social and environmental accounting: a practical demonstration of ethical concern?', *Journal of Business Ethics*, January: 666.

Mintz, M. (1985) *At Any Cost: Corporate greed, women and the Dalkon Shield*, New York: Pantheon Books.

O'Kane, G. (1994) 'Green audits bring savings', *Asian Business*, July: 42.

Peters, R.S. (1975) 'A reply to Kolhberg', *Phi Delta Kappan*, June, 56 (10): 678.

Pincoffs, E. (1986) *Quandaries and Virtues*, Lawrence, KS: University Press of Kansas.

Rest, J. (1979a) *Development in Judging Moral Issues*, Minneapolis, MN: University of Minnesota Press.

—— (1979b) *Revised Manual for the Defining Issues Test*, MMRP Technical Report, Minneapolis, MN: University of Minnesota Press.

—— (1986) *Moral Development: Advances in research and theory*, New York: Praeger.

—— (1988) 'Can ethics be taught in professional schools? The psychological research', *Easier Said Than Done*, Winter: 22–6.

Rubenstein, D. (1991) 'Lessons of love', *CA Magazine*, March: 36.

Sack, Robert J. (1985) 'Commercialism in the profession: a threat to be managed', *Journal of Accountancy*, October: 125.

Scribner, E. and Dillaway, M. (1989) 'Strengthening the ethics content of accounting courses', *Journal of Accounting Education*: 41–55.

Srivastva, S. and Associates (1988) *Executive Integrity: The search for high human values in organizational life*, San Francisco, CA: Jossey-Bass.

Stanga, K. and Turpen, R. (1991) 'Ethical judgements on selected accounting issues: an empirical study', *Journal of Business Ethics*, October: 739–47.

Tinker, T.(1985) *Paper Profits: A social critique of accounting*, New York: Praeger.

Tinker, T. and Okcabol, F. (1991) 'Fatal attractions in the agency relationship', *British Accounting Review*, 23: 329–54.

Tinker, T., Lehman, C. and Neimark, M. (1991) 'Falling down the hole in the middle of the road: political quietism in corporate social reporting', *Accounting, Auditing & Accountability Journal*, 4 (2).

Velasquez, M. (1991) *Business Ethics: Concepts and cases*, Eaglewood Cliffs, NJ: Prentice Hall, 3rd edn.

10

VALUES AND ACCOUNTING

Divergences in ethical thinking on accounting for the environment

Catherine Gowthorpe

> It is in the name of Net Profit, Budget Surplus and Gross National Product that the natural environment in which we all co-exist is being destroyed.
>
> (Hines 1991: 29)

INTRODUCTION

It is widely acknowledged that the earth is in crisis because of the environmental degradation arising from humankind's exploitation of its resources.[1] There exists a measure of agreement that biodiversity is threatened because of the rapid extinction of species, that global warming is a reality which will almost certainly have dire adverse consequences (Leggett 1990: 461) and that the habitats of people and other animals are endangered (Woodwell 1990: 116–32). In this chapter I will examine the role of the accountant in contributing to, and possibly finding a way out of, the environmental problems which surround us.

ACCOUNTING: PART OF THE PROBLEM?

The role of economists and accountants in hastening the end of the world as we know it has been signalled with increasing frequency as the activities of business have become subject to critical examination. Many thinkers have observed a link between neo-classical economics and the blinkered approach to measures of corporate and human satisfaction which have resulted in a very partial accounting for business activities. Others focus upon the related problem of the scientific approach to thinking which has dominated Western thought for the past three hundred years or so. Descartes' philosophy, it is argued, established a division between mind and body which persists to this day and which has resulted in mechanistic, reductionist and analytical approaches to the world; this division 'allowed scientists to treat matter as dead and completely separate from themselves' (Capra 1992: 27). Capra describes the effect upon scientific thought: 'As a consequence of this [Cartesian] division, it was believed that the world could be described objectively, i.e. without ever mentioning the human observer, and such an objective description of nature became the ideal of all science'. Social sciences are equally, if not more, problematic; Flyvbjerg identifies a general difficulty in the social science domain: 'the mainstream social sciences have not come to terms with the fact that despite several hundred years of attempts at establishing themselves as epistemic sciences the epistemic ideal still seems to be an illusion' (1993: 16). More specifically, in the accounting domain, Birkin (1996), while acknowledging that accounting predates Descartes, describes the link between it and the Cartesian idea of the natural world as 'soulless and mechanical'.

It is clear to all with a knowledge of the subject that accounting and its practitioners cling to the ideal of objective description. The approved objectives of accounting described in the conceptual framework projects include objectivity, neutrality and consistency, all attributes which are felt to contribute towards a scientifically rational ideal of accounting. In practice, of course, these objectives are both unattainable and damaging in their reductiveness. However, accountants feel comfortable with the techniques of calculation and the notion of reducing a complex set of transactions to a formalised, manageable statement of affairs is appealing; this picture of the accountant fits well with the prevailing mode of scientific and rational thought.

The neo-classical model of economics has at its centre the notion of an economic being (originally a man)[2] who acts rationally in order to maximise his anticipated utility or happiness. This is an idea rooted firmly in a personalised utilitarianism, which is calculative and apparently rational, functioning well in free markets with no information assymetries; Williams points out that 'utilitarianism is unsurprisingly the value system for a society in which economic values are supreme' (1972: 102). Utilitarian thinking forms the basis of traditional accounting,[3] too, and accountants are familiar with it in its guises of cost–benefit analysis, marginal costing for decision-making and other financial appraisal techniques. But such techniques cannot be applied in a vacuum: according to Gray *et al.*, 'Choice must always have some moral element. . . . That conventional economics and conventional accounting have attempted to strip the explicitly moral from decisions should not blind us to the fact that decisions are still moral choices' (1996: 21).

One of the most convincing objections to utilitarianism is the impossibility of measuring outcomes in advance of events, thus rendering *ex ante* decisions based upon supposed outcomes very dubious. Williams observes: '[utilitarianism] does . . . make enormous demands on supposed empirical information about peoples' preferences, and that information is not only largely unavailable, but shrouded in conceptual difficulty' (Smart and Williams 1973: 137). Thoughtful and critical accountants are well aware of the limitations of their craft; even after the event techniques of accounting render only a very approximate account. The fact that accountants in most parts of the world still use a variant of the deeply unsatisfactory historical cost accounting model for want of the ability to agree some better technique between themselves, underlines the difficulty of producing figures that mean anything very much at all. The problems become vastly greater when we examine the exclusive nature of accounting; only those transactions which can be easily priced are drawn into the accounting equation. Labour and some materials carry a price, an exchange value for use in the market place, but these values are limited in two ways: first, the prices charged may be an undervaluation of the commodity, and second, perhaps more importantly, values are placed only on those items which are subject to easily identifiable ownership. So, a value placed upon a commodity at some time in the past may prove in retrospect to have been mistaken: for example, a company which has failed to enforce, or has been unaware of the need for, safety standards to protect its workers from damage caused by, say, asbestos dust, may find itself obliged many years later to pay compensation to those workers or their dependants. What, in such a case, was the true cost of the labour? In the second case it has meant that businesses have ignored the value of a huge range of items which they 'consume', for example, fresh air, natural habitats and other people's quality of life. Gray pulls no punches: 'In scoring and reporting only priced transactions, accounting is fully implicated in the environmental destruction all around us' (1990a: 383). Even a brief consideration of the possible scale of the costs involved leads us to the supposition (a very uncomfortable one for accountants) that reported profits, which we already know to be often grossly overstated in times of rising prices by reference to models of capital maintenance, are chimerical works of fiction.

A further problem in assessing outcomes arises because of the traditionally short timescale employed in accounting (and economic) decision-making. One of the most challenging aspects of thinking constructively about environmental problems is the proper consideration of inter-generational equity, educated as we are to calculating and predicting effects over a relatively short term. Randers and Meadows exemplify this point by reference to the discounting of costs and benefits over time, calculations which 'assign essentially zero value to anything happening more than twenty years from now' (1993: 473). A significant reason, of course, why accounting measures are focused on the short-term is the near impossibility of making predictions of outcomes more than a short distance into the future. Accounting, for purely practical reasons, is therefore, perhaps ironically, limited in its utilitarian application.

Traditionally, environmental considerations have been given short shrift in accounting and economics; such matters are treated as 'externalities', which means that accountants have felt safe in ignoring them. In a profession which still cannot reach agreement about such relatively straightforward problems as treatment of goodwill on acquisition of a subsidiary this failure to recognise the problem is scarcely surprising. This is not to say that environmental matters have been entirely ignored in published accounts of economic activity; indeed, the incidence and extent of reporting of companies' relationships with the environment have increased substantially, although from a very low base point (see Gray *et al.* 1995: 57). However, reporting by companies has diverse objectives, including improvement in public relations, and the cautious nature and limited extent of the reporting which has so far taken place is unlikely to change the world very rapidly (if at all).

Traditional forms of economic rationality have been attacked by several writers over the last thirty years. One of the most influential writers was one of the first; Schumacher saw the problems of environmental degradation as inextricably linked with economics, and thus with accounting measurement: 'the prevailing creed . . . is that the common good will necessarily be maximised if everybody . . . strives to earn an acceptable "return" on the capital employed' (Schumacher 1974: 35). He sees the problem in moral terms: 'The exclusion of wisdom from economics, science and technology was something which we could perhaps get away with for a little while . . . but now . . . the problem of spiritual and moral truth moves into the central position' (ibid.: 26). The French philosopher Gorz has been widely quoted: 'once you begin to measure wealth in cash, enough doesn't exist . . . . Accounting is familiar with the categories of "more" and "less" but doesn't know that of "enough"!' (1989: 112). Both writers suggest ways of curtailing the Western lifestyle and making do with much less in material terms, ways of redefining our *needs*; they are powerful advocates for a type of environmentalism which requires a radical alteration to our moral and material values.

Ormerod, in challenging the orthodoxy of neo-classical economics, questions the role which Adam Smith is generally assigned as 'the intellectual discoverer of the free market' (1994: 34). Only a part of Smith's work, that relating to the importance of the free market, has generally been made prominent; the other part, his *Theory of Moral Sentiments*, has not. This work made clear the moral context in which individuals should operate. Ormerod also criticises the growth of economics as a calculative academic discipline in which positive as opposed to normative research dominates, and in which the acceptable range of approved methodologies is limited by fashionable orthodoxy.

A further, highly significant, strand of criticism has emerged in the form of feminist economics; Reiter (1995) examines the diverse nature and complexity of some of the recent feminist arguments in economics and accounting, citing a wide range of work to demonstrate the inherent male bias in the disciplines, and the tendency of economic models to disparage characteristics associated with femaleness. She illustrates the poverty of applying prevailing economic models to accounting by looking at what they leave out:

> Economic models underlie accountants' basic view of the world. What we try to account for, what we leave out of our system, who we account for, how we think of values and profits, how we think people act, and how we think the whole system (market) works are all derived from economic thought.
> (Reiter 1995: 41)

ACCOUNTING: PART OF THE SOLUTION?

How, then, should the world, and more specifically, accounting for it, be changed? Much of the academic output in the sphere of environmental accounting has had a normative bias, picking up ideas from a diverse range of interest groups and transplanting them into the accounting domain. However, the normative bias is often limited to generalised approaches; as Gray observes, it proves difficult to 'translate radical insight into suggestions for action' (1992: 400). If we must abandon the old model of accounting, and it seems that it is so unsatisfactory that we must, what is to replace it? This is a moral, as well as a practical and political question.

Two opposing, and perhaps irreconcilable, strands in thinking on this matter are based upon the 'deep' and 'pale' green perspectives which have emerged in the environmental movement. That these stand as mutually exclusive alternatives in the development of accounting is argued by Power: 'Either one adopts variants of an anti-calculative strategy, like Gorz and the post-industrial utopians, or one works with existing regimes of calculation and accounting' (1992: 492). The alternative approaches are described at length elsewhere but a summary is useful here in order to appreciate some of the choices which, perhaps, lie ahead of us.

The 'deep' green approach to imminent ecological disaster is essentially revolutionary, involving a complete rejection of the prevailing economic model, and therefore of accounting; it might (and there can be many variants of the vision) involve an end to anthropocentrism in humankind's priorities, widespread imposed population control, an end to adherence to the ideal of economic growth, and a revision of human 'wants' into human 'needs'. There would appear to be little use for any conventional accounting in such a revolution (see Maunders and Burritt 1991). Reduced to its fundamentals, the argument for the end of accounting would be that accounting has been instrumental in contributing to the environmental problems facing the world; logically, emotionally and morally, we should be able to see that even more accounting is not going to deliver us from the environmental crisis that faces us. Rather than ending accounting, a revolution in thinking might involve a completely different accounting, but we cannot even discuss the form that a radical alternative accounting would take. Gray, for example, raises the issue of language; economics has had such a profound effect on our thinking that contemplation of alternative world views is hampered for lack of appropriate vocabulary: 'we can only think about those things for which we have words and our words and concepts have been dominated by the frameworks of neo-classical economics' (1990b: 35–6). Cooper (1992), examining the issues from a feminine perspective,[4] expands the ideas of the paucity and colonisation of language much further. Moreover, she is quite explicit in her refusal to contemplate a wider role for accounting which would involve forcing nature herself into the traditional accounting model. In the context of the criticisms of neo-classical economics outlined earlier, it is impossible not to have respect and sympathy for the non-participative perspective. Any attempt to value as commodities the so-called 'externalities' represents, from certain perspectives, an immoral desecration and trivialisation of nature. But a significant criticism can be offered here: refusal to participate in a new approach to economics and accounting and to remain deliberately marginalised come perilously close to inaction and thus what appears to be a compact with the status quo.

The 'pale' green perspective involves an attempt at compromise; working within the systems that already exists to achieve change from the inside. The approach is incremental, gradual, relative; for example, emission levels are to be tackled gradually by governments setting a series of small targets. In this perspective accounting will be led through an evolutionary process, to gently adapt it so as to include those things which have been excluded and to count and value those things which hitherto have been uncounted and therefore unvalued. Essentially, this approach extends the capital maintenance models beyond narrow definitions of operating capital to include valuations of a wide range of natural and human resources. It is embodied in the report prepared for the Department of the Environment by Pearce et al. (1989). The Pearce Report is premised upon the ideal of sustainable development; it does not see, necessarily, an end to economic growth, but rather an acceptance that there must be trade-offs between 'narrowly construed economic growth and environmental quality' (1989: 22). The Pearce Report is resolutely practical, offering examples of both physical (presented in units of resource) and monetary environmental accounting.

The pale green model of accounting allows accountants to spread the net of traditional accounting much wider, to incorporate data in terms of both financial and physical quantities, and to contemplate means of 'growing' accounting to include more and more effects; this is an evolving model of accounting. At its best, this is an optimistic and fruitful approach to thinking about accounting and the environment. However, it is open to many criticisms, not the least of which can be expressed in terms of a critique of the utilitarian approach implicit in both the traditional and evolving models. The evolving model is based upon the assumption that all or at least many things, including those things traditionally regarded as 'externalities', can be absorbed into it, and that greater accountability and more realistic decision-making will result. However, one does not have to look far to see the inherent problems in the evolving model. Accountants know, through practice, if not instinctively, that there are some things which cannot be valued,[5] as do the anti-utilitarians: 'In cases of planning, conservation, welfare, and social decisions of all kinds, a set of values which are, at least notionally, quantified in terms of resources, are confronted by values which are not quantifiable in terms of resources' (Williams 1972: 102). Also, as noted earlier, there is the inherent problem that accounting models cannot be reliably extended sufficiently far into the future so as to allow a reasonably informed assessment of outcomes.

A further, related, problem with the evolving model lies in the danger of its being taken too seriously, and thereby excluding other values and criteria. There is already a tendency for the impressionable and uninformed to attach an importance to accounting numbers which they frankly do not merit (earnings per share, return on capital employed, and so on); how much greater would this tendency become if the accounting numbers expanded to colonise previously untouched areas?

A possible way out of the problems of the 'evolving model' is to deny the power of the accounting numbers by accepting their limitations, and improving accountability purely by means of narrative accounts. However, narrative accounts would not avoid all the problems; those making the account would still need to select information from the range of what is available, and the choice would inevitably be conditioned by political, competitive and financial considerations. Moreover, narrative accounts are usually presented alongside numerical accounts, and may suffer both from this proximity and from the belief that numbers give us hard incontrovertible information.

Both the deep green and pale green interpretations of a new accounting are, then, subject to criticism; both approaches present significant problems at the point where we may be running out of time in which to solve the pressing problems of environmental degradation. It is tempting to polarise the positions (which are already, probably falsely, polarised) further by identifying the deep green position as deontological and the pale green as utilitarian.[6] While the descriptions are appealing, this identification may be ultimately unhelpful, as it serves only to reinforce the divergences between the pale green and deep green camps, without offering the prospect of any middle ground in the debate.

VALUES AND ACCOUNTING

We should not, and probably cannot, completely avoid considering the consequences of our actions, whatever critics of utilitarianism may contend, and we certainly should not avoid our moral responsibilities. Accountants may have to be prepared to recognise the limitations of accounting calculation and have the moral courage to make clear those limitations, whatever the cost in terms of lost professional prestige. Efforts to accommodate environmental considerations within the framework of the traditional accounting model may be wasted. According to Williams:

> There is great pressure for research into techniques to make larger ranges of social values commensurable. Some of the effort should rather be devoted to learning – or learning again, perhaps, how to think intelligently about conflicts of values which are incommensurable.
>
> (1972: 103)

Pursuing a similar theme, Flyvbjerg (1993) sees the solution to the problem of sustainability in a rediscovery of the 'lost virtue' of *phronesis*. Aristotle identified 'five ways in which the soul arrives at truth by affirmation or denial, viz: art [*techne*], science [*episteme*], prudence [*phronesis*],[7] wisdom [*sophia*] and intuition [*nous*]' (*Ethics* [1976 trans.]: 206). Aristotle considers *phronesis* to be the greatest of the virtues because it carries with it possession of all the other virtues. (It is a nice irony for accountants that the 'lost' virtue should be the one of prudence, given the importance of this fundamental concept in accounting.) Flyvbjerg contends that 'With the rationalistic turn of the past two or three centuries *phronesis* and value rationality have become marginal practices' (1993: 13). If Flyvbjerg is right, then accounting and economics, along with other social sciences, have taken a wrong turning, have attempted, and have failed, to mimic the attributes of the epistemic sciences, and thus have led us into misapprehension and error. 'The social sciences have much to contribute to social, economic, technological, ecological, political and cultural development when practised as *phronesis*, but little as practised as *episteme*.'

What is demanded, then, is a revolution in the way we think about and conduct in practice the social sciences. Accounting provides a particularly difficult example on which to work, given that its practices are so imbued with (apparently) rational and logical calculation, and that many of both its practitioners and academic theorists (apparently) view it as a scientific discipline akin to the hard sciences. The proposal for what amounts to a paradigm shift in thinking and practising social sciences may, it is true, be weakened by lack of practical advice or direction on how to proceed to achieve it, a weakness recognised by Flyvbjerg: 'it seems that researchers practising phronesis-like methods have a sound instinct for getting on with their research and not getting involved in methodology' (1993: 20). One of the practical orientations he suggests is the enhancement of values in thinking and action, as a means of 'balancing instrumental rationality'.

The role of values is also emphasised by Jamieson, who argues for individual values as the key to finding solutions for apparently intractable problems of global welfare and economics: 'What we need are new values that reflect the interconnectedness of life on a dense, high-technology planet' (1993: 324). He contends that the new values must be accompanied by new conceptions of responsibility, so that we all understand that we have the power to make a contribution for good or ill, and that our own environmental impacts cannot be dismissed because they are individually so tiny. The problems cannot be divested by reference to experts: 'Rather than being "management" problems that governments or experts can solve for us, when seen as ethical problems they become problems for all of us, both as political actors and everyday moral agents.' There are two significant implications in this argument for accountants; first, as individuals they are implicated along with everyone else in the issue of personal moral responsibility and perhaps more so than many in that typically, in the West, they consume relatively large amounts of goods and have a disproportionately significant effect on the environment; second, as professionals they cannot 'manage' environmental problems by the exercise of expertise.

179

A further implication arises when we consider the dichotomy that may exist between the public and private roles of the accountant, or anyone else who has a conventional form of employment. An individual may make virtue-based decisions about private consumption and lifestyle which are incompatible with those decisions in which they are implicated at work; such dichotomies may be particularly pronounced for the accountant, because they may often be involved in producing data for decision-making. Take for example, the case of an accountant who contributes to the decision at work, based upon a fairly narrow set of criteria imposed from above, that the company's waste disposal strategy should avoid the most environmentally friendly option, on the grounds of high cost. This individual may experience moral conflict with a set of personal values relating to the importance of preserving the environment, but may be unable to bring, or even to recognise the possibility of bringing, personal moral values into decisions at work. Some extreme examples of this type of conflict have been examined in the literature on whistleblowing (see Chapters 3 and 4 above), in which it is usually clear that the principled actions of the whistleblower result in profoundly unpleasant consequences for the individual. Gorz recognises the problem: 'These qualities [demanded by professional life] are not connected with personal virtue, and private life is sheltered from the imperative of professional life' (1989: 36). If individual moral values were to prevail new collective values could be forged which could make a truly radical difference to our institutions and the way we solve problems.

The parallel with whistleblowing helps only up to a point; an individual is likely to blow the whistle only in highly confrontational situations where, usually, all other escape routes have been considered and rejected. It is an extreme response to an unusually intense and intractable set of problems. On the other hand, it may be possible for individuals to effect a gradual alteration in moral atmosphere in their professions and organisations without the extremes of confrontation implied in the idea of whistleblowing. A preliminary step in alteration of the moral atmosphere is to at least recognise the issues; accountancy presents particular acute problems in this respect in that its practitioners are highly inclined to view its practices as morally neutral, and fail to make the connection between individual virtues or morality and the professional activity in which they are engaged.

It may be argued that this gradualist approach to the recognition of values is too slow a process, given the urgent nature of the problems. However, the debate on environmental accounting has proceeded for many years now, without producing much radical change to the way accounting information is presented, or to the content and underlying assumptions of that information. In the wider context, democratic governments in the West, especially that of the United States, face apparently insurmountable difficulties in agreeing and implementing targets for reduced environmental impacts of their advanced economies. Individual responsiveness and individual reassessment of values may be the best hope of progress that we have.

CONCLUSION

In this chapter I have described various features of the debate on ethical aspects of accounting for the environment, with particular reference to the dichotomous nature of that debate, which reflects the dichotomy of views in the green movement itself. Underlying the critical ideas about the nature of accounting is the broader theme of the problem of treating the social sciences as epistemic, and the idea that the environmental crisis has arisen at least partly because of a fundamental error in failing to recognise the importance of *phronesis* in economics and accounting.

An attempt is made to identify a middle ground between the polarities of the debate by focusing upon the role of the individual, and upon individual moral values in the practice of accountancy and, indeed, in all other activities practised in working life. Some recent work on the role of values is cited in support of the view that global problems may be susceptible to solutions based upon a recognition and new appreciation of the role of the individual as moral agent. The experience of whistleblowing might suggest that there is little scope for any but the most heroic individuals to make a stand on their moral beliefs, but I suggest, albeit tentatively, that whistleblowing is something of an outlier in the range of moral response, and that individuals may be able to be effective in less overt ways in holding to their own moral beliefs at work. An initial step in the field of accounting would be to make practitioners aware that accounting is far from being a value-free and neutral activity, that it does have significant ethical implications, and that those implications are starkly illustrated in the debate on accounting for the environment.

NOTES

1 But see, for example, Wildavsky (1994) who believes that reports of the destruction of the environment have been greatly exaggerated, and that scientific endeavour and the free market will solve any problems we may encounter. His optimistic faith in these factors leads him to the assertion of ' . . . the likelihood that the future will turn out better than expected' (p. 468). This view cannot be dismissed out of hand; none of us knows the outcome, but it might be appropriate to employ the great accounting virtue of prudence and look at the downside.

2 Ormerod comments: 'even economists are not completely immune to social trends, and in recent years women too have been given the doubtful privilege of being embraced in the definitions of how a rational economic person ought to behave' (1994: 33–4).

3 To the point where accounting may be regarded as synonymous with utilitarianism; Williams refers to 'the unblinking accountant's eye of the strict utilitarian' (Smart and Williams 1973: 113).

4 There is not enough space to deal with Cooper's reasons for using 'feminine' rather than 'feminist'; those interested should certainly read the article.

5 There is a category of things which accountants have contemplated valuing, have even tried to value, but where they have had to concede defeat in the face of immense practical, political and conceptual difficulties.

6 This identification is suggested by Gray (1990b).

7 Phronesis is translatable also as 'practical common sense' (Aristotle, *Ethics* (1976 trans.): 209, footnote 1).

REFERENCES

Aristotle (mid-4th century BC) *Ethics*, trans. J.A.K. Thomson, Harmondsworth: Penguin, 1976.

Birkin, F. (1996) 'The ecological accountant: from the cogito to thinking like a mountain', *Critical Perspectives on Accounting*, 7: 231–57.

Capra, F. (1992) *The Tao of Physics*, London: Flamingo.

Cooper, C. (1992) 'The non and nom of accounting for (m)other nature', *Accounting Auditing & Accountability Journal*, 5 (3): 16–39.

Flyvbjerg, B. (1993) 'Aristotle, Foucault and progressive phronesis: outline of an applied ethics for sustainable development', in E.R. Winkler and J.R. Coombs (ed.) *Applied Ethics: A reader*, Cambridge, MA: Blackwell.

Gorz, A. (1989) *Critique of Economic Reason*, London: Verso.

Gray, R. (1990a) 'Accounting and economics: the psychopathic siblings. A review essay', *British Accounting Review*, 22: 373–88.

—— (1990b) *The Greening of Accountancy: The profession after Pearce*, London: Chartered Association of Certified Accountants, Report no. 17.

Gray, R. (1992) 'Accounting and environmentalism: an exploration of the challenge of gently accounting for accountability, transparency and sustainability', *Accounting, Organizations and Society*, 17 (5): 399–425.

Gray, R., Kouhy, R. and Lavers, S. (1995) 'Corporate social and environmental reporting: a review of the literature and a longitudinal study of UK disclosure', *Accounting, Auditing & Accountability Journal*, 8 (2): 47–77.

Gray, R., Owen, D. and Adams, C. (1996) *Accounting & Accountability: Changes and challenges in corporate social and environmental reporting*, London: Prentice Hall.

Hines, R. (1991) 'On valuing nature', *Accounting, Auditing & Accountability Journal*, 4 (3): 27–9.

Jamieson, D. (1993) 'Ethics, public policy and global warming', in E.R. Winkler and J.R. Coombs (eds) *Applied Ethics: A reader*, Cambridge, MA: Blackwell.

Leggett, J.(1990) 'Global warming: a Greenpeace view', in J. Leggett (ed.) *Global Warming: The Greenpeace report*, Oxford: Oxford University Press.

Maunders, K.T. and Burritt, R.L. (1991) 'Accounting and ecological crisis', *Accounting, Auditing & Accountability Journal*, 4 (3): 9–26.

Ormerod, P. (1994) *The Death of Economics*, London: Faber & Faber.

Pearce, D., Markanya, A. and Barbier, E.B. (1989) *Blueprint For a Green Economy*, London: Earthscan Publications.

Power, M. (1992) 'After calculation? Reflections on *Critique of Economic Reason* by André Gorz', *Accounting, Organizations and Society*, 17 (5): 477–99.

Randers, J. and Meadows, D. (1993) 'The carrying capacity of our global environment – a look at the ethical alternatives', in G.D. Chryssides and J.H. Kaler (eds) *An Introduction to Business Ethics*, London: Chapman & Hall.

Reiter, S.A. (1995) 'Theory and politics: lessons from feminist economics', *Accounting, Auditing & Accountability Journal*, 8 (3): 35–49.

Schumacher, E.F. (1974) *Small is Beautiful: A study of economics as if people mattered*, London: Sphere Books, Abacus edition.

Smart, J.J.C. and Williams, B. (1973) *Utilitarianism: For and Against*, Cambridge: Cambridge University Press.

Wildavsky, A. (1994) 'Accounting for the environment', *Accounting, Organizations and Society*, 19 (4/5): 461–81.

Williams, B. (1972) *Morality: An introduction to ethics*, Cambridge: Cambridge University Press.

Woodwell, G.M. (1990) 'The effects of global warming' in J. Leggett (ed.) *Global Warming: The Greenpeace report*, Oxford: Oxford University Press.

11

CORPORATE SOCIAL REPORTING: AN ETHICAL PRACTICE?

Julia Clarke

INTRODUCTION

The requirement for companies to provide an account of their financial performance is accepted and firmly set out in law. The legal framework of the Companies Act is predicated on the need for directors to account to shareholders for their stewardship of the shareholders' assets and for companies to provide an account to their creditors of the security provided against their debt. Yet a company's activities do not affect only those who have a financial investment in it. Other groups are either directly involved with the company (for example, employees and suppliers) or indirectly involved (for example, consumers and the localities in which the company operates) and so it may be argued that the company should also be accountable to these stakeholders. Indeed, annual reports quite often recognise a broader non-financial or social accountability and provide information on how the company's social responsibilities have been discharged. The term used in this chapter to describe the practice of reporting on the company's social responsibilities is corporate social reporting (CSR) which has been defined as 'the process of communicating the social and environmental effects of organisation's economic actions to particular interest groups within society and to society at large' (Gray *et al.* 1987: ix).

This chapter sets out to consider the ethical foundations for CSR by examining ideas about the nature of the company itself and its relationships with the society in which it operates. The first section provides an introduction to the subject of CSR; the second considers the implications that various theoretical models of the company and theories of corporate social responsibility have for corporate reporting. The third section considers whether CSR itself represents the fulfilment of an ethical responsibility, that is, whether it is motivated by the recognition of a moral accountability; and finally, the fourth section examines how successful it has been in promoting socially responsible behaviour.

THE ELEMENTS OF CORPORATE SOCIAL REPORTING

While social reporting, unlike financial reporting, is not governed by a statutory framework, a limited number of disclosures are required by law. Some companies report only on these areas while others choose to make further voluntary disclosures. This means that in practice CSR has developed in something of a hotchpotch fashion with both large variations in the quality, quantity and type of information, both between companies and over time. Therefore, a brief review of social disclosures by type serves as a useful introduction to the subject.

The 1978 Ernst & Ernst survey identified six areas in which companies might choose to report on social responsibilities (Perks 1993: 85). These were environment, energy (which will be considered together under environmental reporting; separate energy disclosures having received minimal attention in UK company reports (Gray *et al.* 1995: 61), fair business practices, human resources, community involvement and products and other (for example, general social policy statements).

Environmental reporting

This is the element of CSR which has attracted the most attention in recent years, a reflection of the growing importance of environmental issues in political, business and everyday life. Many companies provide environmental information within their annual reports and some (for example, British Telecom) provide separate environmental reports. While there are undoubtedly positive examples of objective and informative reporting much has been criticised for being subjective, selective and lacking quantification and external verification, undertaken primarily as a public relations exercise rather than to render an account (Butler *et al.* 1992: 73).

The selectivity of environmental reporting must raise questions about the ethical motivations of the reporting companies. As Welford (1996) argues, the 'hijacking' of the environmentalist agenda by business may have more to do with 'cherry picking' specific environmental benefits for the short term financial benefit of the company than any concern for the current and future stakeholders of the organisation.

Fair business practices

The Ernst & Ernst surveys and others using their classification (for example, Gray *et al.* 1987) have included both fair business practices with regard to employment (the employment of women, ethnic minorities and people with disabilities) and fair practice with regards to suppliers.

Employees

The Companies Act and the Health and Safety at Work Act set out disclosure requirements in respect of employment practices regarding people with disabilities, numbers of employees and related remuneration and health and safety arrangements. The type and quantity of voluntary disclosures has changed dramatically over the last twenty years, apparently reflecting the changes in the political economy of Britain over the Thatcher years (Gray *et al.* 1995: 63). Value added statements, which highlight the value added to the business by its employees and which were popular during the late 1970s (30 per cent of the three hundred companies surveyed by ICAEW published one in 1980 (Perks 1993: 92)) have virtually disappeared. Instead, the disclosures about employee affairs found in the annual reports of the 1990s tend to be descriptive and non-contentious, highlighting commitments to training, equal opportunities and share ownership schemes.

Suppliers

A 1996 amendment to the Companies Act requires large companies to disclose their policy on payments to suppliers in the forthcoming year. This is a response to the problems caused to many businesses, especially smaller businesses, by the late payments of their customers. Perhaps rather disappointingly for CSR enthusiasts, the opportunity to assess the impact of a disclosure item designed to drive socially responsible behaviour rather than simply reflect it, has been cut short by the 1997 Green Paper which proposes charging interest penalties for late payments. However, the Green Paper may introduce a 'shaming principle' (Warren 1997: 147) into CSR for the first time if it calls for large firms to state in their annual reports how many bills they paid late in the previous year (*Financial Times*, 15 May 1997).

Community involvement

Corporate community involvement (CCI) reporting is required by law to the extent that the Companies Act requires disclosure of monetary gifts for exclusively charitable purposes to persons ordinarily resident in the United Kingdom. This narrow definition excludes much of the community involvement of today's companies which encompasses not just donations to charities but support, both in money and in kind, for environmental projects, for education and a broad range of community initiatives, both in the United Kingdom and overseas. Not surprisingly, as community involvement represents a positive social responsibility, companies are happy to go beyond the minimum reporting requirements. They may devote a relatively large proportion, a page or more, of their annual report to CCI, even though it will usually be a fairly minimal proportion of total annual spend. As with environmental issues reporting tends to be descriptive and selective although companies at the forefront of community affairs have started to examine how more informative reporting, particularly as regards the outcomes of their CCI policies, might be achieved (see for example, the recent report, 'Companies in communities: getting the measure', issued by the London Benchmarking Group).

Products

While product information may well form part of a company's environmental disclosures it does not feature highly in its own right in the practice of CSR in the UK, perhaps because of commercial sensitivities. Customer-related disclosures remained very low throughout the thirteen years from 1979 to 1991 (Gray *et al.* 1995: 59). Moreover, Mathews notes that product safety disclosures often seem to be used as an opportunity for 'self-congratulation or institutional advertising' (1993: 83) rather than to report useful information.

General social policy statements

It is common practice for large companies to have ethical codes or statements of social responsibility yet these, or performance against them, are seldom made public. Gray *et al.* (1995: 61) note that in the UK disclosure of mission statements and statements of social responsibility have remained marginal areas of disclosure and the same findings are reported in a Canadian survey by Rivera and Ruesschoff (Gray *et al.* 1996: 145). Thus CSR does not provide a holistic view of the company's ethical performance; rather it tends to be made up of selective reports on specific areas, either because they are required by law or because the company chooses to report on them.

THE COMPANY AS A MORAL PERSON?

Most discussion on the need for companies to be accountable for their social impact has centred on the debate about the nature of the relationship between business and society. However, before dipping a toe in the waters of this deep and contentious debate it might be useful to consider how the nature of the organisation might affect accountability requirements.

Let us take first the view that companies are controlled by their structures and procedures and that these do not allow for any consideration of objectives outside a specific set of goals (namely profit). This is known as the 'Structural Restraint View'; a company is not a moral being because it is not capable of exercising moral choice and there is no locus of moral decision-making. As Donaldson (1982: 26) points out, such a model has striking (and frightening!) implications (particularly if we stop to think about the extent of corporate power) and would necessitate careful watching and regulation of companies' activities. If the company, by virtue of its nature, cannot include moral considerations in its decisions this implies the need for an external moral watchdog. In such a model CSR could only play a useful role if it was systematic, comprehensive, mandatory and externally imposed.

As discussed above, CSR in practice has not developed in this way. Some elements of CSR which are mandatory would certainly appear to have been conceived of as means of control and regulation (for example, employee disclosures in the UK, certain environmental disclosures in the US). However, rather than following from the structural restraint model these may indicate a pragmatic acceptance that companies will, where able to, trade off moral considerations against financial ones. Companies are not incapable of making moral choices, but like individuals, they may suffer from 'weakness of will' (Beauchamp and Bowie 1988: 122) and they will sometimes make a choice which is morally wrong.

The view that companies can make moral choices, that they are 'moral agents', is the opposite position to the structural restraint view. Goodpaster (quoted in Brummer 1991: 68) sees companies as moral agents, independent from the individuals that comprise them. His position is based on the argument that the company itself, as evidenced by its decision-making and strategy implementation, possesses the two prerequisites for moral agency. These are rationality (the capacity to pursue its objectives with careful attention to ends and means) and respect for others (the ability to consider the interests of other parties). Werhane (1985: 59) argues that companies are secondary or dependent moral agents, they are not metaphysically distinct from their members but rather collective moral intent is dependent upon the collected, individual intentions of those members.

If companies are moral agents then they are morally accountable (Werhane 1985: 76) and by providing information about the company's social and ethical performance then CSR has a role to play in discharging that accountability. However, in contrast to the structural restraint model, this need not be an externally imposed framework – indeed the more ethical a company is the more willing it may be to welcome public scrutiny of its social and ethical performance. This seems to be borne out in practice. Certain companies have specifically identified the furtherance of ethical considerations as being just as, or more, important than wealth maximisation as a corporate objective (for example, the Body Shop, Ben and Jerry's and Traidcraft). It is these companies that have taken a lead in the development of CSR.

MODELS OF CORPORATE RESPONSIBILITY

The model of corporate responsibility based on classical economic theory holds that the company's responsibilities are solely economic. This position was most famously articulated by Friedman, who argued that any social responsibility expenditure was in fact a tax levied by managers on shareholders and that any manager who committed corporate resources to social responsibility was taking on a government function that he was neither elected nor competent to perform (Friedman 1970: 89). As such managers should stick to what they were employed to do, namely, to make profits for shareholders. The corollary of this position is that, since the duties of managers are solely to shareholders and the only duty of the company is to maximise profits, then the only type of report required is an account by managers to shareholders on the financial performance of the company. Information on the company's social performance would only be desirable if it served to aid the decisions of investors, for example, disclosures relating to environmental practices might help readers predict potential liabilities.

In contrast, stakeholder theory holds that companies do have wider responsibilities. While managers are responsible to shareholders they must also consider other groups who are affected by the company's activities. Freeman defines a stakeholder in an organisation as 'any group or individual who can affect or is affected by the achievement of the organisation's objectives' (quoted in Goodpaster 1991: 54); as well as shareholders, examples include employees, suppliers, customers, creditors, governments and communities. Discussion of stakeholding is not limited to academic texts; it has passed into common usage. From an accounting point of view it is particularly interesting to note the articulation of stakeholder concepts within annual reports.

Ullmann (1985) uses stakeholder theory to build a model to explain CSR practice. Stakeholder groups enjoy varying amounts of power over companies, depending on the extent of their control over resources required by the company (for example, secured creditors have a great deal of power, sole suppliers also, local communities much less so). The extent to which a company will note and address stakeholder demands will be positively related to their power. Roberts (1992) tested Ullmann's model empirically and concluded that stakeholder theory was indeed an appropriate model for explaining social reporting practice. However, the demand for CSR from stakeholder groups has often been assumed rather than proven (Tilt 1994: 47). Furthermore, the target audience is seldom specified and CSR disclosures are often located in annual reports, indicating that they are intended primarily for shareholders (Gray et al.1996: 82).

The Corporate Report, a discussion paper on the scope and aims of financial reporting, commissioned by the Accounting Standards Steering Committee in 1974 and published in 1975, endorsed a stakeholder model of financial accounting. It identified seven groups who had a *'reasonable right'* (1975: 17) to information from the reporting entity: the equity investor group, the loan creditor group, the employee group, the analyst-adviser group, the business contact group, the government and the public. *The Corporate Report* shied away from endorsing social reporting, pleading the absence of agreed measurement techniques, but recommended further study into this area. Twenty years on the Accounting Standards Board's draft Statement of Principles also identified seven groups who would be interested in the financial statements but argued that they should be designed to meet the information needs of the providers of risk capital. This group is identified as the primary user and other groups' information needs will only be met by the financial statements so far as these coincide with those of the providers of risk capital (Accounting Standards Board 1995: 36). Thus at a time when the New Labour government is issuing a rallying call to the stakeholder society the accounting profession is turning away from the stakeholder concept as a basis for corporate reporting and instead focusing narrowly on the information needs of direct financial participants.

A third model of corporate social responsibility identified by Brummer (1991: 6) is the social activist model. As its name implies, the social activist theory holds that companies should actively promote social projects, even where these conflict with the pursuit of wealth maximisation. Under this model a company's primary accountability would be for its social impacts and social reporting would replace financial reporting as the primary accounting objective. One company that reflects this theory in practice is Traidcraft plc. Its objective is not to make a profit for its shareholders but 'to do something about redressing the enormous imbalance in wealth and opportunity between poor people in developing countries and us in the rich industrialised countries' (Evans 1991: 874). As a public limited company Traidcraft must comply with the financial reporting requirements of the Companies Act. However, its primary accountability is to its stakeholders, of whom funders are just one group, along with customers, suppliers and staff. It discharges this accountability through a system of social accounting which is defined as *'a systematic approach for businesses to account for their social impact and the extent to which they discharge their public responsibilities*' (Traidcraft Social Accounts 1995–1996: 15). This involves identifying social objectives and ethical values, defining the stakeholders, establishing social performance indicators, measuring performance, keeping records (where possible using a social book-keeping system) and publishing audited accounts (1995–1996: 15). Traidcraft has also provided advice to other companies on social accounting, including Allied Dunbar and the Cooperative Bank (1995–1996: 3). However, social accounting systems based on the social activist model, which demotes wealth maximisation from the position of the primary strategic objective, are unlikely to be adopted widely by more mainstream companies.

CSR AS AN EXPRESSION OF ETHICAL CONCERN

Mathews (1995) considers the arguments for widening accounting beyond its traditional narrow financial focus to encompass social and environmental issues under three broad headings. The first are 'market-related arguments', arguments that social responsibility disclosures may have a positive effect on market performance. Studies into the relationship between CSR and financial performance have provided mixed results (see Mathews 1993: 12–18 for a useful summary). However, whatever the outcome if wealth maximisation is the motive behind a company's social disclosures then this cannot be classified as an ethically motivated practice.

The second group of arguments focuses on ideas of organisational legitimacy. If organisations are to survive and prosper their operations and objectives need to be accepted as legitimate by society (Sutton 1993: 9). Voluntary corporate social reporting may be viewed as a strategy employed by companies in order to help legitimise their existence and their activities. This may be in response to external pressures on business in general from society in general in which case these pressures will change over time (Gray *et al.* 1995: 59) and place (Dierkes and Antal 1986: 113). Additionally organisations may face pressures specific to their industry sector to which certain CSR disclosures are a response (Cowen *et al.* 1987: 111).

CSR may be used as a legitimation tool as it enables organisations to demonstrate that they are in tune with societal values and concerns (environmental reporting is a good example of this). Whether social reporting which is undertaken with the objective of legitimising the organisation represents an ethical practice is debatable. On the one hand it might be argued that if (voluntary) CSR is driven by external factors then this is a moral response in that the company is responding to the value system of the society in which it operates. On the other hand if the motivation in meeting societal expectations is simply to safeguard the company's position and opportunities in order to enhance its own financial performance this is really no different from the market-related position outlined above and so may be seen as amoral. Alternatively, for those taking a radical or Marxist perspective, who do not believe that profit-making private enterprise is a legitimate form of organisation, then CSR is a means of social control (Puxty 1986: 97) used by companies to manage the conflicts which arise from the structural inequalities in capitalist society (Tinker et al. 1991: 30) and as such distinctly unethical.

The third group of arguments is based on the premise that a moral accountability for corporate social and environmental impacts arises from the social contract that exists between business and society. Although much of the early work on CSR was based on the concept of the social contract, ideas of what form such a contract should take (i.e., to whom and for what) and the nature of the accountability consequently arising, remain undeveloped (Gray et al.1988: 12). Nevertheless, the practice of CSR based on the notion of a moral accountability arising from a social contract would represent a moral practice (Mathews 1995: 667) and it is worth exploring this area further.

Donaldson (1982: 39–41) develops the idea of a social contract for business by drawing on the philosophical writings of Hobbes, Rousseau and Locke on social contract theories. Just as these writers distinguished a social contract by which citizens granted the state the right to exist and the government the right to govern, so society has granted companies the right to exist. In return for the legal standing and attributes which have been accorded to them companies have an obligation to enhance the welfare of society through the satisfaction of worker and consumer interests.

> The underlying function of all such organisations from the standpoint of society is to enhance social welfare through satisfying consumer and worker interests, while at the same time remaining within the bounds of justice. When they fail to live up to these expectations, they are deserving of moral criticism.
>
> (Donaldson 1982: 57)

Goodpaster also considers the moral responsibilities of business and the limitations that this sets on how managers controlling businesses behave by reference to different models of stakeholding. The first model he identifies is 'strategic' stakeholding (Goodpaster 1991: 57). This holds that the interests of shareholders are primary and the interests of other stakeholders are considered by management in the context of how they will affect or be affected by the implementation of this primary objective (1991: 57). Under such a system financial reporting to shareholders would remain the primary objective of corporate reporting. In contrast under a 'multi-fiduciary' approach management would assume that all stakeholders should be treated as having equally important rights (1991: 61). Goodpaster rejects the multi-fiduciary approach, arguing that managers cannot set aside their legal obligations to act in the interests of shareholders (it is relevant that Traidcraft, which has adopted a multi-fiduciary approach, has effectively set aside this traditional obligation to shareholders). However, they should recognise that while other stakeholders lack the fiduciary relationship with management that exists between shareholders and management they do not lack a 'morally significant relationship to management' (Goodpaster 1991: 69). Fiduciary obligations to shareholders and other legal obligations of the company obviously cannot be set aside to satisfy these moral obligations (if the company ceased to act in the interests of shareholders then it 'would cease to be a private sector institution' (1991: 69)) but it should be recognised that these moral obligations do set limits on how companies go about fulfilling their fiduciary obligations.

If we accept the moral obligations underpinning both Donaldson's and Goodpaster's models then some mechanism is required so that the company can render an account of its performance in respect of these obligations. Interestingly, *The Corporate Report* used similar terminology to Goodpaster and Donaldson in arguing that companies owe a 'public accountability' (ASSC 1975: 15) that is distinct from their financial reporting obligations to shareholders:

> We consider the responsibility to report publicly . . . is separate from and broader than the legal obligation to report and arises from the custodial role played in the community by economic entities. Just as directors of limited companies are recognised as having as stewardship relationship with share-

holders who have invested their funds, so many other relationships exist both of a financial and non-financial nature.

(ASSC 1975: 15)

And there are indeed plenty of examples of apparent recognition
of such a wider accountability in company reports. A survey of the
studies of the relationship between CSR and social performance
may help to answer the question of whether such statements are
simply rhetoric or whether they represent a moral stance, with CSR
truly reflecting (and reinforcing) ethical behaviour.

REFLECTING AND PROMOTING ETHICAL
BEHAVIOUR

Except where CSR is motivated *solely* by a recognition of a duty of
accountability it would fail as an ethical act in deontological terms.
Such purity of motive can seldom be attributed to a practice which
provides companies with a useful legitimisation and publicity tool.
However, from a utilitarian perspective CSR would be seen as
having worth where it promotes socially responsible behaviour.
Alternatively, if by focusing attention on very limited areas of social
performance it enables companies to 'get away with' increased negative externalities in other respects then it could be argued that CSR
actually reduces overall utility and is hence an unethical practice.

Ullmann (1985) identifies two methods of measuring social
performance used in surveys exploring the relationship between
disclosure and performance. The first is to use reputational indexes
which rate companies according to perceived social performance,
for example, among business students. Studies using this method
have produced mixed results. Bowman and Haire (1975) and Abbott
and Monsen (1979) found a positive correlation, Preston (1978) and
Fry and Hock (1976) found a negative correlation (reported in
Ullmann 1985). Problems arise from this methodology, however,
because reputation is only a proxy of actual performance.
Moreover, it would seem logical that increased social reporting
would heighten *perceptions* of the company's social performance.

The second, more objective method is to compare the company's
self-reporting with how its social performance is rated by an
external body. The three studies using this method reported by
Ullmann all used the Council for Economic Priorities (CEP) pollution performance rankings and they all concluded that there was no

correlation between social disclosure and pollution performance. This contrasts with the findings of a later study which found a positive relationship between disclosure and performance leading them to conclude that 'social improvements by a firm are quickly capitalised by social disclosure in an attempt to create an impression of sensitivity to non-market influences that may be in the long-term interests of the shareholders' (Belkaoui and Karpik 1989: 46).

Yet even if increased reporting reflects greater social responsibility there are no studies which have found that it *drives* improved social performance. Indeed, there are instances where it seems purposely to have been used to distract attention away from socially irresponsible behaviour. Patterson (in Gray *et al.* 1996: 112) cites the case of the American company, Atlantic Richfield, which produced a Social Report in 1977 that failed to mention that it had been responsible for a major environmental catastrophe involving nuclear waste! Deegan and Rankin compared the environmental disclosures of twenty Australian companies that had been successfully prosecuted by the Environmental Protection Authorities with twenty that had not. They found that companies that had been prosecuted made significantly more positive environmental disclosures than their non-prosecuted counterparts (Deegan and Rankin 1996: 59).

On the other hand, corporate community involvement might be an area where reporting encourages a greater commitment, since this is a positive social responsibility which reflects well on the company. However, it is seldom that CCI is motivated purely by altruism (Clarke 1997: 202) and indeed the link between the benefit to the community and to the company is often openly acknowledged in company reports (Vyakarnam 1992: 7). Thus there is a problem of identification; by dressing up a business decision as an altruistic action the organisation may gain the kudos without the cost. A profit-seeking policy that can *also* be used as a legitimation tactic may mean that the organisation avoids having to implement alternative non-profit seeking actions as evidence of socially responsible (or acceptable) corporate behaviour.

Moreover disclosure requirements could act as a deterrent to socially responsible behaviour where this is seen to be contrary to shareholders' financial interests (Ullmann). In the USA, Mills and Gardner found that management tend to disclose CCI expenditure 'at times when the financial statements of the firm otherwise look favourable to the firm' (Mills and Gardner 1984: 407).

CONCLUSION

This chapter has provided a brief overview of the elements of corporate social reporting in the United Kingdom. It is hoped that this element by element approach has emphasised the fragmentary development of CSR. It is extremely rare for companies to provide comprehensive social reports covering all aspects of their social performance. Rather, CSR tends to be limited, either to a mixture of mandatory and selected disclosures in the annual report, the main focus of which remains to provide financial information to shareholders, or to reports on specific aspects of social responsibility, such as the environment or community involvement.

This pattern of development indicates that CSR practice has followed the stakeholder model identified by Ullmann and Roberts. Companies are using CSR to manage stakeholder relationships, emphasising areas where stakeholders have particular power or are important in order to reassert the company's legitimacy. Thus, the 1970s, a decade of considerable union power, saw the heyday of employee reporting while the 'green' 1990s have witnessed a strong growth in environmental reporting. As Goodpaster points out, it has to be questioned to what extent such strategic stakeholder management is ethical, motivated as it is by the advancement of the company's own economic interests.

Nevertheless, from a utilitarian perspective, CSR might be seen as an 'ethical practice' if it encourages companies to behave in a socially responsible manner. Unfortunately, studies into the relationship between social reporting and social performance have not provided a clear and consistent answer to the question of cause and effect between these two variables. Indeed it has to be asked whether CSR, by emphasising positive aspects of corporate social performance, allows companies to reduce their performance in other areas. Certainly selective reporting may provide such opportunities. If CSR is to drive ethical behaviour then more comprehensive, careful and informative reporting has to be encouraged. While there have been calls for compulsory CSR (for example, Parker (1986: 88) recommends a system for social reporting standards similar to that for financial reporting) it would seem that comprehensive regulation is inappropriate for a practice that is still in such a developmental stage. In the meantime it will be interesting to monitor how mandatory reporting affects performance in specific areas: suggestions that New Labour will implement requirements for companies to report on instances of late payment may provide an excellent opportunity to see whether CSR can help drive ethical practice towards suppliers.

REFERENCES

Accounting Standards Board (1995) *Statement of Principles for Financial Reporting, Exposure Draft*, London: ASB.

Accounting Standards Steering Committee (1975) *The Corporate Report*, London: Accounting Standards Steering Committee.

Beauchamp, T.L. and Bowie, N.E. (1988) *Ethical Theory and Business*, Englewood Cliffs, NJ: Prentice Hall.

Belkaoui, A. and Karpik, P.G. (1989) 'Determinants of the corporate decision to disclose social information', *Accounting, Organizations and Society*, 2 (1): 36–51.

Brummer, J.J. (1991) *Corporate Responsibility and Legitimacy*, Westport, VA: Greenwood Press.

Butler, D., Frost, C. and MacVe, R. (1992) 'Environmental reporting', in D.J. Tonkin and L.C.L. Skerratt (eds) *Financial Reporting 1991–1992: A survey of UK reporting practice*, London: Institute of Chartered Accountants in England and Wales.

Clarke J. (1997) 'Shareholders and corporate community involvement', *Business Ethics: A European Review*, 6 (4): 201– 7.

Cowen, S.S., Ferreri, L.B. and Parker, L.D. (1987) 'The impact of corporate characteristics on social responsibility disclosure: a typology and frequency-based analysis', *Accounting, Organizations and Society*, 12 (2): 111–22.

Deegan, C. and Rankin, M. (1996) 'Do Australian companies report environmental news objectively?', *Accounting, Auditing & Accountability Journal*, 9 (2): 50–67.

Dierkes, M. and Antal, B.A. (1986) 'Whither corporate social reporting: is it time to legislate?', *California Management Review*, 28 (3): 106–21.

Donaldson, T. (1982) *Corporate Morality*, Englewood Cliffs, NJ: Prentice Hall.

Evans, R. (1991) 'Business ethics and changes in society', *Journal of Business Ethics*, 10: 871–6.

Friedman, M. (1988) 'The social responsibility of business is to increase its profits', in T.L. Beauchamp and N.E. Bowie (eds) *Ethical Theory and Business*, Englewood Cliffs, NJ: Prentice Hall.

Goodpaster, K.E. (1991) 'Business ethics and stakeholder analysis', *Business Ethics Quarterly*, 1 (1): 53–73.

Gray, R.H., Kouhy, R. and Lavers, S. (1995) 'Corporate social and environmental reporting: a review of the literature and a longitudinal study of UK disclosure', *Accounting, Auditing & Accountability Journal*, 8 (2): 47–77.

Gray, R.H., Owen, D. and Adams, C. (1996) *Accounting and Accountability*, Hemel Hempstead: Prentice Hall.

Gray, R.H., Owen, D. and Maunders, K. (1987) *Corporate Social*

Reporting: Accounting and accountability, Hemel Hempstead: Prentice Hall.

—— (1988) 'Corporate social reporting: emerging trends in accountability and the social contract', *Accounting, Auditing & Accountability Journal*, 1 (1): 6–20.

London Benchmarking Group (1997) *Companies in the Community: Getting the measure*, London: Corporate Citizen International.

Mathews, M.R. (1993) *Socially Responsible Accounting*, London: Chapman & Hall.

—— (1995) 'Social and environmental accounting: a practical demonstration of ethical concern?', *Journal of Business Ethics*, 14: 663–71.

Mills D.L. and Gardner M.J. (1984) 'Financial profiles and the disclosure of expenditures for socially responsibility', *Journal of Business Research*, 12 (4): 407–24.

Parker, L.D. (1986) 'Polemical themes in social accounting: a scenario for standard setting', *Advances in Public Interest Accounting*, 1: 67–93.

Perks, R.W. (1993) *Accounting and Society*, London: Chapman & Hall.

Puxty, A.G. (1986) 'Social accounting as immanent legitimation: a critique of technist ideology', *Advances in Public Interest Accounting*, 1: 95–111.

Roberts, R.W. (1992) 'Determinants of corporate social responsibility disclosure', *Accounting, Organizations and Society*, 17 (6): 595–612.

Sutton, B. (ed.) (1993) *The Legitimate Corporation*, Cambridge, MA: Blackwell Business.

Tilt, C.A. (1994) 'The influence of external pressure groups on corporate social disclosure, some empirical evidence', *Accounting, Auditing & Accountability Journal*, 7 (4): 47–72.

Tinker, A.M., Lehman, C. and Neimark, M. (1991) 'Corporate social reporting: falling down the hole in the middle of the road', *Accounting, Auditing & Accountability Journal*, 4 (1): 28–54.

Traidcraft plc (1996) *Social Accounts, 1995–1996*, Gateshead: Traidcraft.

Ullmann, A.E. (1985) 'Data in search of a theory: a critical examination of relationships among social performance, social disclosure and economic performance of U.S. firms', *Academy of Management Review*, 10 (3): 540–47.

Vyakarnam, S. (1992) 'Social responsibility in the UK top 100 companies', *Cranfield School of Management Research Papers*, July.

Warren, R. (1997) 'Corporate punishment, is shame enough?', in G. Moore (ed.) *Business Ethics: Principle and Practice*, Sunderland: Business Education Publishers.

Welford R. (1996) *Hijacking Environmentalism: The industrial response to the environmental agenda*, paper presented at the 1996 Business Strategy and Environment Conference, Leeds.

Werhane, P. (1985) *Persons, Rights and Corporations*, Englewood Cliffs, NJ: Prentice Hall.

INDEX

Abbott, A. 127; and Monsen, 195
ACCA *see* Chartered Institute of
  Certified Accountants
accountants: and codes of conduct
  155–8; and commitment to
  morality 158–63; criticism of
  76–7, 80; and ethics 154–5;
  failure of 98, 99–100; and
  integrity 153–4, 158–9, 163–4;
  and Joint Monitoring Unit 110;
  reforms for 100; role of 1–2, 6,
  7–9; and social disclosures 101;
  tensions/conflicts in the NHS
  72–7; and trust 153; *see also*
  radical critics case
accounting: and assessment of
  outcomes 172–3; and change
  134; and conflicts of interest
  139–40; critique of 118–19; and
  cult of personalities 124; and
  defence of *status quo* in 133;
  democracy in 121–4; and
  disciplinary processes 130; and
  environmental destruction
  172–3; ethical aspects of 1–2;
  evolving model of 177–8;
  exclusive nature of 172–3;
  impact of 134; and independent
  regulation 131–3; influences of
  118; and moral choice 2–4; as
  neutral and value-free 1–2; and
  objective description 171; and
  opposition to change 125–9;
  partisanship in 119–21; politics
  of 119–24; and politics of

soothing reports 124–5; as
  professional activity 138–41;
  recurring failures of 133–4;
  reform of 124–33; and self-
  regulation 129–31; and values
  178–81; visible/invisible hand of
  118, 134
Accounting Education Change
  Commission (AECC, USA)
  161–2, 167
Accounting Principles Board (APB,
  USA) 7, 8
accounting regulation 6–7; and
  audit firm lobbying 9; and
  certainty of outcome 15–16;
  economic impact issues 9–10;
  ethical perspective 11–13; and
  issue of relentlessness 13–15, 15,
  18; mechanistic/judgemental
  issues 9–10, 16; and provision of
  level playing field 10;
  public/private sector differences
  7–8; role of practitioner in 7–9;
  and sex differences 18–21; and
  substance over form 15–16; and
  temporal vs closing rate method
  13–14; and unconventional
  treatments 16–18
Accounting Standards Board (ASB)
  7, 15, 27, 191
Accounting Standards Committee
  (ASC) 7, 16
Accounting Standards Steering
  Committee (ASSC) 194–5

200